NOTES ON LIFE INSURANCE.

PART FIRST—THEORETICAL.

PART SECOND—PRACTICAL.

WITH APPENDIX.

"The rate of premium which must be charged in order to carry out an insurance contract, is the problem which stands at the threshold of Life Assurance."

DR. FARR.

SECOND EDITION

REVISED, ENLARGED, AND RE-ARRANGED.

BY

GUSTAVUS W. SMITH.

NEW-YORK:
S. W. GREEN, PRINTER, Nos. 16 & 18 JACOB STREET.
1875.

"DOES the system itself rest on principles and laws so certain and stable as to justify a reasonable conviction that if the system is fairly and honestly administered, the bread that is cast on its waters will be surely found, though after many days?" (JOHN E. SANFORD, 1868.)

"WHAT is wanted is that the school-house and the press, the universal educators, shall take up the matter, not in the interests of companies or their agents, but in that of the public and its coming generations. The companies have nothing to fear but every thing to hope from the most thorough discussion of their plans and the exposure of all the details of their management."

(ELIZUR WRIGHT, 1872.)

In case a renewal premium is not paid, the policy-holder has no right in equity, at his own option, to demand the return to him of any portion of the reserve. The original contract was for insurance: the policy-holder's contributions to the reserve fund are intended to provide for future insurance, and all that he is in equity entitled to is the insurance that these contributions will at that time effect. (See page 139 of this work.)

In case a policy-holder does not pay his renewal premium: "The company ought to give him paid-up insurance, and can base it upon his contribution to the reserve fund." "This being done, the policy-holder has received the full value of his payments, in the commodity in which the company deals." "The theory that all the computed reserve is the individual property of the insured, to be demanded and received at will, is unsound and unsafe."

(Prof. Bartlett, 1875.)

PUBLISHERS' NOTICES.

THE following extracts are from some of the many letters addressed to the author of *Notes on Life Insurance*, soon after the publication of the first edition, 1870.

Mr. JOHN PATERSON, mathematician, Insurance Department, State of New-York, writes :

"I hesitate not to say that, in matter and manner, the work opportunely meets a great public want. To the unmathematical portion of the business community, who may feel interested, or even only curious, about this great financiering speculation, which has so recently, as it were, flooded almost the entire continent, it reveals in plain words, by successive steps, the entire process of management, and dispels all the presupposed mystery in which the question was involved—all this by ordinary arithmetic, the well-selected examples in which are clearly solved. Further than this, the algebraic deductions will bear the strictest scrutiny, and might well serve to initiate the tyro in actuarial science, while the advanced student may find some corroboration in the author's critical views. It is a household word with him, that what is usually termed the reserve is a 'Trust Fund Deposit,' does not in any sense belong to the company, but is a debt due to the policy-holder.

"The comments in the second part of the treatise deserve the thoughtful consideration of all officials, as well as incumbents, who stand under the banner of this mammoth institution of the age."

Mr. H. A. GRISWOLD, of Louisville, Ky., writes:

"I have read your *Notes on Life Insurance* with the greatest interest, and congratulate you on the ability with which a subject, usually so intricate and incomprehensible, is made intelligible to ordinary minds. No great mathematical knowledge is required : the algebra is within the scope of ordinary school instruction, and even this moderate amount is not necessary, provided the inquirer will assume the accuracy of a few formulæ."

Professor WILLIAM H. C. BARTLETT, Actuary of the Mutual Life Insurance Company of New-York, says:

"It gives me great pleasure to say that the *Notes on Life Insurance*, by General G. W. Smith, is a very valuable contribution to our stock of information on the subject, and I very heartily commend the work to public favor. It should be in the hands of every insurance agent in the country."

General ROBERT TOOMBS, Georgia, says:

"I have read your book with great pleasure, and consider it a very valuable addition to the science of Life Insurance, now greatly needed, especially by the people—I mean policy-holders—and I doubt not will be of incalculable benefit to them.

"You have given a simple rule, simplified, by which to enable thousands of policy-holders to know something of the condition of companies in which such vast amounts of their annual earnings are invested for the noblest of purposes, and with the means of arresting gradual decay and ruin of such of these companies as may be badly managed. I am very anxious to see it largely circulated."

Hon. OLIVER PILLSBURY, Insurance Commissioner of New-Hampshire, says:

"I have been much interested in your 'Notes.' They are all that I expected and more. I wish they could be scattered as leaves of the forest, all abroad. You have literally turned the mysteries of Life Insurance inside out, and rendered them susceptible of comprehension by ordinary reflecting minds. I consider the unpretending pamphlet worth more to me than all the elaborated volumes I have ever purchased. Your style is peculiarly adapted to the common people."

Prof. A. L. PERRY, of Williams College, says:

"I have read this work with great care, and I may add, with great interest. It has cleared up to my mind a subject of which I was almost totally ignorant before, although I have had three policies on my life for several years. In taking them out, and paying the annual premiums, I have walked by faith and not by sight. I believe I know now the whys and wherefores, as well as the *modus operandi.*"

The Hon. LINTON STEPHENS, Georgia, says:

"Your *Notes on Life Insurance* go to the very bottom of a knowledge which has heretofore been a sealed book to all but the *initiated few*, and places it within the easy comprehension of all intelligent men of business. Even persons of quite limited education can acquire from this most useful little work a sufficient acquaintance with the principles of insurance to enable them to judge for themselves of the trustworthiness of the multitude of different insurance institutions which are now claiming the confidence and struggling for the patronage of the public. The importance of this timely work is to be measured only by the present vast and still-increasing magnitude of the business of Life Insurance."

Prof. DAVID MURRAY, of Rutgers College, New-Brunswick, N. J., says:

"I have read the *Notes on Life Insurance* with the greatest interest. I am free to say that I consider it the best popular explanation of the theory and practice of Life Insurance that I know. I have examined, with constantly increasing admiration, the lucid development of, to most, a complicated and difficult subject. It seems to me exactly fitted to be put into the hands of the officers and agents of all our life companies, in order that they may be furnished with something more than a mere 'routine' knowledge of their business."

General A. P. STEWART, Assistant Actuary of the St. Louis Mutual Life Insurance Company, says :

"I have read the 'Notes' very carefully. The discussion of the mathematical theory of Life Insurance is the simplest and clearest I have seen, and would be a good text-book on the subject for schools and colleges. The practical part of the 'Notes' is also very valuable, and should be read by every one who is insured or who contemplates insuring."

Hon. WILLIAM BARNES, former Superintendent of the Insurance Department of the State of New-York, says :

"In my opinion, it is the most useful and valuable work ever issued in this country for the purpose of popular information in the mathematics and fundamental principles of Life Insurance. Indeed, I am not familiar with any foreign book which attains the object so fully and completely."

General S. B. BUCKNER, Louisville, Ky., says :

"I can not adequately commend your *Notes on Life Insurance.* Though not addressed to insurance people, I consider them, in the present condition of the business, almost indispensable to agents. Nowhere else in the English language can be found so complete and so intelligible an epitome of all the principles which constitute the basis of Life Insurance. In the hands of any intelligent reader, they will unlock the mysteries in which some seek to vail the business which should be exposed in the clearest light."

CONTENTS.

PART I. THEORY. (ARITHMETICAL DISCUSSION.)

PART I. CONTINUED. (ALGEBRAIC DISCUSSION.)

PART II. PRACTICAL LIFE INSURANCE.

APPENDIX.

PREFACE.

THE numerical examples and tables in the text are simply illustrative; they are *not* intended as "*sums* to be worked and the results committed to memory." After the general principles are understood, the accuracy of the illustrations may be tested by those who have time and taste for such calculations. A good computer who has learned the theory will then be able to detect and correct any arithmetical errors.

There is nothing in the theory, the principles, or in the method of calculating values in Life Insurance, that is not within the easy comprehension of men who have a thorough knowledge of the single rule of three, and a *mere acquaintance* with the simplest principles of elementary algebra. The intelligent, general business sense of the country should be informed definitely what Life Insurance is, and what it is not; and it is hoped that the following *Notes* may tend, in some degree, to promote this end.

The rather complex equations given in the discussions for determining the deposit on certain "return premium" policies may well be merely glanced over by those not directly interested in this *peculiar* kind of contract for insurance. The same may be said in regard to joint lives. But the *principles* used in constructing the commutation columns and the *meaning* of the values given in these tables should be closely studied.

PART I.–THE THEORY.

CHAPTER I.

NET PREMIUMS.

After a table of mortality and a rate of interest are designated, the method of calculating net values in life insurance is simple when carefully explained. The net premium is the amount that will, on the designated data—namely, rate of interest and table of mortality—exactly effect the insurance. In this calculation, expenses and profits are left out of consideration.

Life insurance calculations are made, first on the supposition that the amount insured is $1. Having obtained the net premium that will insure $1, the net premium that will effect similar insurance for $100, $1000, or any other named sum, is found by multiplying the net premium that will insure $1 by the sum actually insured. It is assumed that the payment of the premium is made at the time the insurance is effected; this is called the beginning of the policy-year, and the amount insured is to be paid at the end of that policy-year, in which the insured may die.

Interest.—The first thing to be considered, in making calculations for net premiums, is the method by which we determine the amount of money that will, when increased by interest at a given rate per annum, compounded annually, produce $1 in any designated number of years. Suppose that the rate of interest is 4 per cent per annum. The amount that will at this rate produce $1 in one year, when the principal and interest thereon for one year are added together, is expressed by $\frac{1}{1\cdot04} = \frac{100}{104}$ = $0.961538, plus other decimal figures.

If the rate of interest is $4\frac{1}{2}$ per cent per annum, the amount in hand that will, at this rate, produce $1 in one year is expressed by $\frac{\$1}{1\cdot045} = \frac{1000}{1045}$ = $0.956938. In general, divide one dollar by *one* plus the rate of interest in order to obtain the amount that will, if invested at this rate of interest, produce $1 in one year.

Having obtained the amount that will, at the given rate of interest, produce \$1 in one year, in order to obtain the amount that will, at the same rate of interest per annum, produce \$1 in two years, interest being compounded annually, we multiply the amount that will produce \$1 in one year by itself. For instance, the amount that will produce \$1 in one year at 4 per cent being expressed by $\frac{\$1}{1.04}$, the amount that will, at the same rate of interest, compounded annually, produce \$1 in two years, is expressed by $\frac{\$1}{1.04} \times \frac{1}{1.04} = \$0.924556$.

If the rate of interest is $4\frac{1}{2}$ per cent, the expression becomes $\frac{\$1}{1.045} \times \frac{1}{1.045} = \$0.915730$.

The amount that will, at 4 per cent, produce \$1 in three years is expressed by $\frac{\$1}{1.04} \times \frac{1}{1.04} \times \frac{1}{1.04} = \$0.888996$. Interest being $4\frac{1}{2}$ per cent, the expression becomes $\frac{\$1}{1.045} \times \frac{1}{1.045} \times \frac{1}{1.045} = \$0.876297$.

In general, to obtain the amount that will, if invested at any given rate of interest, compounded annually, produce \$1 in any designated number of years, the rule is: *Divide* \$1 *by one plus the rate of interest, and multiply the quotient by itself a number of times equal to the number of years less one.* That is to say, for two years, multiply once; for three years, twice; for four years, three times, and so on.

These calculations have been made, and the results, at various rates of interest, have been placed in appended tables.

Tables of Mortality.—There are at present two tables of mortality in quite general use in the United States. It is not claimed that either of them is in exact accordance with the rate of mortality among insured lives in this country. It is, however, maintained by life-insurance experts that either of the tables referred to is sufficiently accurate for practical purposes. The tables are given below. It will be noticed that in both it is assumed that there are 100,000 persons living at age 10. In the column headed "number of deaths" will be found opposite age 10 the number that will die between age 10 and age 11. This will leave a certain number living at age 11. This number is placed opposite age 11, in the column headed "number living;" and opposite age 11 in the column headed "number of deaths" is placed the number that die between age 11 and age 12.

For example, in the American Experience Table of Mortality, among insured lives, we find opposite age 10 in the column headed "number living," 100,000. Opposite same age we find, in the column headed "number of deaths," 749. This is the number, according to this table, that will die between age 10 and age 11, and it will leave 99,251 living at age 11, of which number 746 will die between age 11 and age 12.

American Experience Table of Mortality.

Age.	Number living.	Num. of deaths.	Age.	Number living.	Num. of deaths.
10	100,000	749	53	66,797	1091
11	99,251	746	54	65,706	1143
12	98,505	743	55	64,563	1199
13	97,762	740	56	63,364	1260
14	97,022	737	57	62,104	1325
15	96,285	735	58	60,779	1394
16	95,550	732	59	59,385	1468
17	94,818	729	60	57,917	1546
18	94,089	727	61	56,371	1628
19	93,362	725	62	54,743	1713
20	92,637	723	63	53,030	1800
21	91,914	722	64	51,230	1889
22	91,192	721	65	49,341	1980
23	90,471	720	66	47,361	2070
24	89,751	719	67	45,291	2158
25	89,032	718	68	43,133	2243
26	88,314	718	69	40,890	2321
27	87,596	718	70	38,569	2391
28	86,878	718	71	36,178	2448
29	86,160	719	72	33,730	2487
30	85,441	720	73	31,243	2505
31	84,721	721	74	28,738	2501
32	84,000	723	75	26,237	2476
33	83,277	726	76	23,761	2431
34	82,551	729	77	21.330	2369
35	81,822	732	78	18,961	2291
36	81,090	737	79	16,670	2196
37	80,353	742	80	14,474	2091
38	79,611	749	81	12,383	1964
39	78,862	756	82	10,419	1816
40	78,106	765	83	8,603	1648
41	77,341	774	84	6,955	1470
42	76,567	785	85	5,485	1292
43	75,782	797	86	4,193	1114
44	74,985	812	87	3,079	933
45	74,173	828	88	2,146	744
46	73,345	848	89	1,402	555
47	72,497	870	90	847	385
48	71,627	896	91	462	246
49	70,731	927	92	216	137
50	69,804	962	93	79	58
51	68,842	1001	94	21	18
52	67,841	1044	95	3	3

Actuaries' Table of Mortality.

Age.	Number living.	Num. of deaths.	Age.	Number living.	Num. of deaths.
10	100,000	676	21	92,588	683
11	99,324	674	22	91,905	686
12	98,650	672	23	91,219	690
13	97,978	671	24	90,529	694
14	97,307	671	25	89,835	698
15	96,636	671	26	89,137	703
16	95,965	672	27	88,434	708
17	95.293	673	28	87.726	714
18	94,620	675	29	87,012	720
19	93.945	677	30	86,292	727
20	93,268	680	31	85,565	734

Actuaries' Table of Mortality—continued.

Age.	Number living.	Num. of deaths.	Age.	Number living.	Num. of deaths.
32	84,831	742	66	44,693	2128
33	84,089	750	67	42,565	2191
34	83,339	758	68	40,374	2246
35	82,581	767	69	38,128	2291
36	81,814	776	70	35,837	2327
37	81,038	785	71	33,510	2351
38	80,253	795	72	31,159	2362
39	79,458	805	73	28,797	2358
40	78,653	815	74	26,439	2339
41	77,838	826	75	24,100	2303
42	77,012	839	76	21,797	2249
43	76,173	857	77	19,548	2179
44	75,316	881	78	17,369	2092
45	74,435	909	79	15,277	1987
46	73,526	944	80	13.290	1866
47	72,582	981	81	11,424	1730
48	71,601	1021	82	9,694	1582
49	70,580	1063	83	8,112	1427
50	69,517	1108	84	6,685	1268
51	68,409	1156	85	5,417	1111
52	67,253	1207	86	4,306	958
53	66,046	1261	87	3,348	811
54	64,785	1316	88	2,537	673
55	63,469	1375	89	1,864	545
56	62,094	1436	90	1,319	427
57	60,658	1497	91	892	322
58	59,161	1561	92	570	231
59	57,600	1627	93	339	155
60	55,973	1698	94	184	95
61	54,275	1770	95	89	52
62	52,505	1844	96	37	24
63	50,661	1917	97	13	9
64	48,744	1990	98	4	3
65	46,754	2061	99	1	1

Various other tables of mortality are sometimes used in making life insurance calculations, but it is not necessary to give them here. Mortality tables are all based upon statistical information, obtained by observation and experience. It is assumed that each insured person at any particular age has the average chance of living for one year that is indicated by the table at that age.

Manner of using the Mortality Table.—In illustration of the calculation of the chance that a person may die during any given time, let us suppose that out of one hundred persons condemned to be shot on a given day, all are reprieved for the day, except one, and the one to be shot is to be the one who draws the black ball out of a box containing ninety-nine white balls and one black one. The chance, before the drawing, of any particular man's getting the black ball, and, therefore, his chance of being shot that day is one only out of one hundred. If two men had to die that day, each individual's chance, before the drawing, of getting a black ball, would be twice as great as it was before ; for now there are two black balls and only ninety-eight white ones in the box. The chance, in this case, would be two out of one hundred ; for three persons, three out of one hundred ; and so on to the limit of one hundred out of one hundred—which would make it certain that each man would be shot.

To apply this principle to life insurance, and to show that the amount that will insure one dollar, to be paid certain at the end of any year, when multiplied by the fraction which represents the chance that the person will die during the year, gives what it is worth to insure one dollar, to be paid at the end of the year, in case the insured dies during the year : let us suppose that out of one hundred persons alive at the beginning of the year, it is known that one of them, and one only, will die during the year. The value of one dollar, to be paid certain at the end of one year, in the particular case of interest at four and one half per cent, is $0.956938. The chance that the person will die during the year is one out of one hundred. To make it certain that his heirs will obtain one dollar at the end of the year, he must advance $0.956938 at the beginning of the year. But the one dollar is not to be paid certain ; it is to be paid only in case he dies. Suppose the whole one hundred persons are insured ; then, since there is but one to die, and but one dollar to be paid, each person will have to give only the one hundredth part of $0.956938 in order to make up what is necessary to pay this one dollar at the end of the year. Therefore, $0.956938 divided by 100 is what each man would have to pay. In case it is known that two persons out of the one hundred will die, the amount requisite to effect the insurance will be twice as much as before, because two dollars must be paid certain at the end of the year. The chance that each person may die during the year is twice as great as in the first case, and is therefore two out of one hundred ; and the amount that each person will have to pay for his insurance is $0.956938, divided by 100, and the result multiplied by two. In case it is known that all of them will die during the year, the fraction which represents the chance that any particular individual will die becomes $\frac{100}{100}$, or unity. This represents the certainty ; and to insure one dollar, to be paid at the end of the year to the heirs of the insured, in case he dies during the year, each person will now have to pay $\frac{100}{100}$ of $0.956938—that is to say, each must, in this case, pay enough to make, with interest at four and one half per cent added, the full amount for which he is insured.

To insure One Dollar for One Year at Age 30.—The American Experience table shows that out of 100,000 persons living at age ten, there will be 85,441 living at age thirty. The number of deaths between age thirty and age thirty-one is 720. Therefore,

$\frac{720}{85441}$ is the fraction which represents the chance that the insured will die before he is thirty-one years of age.

The present value of one dollar to be paid *certain* at the end of one year has, in the case of interest at four and one half per cent, been found to be equal to $0.956938. Multiply this by the fraction $\frac{720}{85441}$, which represents the chance that the insured will die during the year between age thirty and age thirty-one, and we have $0.0081064. This is *the value of the risk on one dollar*, or what it is worth to insure one dollar to be paid to the heirs of a person at the end of one year, in case he dies during the year, the age of the insured being thirty years at the time he takes out the policy. It would require one thousand times as much to insure one thousand dollars as it does to insure one dollar, and half as much to insure half a dollar as it does a whole dollar. We can obtain, by using the mortality table, the fraction representing the chance that a person of any given age will die during the succeeding year, just as we did in this case for age thirty. We have, therefore, already determined the means for calculating the sum that will at any age insure one dollar to be paid to the heirs of the insured in one year, in case he dies during the year ; but we must know the age of the person, the rate of interest must be fixed, and a mortality table must be available for use in the calculations.

The following table shows the *net* amount that will insure $1000 for one year at different ages from 20 to 70 inclusive, the calculations being all based upon the American Experience Table of Mortality, but at different rates of interest, 4, 4½, 5, and 6 per cent.

Cost of Insurance on $1000, for one year, at different Ages—American Experience—Various Rates of Interest.

Age.	Four per cent.	Four and a half per cent.	Five per cent.	Six per cent.	Age.
20	$7.504	$7.469	$7.433	$7.363	20
21	7.553	7.517	7 481	7.411	21
22	7.602	7.566	7.530	7.459	22
23	7.652	7.616	7.579	7.508	23
24	7.703	7.666	7.630	7.558	24
25	7.754	7.717	7.680	7.608	25
26	7.815	7.780	7.743	7.670	26
27	7.881	7.844	7.806	7.733	27
28	7.947	7.909	7.871	7.797	28
29	8.024	7.986	7.948	7.873	29
30	8.103	8.064	8.026	7.950	30
31	8.183	8.144	8.105	8.029	31
32	8.276	8.237	8.197	8.120	32
33	8.383	8.342	8.303	8.224	33
34	8.491	8.451	8.410	8.331	34
35	8.602	8.561	8.520	8.440	35
36	8.739	8.697	8.656	8.574	36
37	8.879	8.837	8.795	8.712	37
38	9.046	9.003	8.960	8.876	38

Cost of Insurance on $1000—continued

Age.	Four per cent.	Four and a half per cent.	Five per cent.	Six per cent.	Age.
39	$9.218	$9.174	$9.130	$9.044	39
40	9.418	9.373	9.328	9.240	40
41	9.623	9.577	9.531	9.441	41
42	9.858	9.811	9.764	9.672	42
43	10.113	10.064	10.016	9.922	43
44	10.412	10.363	10.313	10.216	44
45	10.734	10.682	10.632	10.531	45
46	11.117	11.064	11.011	10.907	46
47	11.539	11.484	11.429	11.321	47
48	12.028	11.971	11.914	11.801	48
49	12.602	12.542	12.482	12.364	49
50	13.251	13.188	13.125	13.001	50
51	13.981	13.914	13.848	13.717	51
52	14.797	14.726	14.656	14.518	52
53	15.705	15.629	15.555	15.409	53
54	16.727	16.647	16.567	16.411	54
55	17.857	17.771	17.687	17.520	55
56	19.120	19.029	18.938	18.760	56
57	20.515	20.416	20.319	20.128	57
58	22.053	21.948	21.843	21.637	58
59	23.769	23.656	23.543	23.321	59
60	25.667	25.544	25.422	25.182	60
61	27.769	27.636	27.503	27.245	61
62	30.088	29.944	29.802	29.520	62
63	32.638	32.481	32.327	32.022	63
64	35.455	35.285	35.117	34.786	64
65	38.585	38.401	38.218	37.857	65
66	42.026	41.825	41.626	41.233	66
67	45.815	45.596	45.379	44.950	67
68	50.002	49.763	49.526	49.058	68
69	54.579	54.318	54.060	53.549	69
70	59.608	59.323	59.041	58.484	70

For the purpose of comparison, the following table is inserted :

Cost of Insurance on $1000, for one year, at different Ages—Actuaries' Table—Various Rates of Interest.

Age.	Four per cent.	Four and a half per cent.	Five per cent.	Six per cent.	Age.
20	$7.010	$6.977	$6.944	$6.878	20
21	7.093	7.059	7.026	6.959	21
22	7.177	7.143	7.109	7.042	22
23	7.273	7.238	7.204	7.136	23
24	7.371	7.336	7.301	7.232	24
25	7.471	7.435	7.400	7.330	25
26	7.583	7.547	7.511	7.440	26
27	7.698	7.661	7.625	7.553	27
28	7.826	7.788	7.751	7.678	28
29	7.956	7.918	7.881	7.807	29
30	8.101	8.062	8.024	7.948	30
31	8.248	8.209	8.170	8.093	31
32	8.410	8.370	8.330	8.252	32
33	8.576	8.535	8.494	8.414	33
34	8.746	8.704	8.662	8.581	34
35	8.931	8.888	8.845	8.762	35
36	9.122	9.076	9.033	8.948	36
37	9.314	9.270	9.225	9.138	37
38	9.525	9.480	9.435	9.346	38
39	9.741	9.695	9.649	9.558	39
40	9.963	9.916	9.869	9.775	40
41	10.204	10.155	10.106	10.011	41
42	10.476	10.425	10.375	10.278	42
43	10.818	10.766	10.715	10.614	43
44	11.247	11.194	11.140	11.035	44

Cost of Insurance on $1000—continued.

Age.	Four per cent.	Four and a half per cent.	Five per cent.	Six per cent.	Age.
45	$11.742	$11.686	$11.630	$11.521	45
46	12.345	12.286	12.227	12.112	46
47	12.996	12.934	12.872	12.751	47
48	13.711	13.646	13.580	13 452	48
49	14.482	14.412	14.344	14.209	49
50	15.326	15.252	15.180	15.036	50
51	16.248	16.171	16.093	15.941	51
52	17.257	17.174	17.093	16.931	52
53	18.359	18.271	18.183	18.012	53
54	19.532	19.439	19.346	19.163	54
55	20.831	20.731	20.633	20.438	55
56	22.237	22.130	22.025	21.817	56
57	23.730	23.617	23.504	23.282	57
58	25.371	25.249	25.129	24.892	58
59	27.160	27.030	26.901	26.647	59
60	29.169	29.030	28.891	28.619	60
61	31.357	31.207	31.059	30.765	61
62	33.770	33.608	33.448	33.132	62
63	36.384	36.210	36.038	35.698	63
64	39.255	39.068	38.882	38.515	64
65	42.386	42.184	41.983	41.586	65
66	45.782	45.563	45.346	44.919	66
67	49.494	49.258	49.023	48.560	67
68	53.490	53.234	52.981	52.481	68
69	57.776	57.500	57.226	56.686	69
70	62.436	62.137	61.841	61.257	70

In further illustration of the question of net premiums and net values of life policies in case the insurance is for one year only; we will suppose that the age of the person applying for insurance is 40, the mortality table used the Actuaries', the rate of interest is four per cent, the insurance to be for one year, the amount of the policy $10,000, and the policy-holder is a *fair average* of insured lives. What amount in hand ought to be paid to insure $10,000 as above, leaving out all consideration of expenses, and having neither gain nor loss represented in the chances of the transaction?

We will first determine the amount that will insure $1. The present value of $1, to be paid *certain* at the end of one year, interest being assumed at four per cent per annum, is equal to $0.961538. From the mortality table we find that out of 100,000 persons living at age 10, there are 78,653 living at age 40, and that 815 of these will die during the year between age 40 and age 41. Therefore, $\frac{815}{78653}$ is the fraction which represents the chance that the insured will die during the year; and this multiplied by $0.961538, which is the present value of $1, to be paid *certain* at the end of one year, will give what it is now worth to insure the $1, to be paid in case the insured dies during the year, or $\$0.961538 \times \frac{815}{78653} = \$0.009963432$. This, multiplied by 10,000, makes $99.63, plus a fraction of a cent, which is the net premium that will insure

$10,000, to be paid to the heirs of the person insured at the end of one year ; provided he dies during the year.

If every one of the whole 78,653 had been insured for one year in the sum of $10,000 each, the heirs of the 815 who died were respectively entitled to, and were paid, $10,000 each. The aggregate payment of losses by death, for the year, amounted, therefore, to $8,150,000. The net annual premiums, $99.63 each, on 78,653 policies, when increased by four per cent interest, amounted at the end of the year to $8,149,996.43.

It is seen from this, that the fraction of a cent omitted in each of the 78,653 premiums amounted, in the aggregate, to a deficiency of $3.57, in paying $8,150,000 losses by death. The 77,838 persons who did not die during the year, in this case receive nothing. They are not entitled to any thing ; they had their lives insured during the year ; they each paid in advance a *net* premium amounting to $99.63 ; the whole of this, and net interest on it, has gone to pay at the end of the year $10,000 to the heirs of each of the 815 policyholders that died during the year.

Net Single Premium for Insurance for Whole Life.—What sum paid in hand will, "*on the supposition that the mortality table and rate of interest designated as the basis of the calculations are correct,*" be the exact equivalent of $1 insured, to be paid at the end of any year in which the insured may die? In other words, we have now to determine the amount that, if paid in hand, will exactly insure $1 for whole life. The problem before us reduces to this, namely: *First,* calculate the present value of the amount requisite to effect the insurance each separate year that the insured may live, as indicated by the designated table of mortality. Then add together the respective amounts that are found to be necessary to effect the insurance each year, and their sum will give the amount that, if paid in hand, will effect the insurance for whole life.

Assume that the age of the person at the time he insures is 40, that he is a fair average of insured lives, the table of mortality is the Actuaries', and the rate of interest four per cent, compounded annually. We have already found that the amount necessary in this case to insure $1 to be paid to the heirs of the insured in case he dies during the first year—that is, between age 40 and age 41—is $0.009963432. Now, let us see what amount of money, if paid in hand at the time the policy is issued (age 40), will secure $1 to be paid to the heirs of the insured at the end of two years, in case he dies in the second year from the date of the policy. This problem is solved separately, and the amount we are now to find insures only against death in the second year.

Find the amount that will, if invested at 4 per cent per annum, compound interest, produce $1 in two years. To do this, we have to divide 100 by 104 ; this gives $0.961538, and this is the amount that will produce $1 in one year at 4 per cent per annum. Multiply this by itself, and we have $0.924556, which is the amount that will produce $1 in two years at 4 per cent compounded annually.

Now, the question is, What fraction, at age 40 (the time at which the insurance is effected), represents the chance that the insured will die during the second year—that is, between age 41 and age 42 ?

By the Actuaries' Table of Mortality, we see that out of 78,653 insured persons living at age 40, the number that will die between age 41 and age 42 is 826. Therefore, the fraction 826 divided by 78,653 represents at the time this insurance is effected, age 40, the chance that the insured will die between age 41 and age 42.

Multiply the amount, $0.924556, that will, at the designated rate of interest, produce $1 certain in two years, by the fraction $\frac{826}{78653}$, which represents the chance that the $1 insured will have to be paid, and we have $0.009705, which is the amount that will, if paid in hand at age 40, insure $1 to be paid to the heirs of the insured in case he dies in the second year.

In like manner, we can find the amount that, if paid in hand at age 40, will insure $1 to the heirs of the insured in case he dies in the third year—and for each and every year up to and including the table limit.

Add together these respective yearly amounts, and the result gives the *net single premium* that will, if paid in hand at age 40, insure $1 for whole life.

The amount in this case is $0.38104 ; multiply this by 1000, and we have $381.04, which is the *net* single premium that will at age 40 insure $1000, to be paid to the heirs of the insured at the end of any year in which he may die.

Detailed Calculation of Net Single Premium for Whole-Life Policies.—In illustration of this subject, we will assume that the age of the insured is 50. The amount insured is $1. The table of mortality used is the American Experience, and the rate of interest is 4½ per cent per annum, compounded yearly. Opposite age 50 in the following table, in the column headed, " *Value in hand at age*

50 *of* $1 *to be paid certain at the end of each respective year,"* we find the amount $0.956938. This is the amount that at $4\frac{1}{2}$ per cent will produce $1 in one year, and it is obtained by dividing 100 by $104\frac{1}{2}$. This is to be multiplied by the number of deaths during the year between age 50 and age 51 ; this number, as shown by the mortality table, is 962, and it is placed in the following table opposite age 50, in the column headed, "Number of Deaths." In the next column, which is headed, "Number Living at Age 50," we find the number 69804 ; this, too, is taken from the table of mortality. The product arising from multiplying $0.956938 by 962 is divided by 69804, and the result is $0.013188. This is the amount that at age 50 will insure $1, to be paid to the heirs of the insured at the end of the year, in case he dies between age 50 and age 51.

Opposite age 51, in the same table, in the column headed, "Value in hand at age 50 of $1, to be paid *certain* at the end of each respective year," we find the amount $0.915730. This is the amount that will produce $1 certain in two years, when invested at $4\frac{1}{2}$ per cent per annum, compounded annually, and it was obtained by multiplying $\frac{1}{1.045}$ by $\frac{1}{1.045}$. Multiplying this by 1001, which is the number of deaths between age 51 and age 52, and divide the product by 69804, which is the number living at age 50, and we have $0.013132. This is the amount that, if paid in hand at age 50, will insure $1, to be paid to the heirs of the insured at the end of the second year, in case the insured dies in that year—that is, between age 51 and age 52.

In a similar manner, the calculations as shown in the table are made each respective year to include age 95, which is the limit of the table of mortality we are now using, and the sum of all these respective yearly values gives us $0.430037. This amount, if paid in hand at age 50, will insure $1 for whole life on the data assumed —namely, the American Experience Table of Mortality, and $4\frac{1}{2}$ per cent per annum, compounded yearly.

In an entirely similar manner, the calculations can be made at any age included in the table of mortality, and at any designated rate of interest.

Having found the net single premium that will insure $1 at any age, the net single premium that will insure any other amount at the same age is found by a simple proportion.

TABLE.—*Illustrating the manner of calculating the net Single Premium for a Whole-Life Policy for $1; issued at age 50—American Experience, four and a half per cent.*

Age.	Value in hand, at age 50, of $1, to be paid *certain* at the end of each respective year.		Number of Deaths.		Number living at age 50.		Value, in hand, at age 50, of $1, to be paid at the end of each respective year, *provided* the insured dies during the year.	Age.
50	$0.956938	×	962	÷	69804	=	$0.013188	50
51	0.915730	×	1001	÷	69804	=	.013132	51
52	0.876297	×	1044	÷	69804	=	.013106	52
53	0.838561	×	1091	÷	69804	=	.013106	53
54	0.802451	×	1143	÷	69804	=	.013140	54
55	0.767896	×	1199	÷	69804	=	.013190	55
56	0.734828	×	1260	÷	69804	=	.013264	56
57	0.703185	×	1325	÷	69804	=	.013348	57
58	0.672904	×	1394	÷	69804	=	.013438	58
59	0.643928	×	1468	÷	69804	=	.013542	59
60	0.616199	×	1546	÷	69804	=	.013647	60
61	0.589664	×	1628	÷	69804	=	.013752	61
62	0.564272	×	1713	÷	69804	=	.013847	62
63	0.539973	×	1800	÷	69804	=	.013924	63
64	0.516720	×	1889	÷	69804	=	.013983	64
65	0.494469	×	1980	÷	69804	=	.014026	65
66	0.473176	×	2070	÷	69804	=	.014032	66
67	0.452800	×	2158	÷	69804	=	.013998	67
68	0.433302	×	2243	÷	69804	=	.013923	68
69	0.414643	×	2321	÷	69804	=	.013787	69
70	0.396787	×	2391	÷	69804	=	.013591	70
71	0.379701	×	2448	÷	69804	=	.013316	71
72	0.363350	×	2487	÷	69804	=	.012946	72
73	0.347703	×	2505	÷	69804	=	.012478	73
74	0.332731	×	2501	÷	69804	=	.011921	74
75	0.318402	×	2476	÷	69804	=	.011294	75
76	0.304691	×	2431	÷	69804	=	.010611	76
77	0.291571	×	2369	÷	69804	=	.009895	77
78	0.279015	×	2291	÷	69804	=	.009157	78
79	0.267000	×	2196	÷	69804	=	.008400	79
80	0.255502	×	2091	÷	69804	=	.007654	80
81	0.244500	×	1964	÷	69804	=	.006879	81
82	0.233971	×	1816	÷	69804	=	.006087	82
83	0.223896	×	1648	÷	69804	=	.005286	83
84	0.214254	×	1470	÷	69804	=	.004512	84
85	0.205028	×	1292	÷	69804	=	.003[illegible]95	85
86	0.196199	×	1114	÷	69804	=	.003131	86
87	0.187750	×	933	÷	69804	=	.002509	87
88	0.179665	×	744	÷	69804	=	.001915	88
89	0.171929	×	555	÷	69804	=	.001367	89
90	0.164525	×	385	÷	69804	=	.000907	90
91	0.157440	×	246	÷	69804	=	.000555	91
92	0.1[illegible]0661	×	137	÷	69804	=	.000296	92
93	0.144173	×	58	÷	69804	=	.000120	93
94	0.137964	×	18	÷	69804	=	.000036	94
95	0.132023	×	3	÷	69804	=	.000006	95
	Total..						$0.430037	

If the insurance is for a limited number of years only, the calculation is made for each year of the term, and the sum of these yearly amounts will give the net single premium that will, if paid at the time the policy is issued, insure $1 to be paid to the heirs of the insured at the end of the year in which the policy-holder may die; *provided* he dies before the expiration of the term. For instance, suppose the insurance at age 50 is to continue for ten years only;

take in the above table the amounts for the first ten years, their sum will be the net single premium required.

If insurance is paid for at age 50, to begin only at the end of ten years from that time, and then continue for life; the net single premium is obtained by subtracting the amount that will at age 50 insure $1 until age 60, from the amount that will at age 50 insure $1 for life.

If insurance is paid for at age 50 to begin at age 60, and then continue for ten years only: subtract the net single premium that will at age 50 insure $1, to begin at age 70 and continue for life, from the net single premium that will at age 50 insure $1, to begin at age 60 and continue for life.

The net single premium that will at any age insure $1, to be paid at the end of any designated year, provided the insured dies in that year, is found, as before stated, by first determining the amount that will at the named rate of interest produce $1 at the end of the designated year, and then multiplying this amount by the fraction (obtained from the mortality table), which represents, at the time the insurance is effected, the chance that the insured will die in the designated year.

For purposes of comparison and general illustration, the following tables are given, showing the net single premiums that will insure $1000 for whole life, at ages from 20 to 70 inclusive, at 4, 4½, 5, and 6 per cent respectively:

Net Single Premiums—American Experience—Various Rates of Interest.

Age.	Four per cent.	Four and a half per cent.	Five per cent.	Six per cent.	Age.
20	247.798	217.448	192.545	154.766	20
21	251.846	221.155	195.896	157.476	21
22	256.076	225.019	199.402	160.329	22
23	260.472	229.049	203.071	163 334	23
24	265.042	233.255	206.913	166.501	24
25	269.704	237.644	210.937	169.840	25
26	274.737	242.227	215.155	173.364	26
27	279.872	247.005	219.568	177.075	27
28	285.207	251.989	224.187	180.987	28
29	290.754	257.189	229.025	185.111	29
30	296.514	262.609	234.084	189.454	30
31	302.497	268.261	239.378	194.029	31
32	308.713	274.155	244.922	198.853	32
33	315.167	280.298	250.718	203.933	33
34	321.862	286.692	256.775	209.275	34
35	328.809	293.353	263.107	214.898	35
36	336.022	300.294	269.728	220.822	36
37	343.088	307.514	276.552	227.046	37
38	351.245	315.027	283.859	233.591	38
39	359.266	322.832	291.385	240.458	39
40	367.575	3 0.946	299.237	247.676	40
41	376.167	339.368	308.371	255.242	41

Net Single Premiums—continued

Age.	Four per cent.	Four and a half per cent.	Five per cent.	Six per cent.	Age.
42	385.060	348.115	315.940	263.183	42
43	394.252	357.190	324.815	271.505	43
44	403.751	366.602	334.051	280 225	44
45	413.551	376.346	343.646	289.343	45
46	423.659	386.432	353.613	298.877	46
47	434.063	396.848	363.939	308.818	47
48	444.762	407.597	374.632	319.178	48
49	455.744	418.667	385.679	329.947	49
50	467.046	430.037	397.060	341.108	50
51	478.480	441.695	408.767	352.653	51
52	490.207	453.626	420.781	364.572	52
53	502.154	465.819	433.096	376.857	53
54	514.307	478.259	445.698	389.497	54
55	526.645	490.925	458.564	402.473	55
56	539.153	503.802	471.681	415.771	56
57	551.806	516.866	485.024	429.371	57
58	564.589	530.099	498.578	443.255	58
59	577.482	543.484	512.321	457.405	59
60	590.457	556.989	526.226	471.792	60
61	603.491	570.591	540.266	486.390	61
62	616.557	584.261	553.566	501.166	62
63	629.630	597.973	568.631	516.094	63
64	642.687	611.702	582.906	531.146	64
65	655.699	625.416	597.198	546.284	65
66	668.630	639.076	611.467	561.464	66
67	681.452	652.653	625.679	576.648	67
68	694.137	666.114	639.801	591.797	68
69	706.647	679.418	653.787	606.861	69
70	718.960	692.540	667.610	621.805	70

Net Single Premiums—Actuaries' Table—Various Rates of Interest.

Age.	Four per cent.	Four and a half per cent.	Five per cent.	Six per cent.	Age.
20	251.907	221.069	195.651	156.926	20
21	256.564	225.373	199.598	160.219	21
22	261.377	229.830	203.703	163.662	22
23	266.357	234.458	207.977	167.266	23
24	271.500	239.254	212.418	171.032	24
25	276.816	244.226	217.037	174.969	25
26	282.312	249.384	221.843	179.089	26
27	287.990	254.728	226.837	183.394	27
28	293.856	260.269	232.030	187.896	28
29	299.913	266.007	237.425	192.598	29
30	306.168	271.952	243.033	197.513	30
31	312.624	278.108	248.856	202.646	31
32	319.289	284.485	254.907	208.011	32
33	326.167	291.086	261.191	213.614	33
34	333.267	297.922	267.719	219.469	34
35	340.600	304.443	274.506	225.593	35
36	348.170	312.346	281.559	231.996	36
37	355.989	319.951	288.892	238.695	37
38	364.065	327 838	296.522	245.710	38
39	372.414	336.012	304.458	253.053	39
40	381.040	344.491	312.718	260.747	40
41	389.960	353.292	321.321	268.815	41
42	399.183	363.425	330 283	277.275	42
43	408.709	371.891	339.600	286 134	43
44	418.515	381.668	349.258	295.374	44
45	428.571	391.729	359.226	304.967	45
46	438.862	402.054	369.487	314.899	46
47	449.346	412.604	380.002	325.128	47
48	460.022	423.390	390.767	335.656	48

Net Single Premiums—continued.

Age.	Four per cent.	Four and a half per cent.	Five per cent.	Six per cent.	Age.
49	470.878	434.364	401.775	346.477	49
50	481.906	445.560	413.024	357.590	50
51	493.107	456.955	424.502	368.988	51
52	504.460	468.537	436.200	380.661	52
53	515.949	480.293	448.105	392.600	53
54	527.567	492.211	460.204	404.792	54
55	539.312	504.291	472.498	417.241	55
56	551.157	516.509	484.966	429.926	56
57	563.103	528.856	497.596	442.836	57
58	575.142	541.335	510.392	455.980	58
59	587.257	553.925	523.335	469.337	59
60	599.433	566.610	536.407	482.891	60
61	611.628	579.346	549.564	496.593	61
62	623.826	592.115	562.783	510.423	62
63	635.995	604.883	576.032	524.343	63
64	648.120	617.633	589.292	538.334	64
65	660.171	630.335	602.530	552.359	65
67	672.124	642.961	615.716	566.386	66
67	683.968	655.491	628.830	580.390	67
68	695.654	667.892	641.835	594.332	68
69	707.192	680.154	654.713	608.196	69
70	718.569	692.271	667.474	621.973	70

Net Annual Premium for Whole-Life Policies.—Having shown how to calculate the net *single* premium that will insure one dollar for whole life at any age included in the table of mortality, it is now proposed to see how the exact equivalent can be determined when the payments are made by installments instead of one sum in advance. It is usual, in ordinary whole-life policies, for the companies to charge, and the insured to pay, equal annual premiums, the first in advance, and one at the beginning of each following year, as long as the insured is alive. When the net single premium at any age has been accurately calculated, the question arises, What is the net *annual* premium, under the conditions just named, that will be the precise equivalent of this net *single* premium at the time the policy issued?

When this net *annual* premium is accurately determined, it being the precise money equivalent of the net single premium, and the net single premium being just sufficient, on the data designated, to effect the insurance, it follows that its precise equivalent, paid in equal annual premiums, will also be just sufficient to effect the insurance.

To solve this problem, first find the value, at any named age, of a whole-life series of annual premiums of $1 each, the condition being that the first payment of $1 is to be made at the time the policy is issued, and that $1 is to be paid at the beginning of each following year, as long as the person is alive to make the payment. When this is done, the problem we wish to solve becomes simple, because, after we have found, at any named age, the value in hand of this life series of premiums of $1 each, *this amount will be to the net single premium at that age as* $1 *is to the annual premium required.* We will use the American Experience Table of Mortality and $4\frac{1}{2}$ per cent interest.

The first thing, then, is to find the value at any age—say 50—of a life series of annual premiums of $1 each, the first to be paid in advance, and $1 to be paid at the beginning of each following year, as long as the insured is alive to make the payments.

The first annual payment is to be made in hand, and its value, at the time the policy is issued, is $1. The value in hand of $1, to be paid at the end of one year, interest being $4\frac{1}{2}$ per cent per annum, is 100 divided by $104\frac{1}{2}$; but this second payment is not to be made *certain*, but only on condition that the insured, aged 50, will be alive at age 51. The fraction which, at age 50, represents the chance that the insured will be alive at age 51, is equal to the number living at age 51, divided by the number living at age 50. From the table of mortality, we find the number living at age 51 is 68,824, and the number living at age 50 is 69,804. The fraction in this case is, therefore, $\frac{68824}{69804}$. The value, at age 50, of this second payment of $1 to be made at age 51, in case the insured is alive to make the payment, is equal to $\frac{1}{1.045} \times \frac{68824}{69804}$. In like manner, the value of the third payment, which is to be made at the end of two years, in case the insured is alive at that time to make the payment, is equal to $\frac{1}{1.045} \times \frac{1}{1.045}$, multiplied by the fraction which, at age 50, represents the chance at that time that the insured will be alive at age 52 to make the third payment. This fraction is equal to the number living at 52, divided by the number living at 50, which we see, from the table of mortality, is $\frac{67841}{69804}$; therefore the value in hand, at age 50, of the third payment of $1, to be paid only on condition that the insured is alive at age 52, is expressed by $\frac{1}{1.045} \times \frac{1}{1.045} \times \frac{67841}{69804}$.

In a manner entirely similar, we can calculate at age 50 the value in hand of the fourth and every payment of the whole-life series to the limit of the table. This has been done, and the sum of the respective values in hand, at age 50, of the whole-life series of annual premiums of $1 each, is found to be $13.235802.

Table, illustrating the manner of calculating the value, at age 50, of a Whole-Life Series of Annual Payments of $1 each—the first payment to be made in hand, and one at the beginning of each following year, as long as the person is alive to make the payment. American Experience—four and a half per cent.

Age.	Value in hand, at age 50, of $1, to be paid *certain* at the beginning of each year.		Number living at beginning of each year. *Numerator.*		Number living at age 50. *Denominator.*		Value in hand, at age 50, of $1, to be paid at the beginning of each respective year, provided the person is alive to make the payment.	Age.
50	$1.000000	×	69804	÷	69804	=	$1.000000	50
51	0.956938	×	68842	÷	69804	=	0.943750	51
52	0.915730	×	67841	÷	69804	=	0.889978	52
53	0.876297	×	66797	÷	69804	=	0.838548	53
54	0.838561	×	65706	÷	69804	=	0.789331	54
55	0.802451	×	64563	÷	69804	=	0.742202	55
56	0.767896	×	63364	÷	69804	=	0.697051	56
57	0.734828	×	62104	÷	69804	=	0.653770	57
58	0.703185	×	60779	÷	69804	=	0.612270	58
59	0.672904	×	59385	÷	69804	=	0.572466	59
60	0.643928	×	57917	÷	69804	=	0.534273	60
61	0.616199	×	56371	÷	69804	=	0.497619	61
62	0.589664	×	54743	÷	69804	=	0.462437	62
63	0.564272	×	53030	÷	69804	=	0.428677	63
64	0.539973	×	51230	÷	69804	=	0.396293	64
65	0.516720	×	49341	÷	69804	=	0.365244	65
66	0.494469	×	47361	÷	69804	=	0.335490	66
67	0.473176	×	45291	÷	69804	=	0.307011	67
68	0.452800	×	43133	÷	69804	=	0.279792	68
69	0.433302	×	40890	÷	69804	=	0.253821	69
70	0.414643	×	38569	÷	69804	=	0.229104	70
71	0.396787	×	36178	÷	69804	=	0.205647	71
72	0.379701	×	33730	÷	69804	=	0.183475	72
73	0.363350	×	31243	÷	69804	=	0.162629	73
74	0.347703	×	28738	÷	69804	=	0.143148	74
75	0.332731	×	26237	÷	69804	=	0.125063	75
76	0.318402	×	23761	÷	69804	=	0.108383	76
77	0.304691	×	21330	÷	69804	=	0.093104	77
78	0.291571	×	18961	÷	69804	=	0.079200	78
79	0.279015	×	16670	÷	69804	=	0.066632	79
80	0.267000	×	14474	÷	69804	=	0.055363	80
81	0.255502	×	12383	÷	69804	=	0.045325	81
82	0.244500	×	10419	÷	69804	=	0.036494	82
83	0.233971	×	8603	÷	69804	=	0.028836	83
84	0.223896	×	6955	÷	69804	=	0.022308	84
85	0.214254	×	5485	÷	69804	=	0.016835	85
86	0.205028	×	4193	÷	69804	=	0.012316	86
87	0.196199	×	3079	÷	69804	=	0.008654	87
88	0.187750	×	2146	÷	69804	=	0.005772	88
89	0.179665	×	1402	÷	69804	=	0.003609	89
90	0.171929	×	847	÷	69804	=	0.002086	90
91	0.164525	×	462	÷	69804	=	0.001089	91
92	0.157440	×	216	÷	69804	=	0.000487	92
93	0.150661	×	79	÷	69804	=	0.000171	93
94	0.144173	×	21	÷	69804	=	0.000043	94
95	0.137964	×	3	÷	69804	=	0.000006	95
	Total						$13.235802	

NOTE.—The remarks that follow the table illustrating the calculation of the net single premium that will insure $1 for life, apply to the value, at any age, of a series of annual payments of $1 for a designated term of years.

Having shown, in the foregoing table, how we calculate the value, at age 50, of a whole-life series of annual premiums of $1 each, attention is called to the fact that the calculation of the net value at any other age of a similar series of premiums can be made, in a like manner, from any table of mortality, and at any rate of interest

Value at different Ages of a Life Series of Annual Payments of $1 *each—American Experience Table of Mortality—Various Rates of Interest.*

Age.	Four per cent.	Four and a half per cent.	Five per cent.	Six per cent.	Age.
20	$19.5579	$18.1726	$16.9566	$14.9325	20
21	19.4520	18.0665	16.8862	14.8846	21
22	19.3420	17.9968	16.8126	14.8342	22
23	19.2277	17.9032	16.7355	14.7811	23
24	19.1089	17.8055	16.6548	14.7252	24
25	18.9854	17.7036	16.5703	14.6662	25
26	18.8568	17.5972	16.4818	14.6039	26
27	18.7233	17.4862	16.3891	14.5383	27
28	18.5846	17.3705	16.2921	14.4692	28
29	18.4404	17.2497	16.1905	14.3964	29
30	18.2906	17.1238	16.0842	14.3129	30
31	18.1351	16.9926	15.9731	14.2388	31
32	17.9735	16.8557	15.8567	14.1536	32
33	17.8056	16.7131	15.7349	14.0639	33
34	17.6316	16.5646	15.6077	13.9695	34
35	17 4510	16.4099	15.4748	13.8701	35
36	17.2634	16.2487	15.3357	13.7655	36
37	17.0691	16.0811	15.1906	13.6555	37
38	16.8676	15.9066	15.0390	13.5399	38
39	16.6591	15.7253	14.8809	13.4185	39
40	16.4431	15.5369	14.7160	13.2911	40
41	16.2196	15.3413	14.5443	13.1574	41
42	15.9884	15.1382	14.3653	13.0171	42
43	15.7494	14.9275	14.1789	12.8701	43
44	15.5025	14.7089	13.9849	12.7160	44
45	15.2477	14.4826	13.7834	12.5549	45
46	14.9849	14.2484	13.5741	12.3865	46
47	14.7144	14.0065	13.3573	12.2109	47
48	14.4362	13.7569	13.1327	12.0279	48
49	14.1507	13.4998	12.9008	11.8327	49
50	13.8583	13.2358	12.6617	11.6404	50
51	13.5595	12.9651	12.4159	11.4365	51
52	13.2546	12.6880	12.1636	11.2259	52
53	12.9440	12.4049	11.9050	11.0089	53
54	12.6280	12.1160	11.6404	10.7856	54
55	12.3072	11.8218	11.3702	10.5563	55
56	11.9820	11.5228	11.0947	10.3214	56
57	11.6530	11.2194	10.8145	10.0811	57
58	11.3207	10.9121	10.5299	9.8358	58
59	10.9855	10.6013	10.2413	9.5858	59
60	10.6481	10.2877	9.9493	9.3317	60
61	10.3092	9 9718	9.6544	9.0738	61
62	9.9695	9 6544	9.3574	8.8127	62
63	9.6296	9.3360	9.0587	8.5490	63
64	9.2901	9.0172	8.7590	8.2831	64
65	8.9518	8.6987	8.4588	8.0156	65
66	8.6156	8.3814	8.1592	7.7475	66
67	8.2822	8.0662	7.8607	7.4792	67
68	7.9524	7.7536	7.5642	7.2116	68
69	7.6272	7.4446	7.2705	6.9455	69
70	7.3070	7.1399	6.9802	6.6814	70

Value at different Ages of a Life Series of Annual Payments of $1 *each—Actuaries' Table of Mortality—Various Rates of Interest.*

Age.	Four per cent.	Four and a half per cent.	Five per cent.	Six per cent.	Age.
20	$19.4504	$18.0886	$16.8913	$14.8943	20
21	19.3293	17.9887	16.8084	14.8361	21
22	19.2042	17.8852	16.7222	14.7753	22
23	19.0747	17.7777	16.6325	14.7116	23
24	18.9410	17.6663	16.5391	14.6451	24
25	18.8027	17.5508	16.4422	14.5756	25
26	18.6598	17.4311	16.3416	14.5028	26
27	18.5122	17.3069	16.2364	14.4267	27
28	18.3597	17.1783	16.1274	14.3472	28
29	18.2022	17.0450	16.0141	14.2641	29
30	18.0397	16.9070	15.8963	14.1772	30
31	17.8718	16.7640	15.7739	14.0866	31
32	17.6985	16.6159	15.6469	13.9918	32
33	17.5196	16.4626	15.5149	13.8928	33
34	17.3350	16.3039	15.3778	13.7894	34
35	17.1443	16.1393	15.2354	13.6812	35
36	16.9476	15.9689	15.0880	13.5681	36
37	16.7443	15.7923	14.9333	13.4497	37
38	16.5342	15.6092	14.7730	13.3258	38
39	16.3172	15.4193	14.6064	13.1961	39
40	16.0929	15.2224	14.4329	13.0601	40
41	15.8610	15.0181	14.2523	12.9176	41
42	15.6212	14.8060	14.0641	12.7681	42
43	15.3736	14.5862	13.8684	12.6116	43
44	15.1186	14.3591	13.6656	12.4484	44
45	14.8571	14.1255	13.4562	12.2789	45
46	14.5896	13.8857	13.2408	12.1035	46
47	14.3170	13.6407	13.0200	11.9227	47
48	14.0394	13.3905	12.7939	11.7367	48
49	13.7572	13.1354	12.5627	11.5456	49
50	13.4703	12.8754	12.3265	11.3493	50
51	13.1792	12.6108	12.0855	11.1479	51
52	12.8841	12.3418	11.8398	10.9416	52
53	12.5853	12.0688	11.5898	10.7307	53
54	12.2832	11.7920	11.3357	10.5153	54
55	11.9779	11.5115	11.0775	10.2954	55
56	11.6698	11.2278	10.8157	10.0713	56
57	11.3593	10.9411	10.5505	9.8432	57
58	11.0463	10.6513	10.2818	9.6110	58
59	10.7311	10.3589	10.0100	9.3751	59
60	10.4147	10.0643	9.7355	9.1356	60
61	10.0977	9.7686	9.4592	8.8935	61
62	9.7805	9.4721	9.1815	8.6492	62
63	9.4641	9.1755	8.9033	8.4033	63
64	9.1489	8.8794	8.6249	8.1561	64
65	8.8356	8.5845	8.3520	7.9083	65
66	8.5248	8.2913	8.0700	7.6605	66
67	8.2170	8.0003	7.7946	7.4131	67
68	7.9130	7.7123	7.5215	7.1668	68
69	7.6130	7.4276	7.2509	6.9219	69
70	7.3172	7.1462	6.9831	6.6785	70

To obtain the net Annual Premium.—When the net single premium that will insure $1 for whole life has been calculated, and the value at the designated age of a whole-life series of annual payments of $1 each is known, we obtain the *net* annual premium that will insure $1 for whole life at that age by the following rule: Divide the net single premium at any age by the value at that age of a whole-life series of annual payments of $1 each, and the result is the net annual premium that will insure $1 for whole life at that age. For instance (American Experience, 4½ %), at age 30, the net *single* premium to insure $1 is $0.262609, the value at age 30 of the series of $1 premiums is $17.1238, therefore we have the proportion:

$17.1238 : $0.262609 :: $1 is to the net annual premium that at age 30 will insure $1 for whole life.

NOTE.—It follows, too, from this general reasoning, that if it is desired to convert the net single premium into a limited number of annual premiums, or equal installments, for a specified number of years, we first find the value at the age in question of a series of annual payments of $1 each for the designated term of years, and divide the net single premium by this value.

The following table shows the *net* annual premiums that will insure $1000 at different ages, from 20 to 70 inclusive:

Net Annual Premiums—American Experience—Various Rates of Interest.

Age.	Four per cent.	Four and a half per cent.	Five per cent.	Six per cent.	Age.
20	$12.669	$11.966	$11.355	$10.364	20
21	12.947	12.228	11.601	10.580	21
22	13.239	12.503	11.860	10.808	22
23	13.547	12.794	12.134	11.050	23
24	13.870	13.100	12.424	11.307	24
25	14.211	13.423	12.730	11.580	25
26	14.570	13.765	13.054	11.871	26
27	14.948	14.126	13.397	12.180	27
28	15.346	14.507	13.760	12.508	28
29	15.767	14.910	14.146	12.858	29
30	16.211	15.336	14.554	13.230	30
31	16.680	15.787	14.986	13.627	31
32	17.176	16.265	15.446	14.050	32
33	17.700	16.771	15.934	14.500	33
34	18.255	17.308	16.452	14.975	34
35	18.842	17.877	17.002	15.494	35
36	19.464	18.481	17.588	16.042	36
37	20.124	19.123	18.211	16.627	37
38	20.824	19.805	18.875	17.252	38
39	21.566	20.529	19.581	17.920	39
40	22.354	21.301	20.334	18.635	40
41	23.192	22.121	21.136	19.399	41
42	24.084	22.996	21.993	20.218	42
43	24.988	23.928	22.908	21.096	43
44	26.044	24.924	23.886	22.037	44
45	27.122	25.986	24.932	23.046	45
46	28.273	27.121	26.050	24.129	46
47	29.499	28.333	27.247	25.310	47
48	30.809	29.629	28.527	26.536	48
49	32.207	31.013	29.896	27.873	49
50	33.698	32.490	31.359	29.304	50
51	35.288	34.068	32.923	30.836	51
52	36.984	35.752	34.593	32.476	52
53	38.794	37.551	36.379	34.232	53
54	40.728	39.473	38.289	36.113	54
55	42.792	41.527	40.330	38.126	55
56	44.997	43.722	42.514	40.282	56
57	47.353	46.069	44.849	42.592	57
58	49.872	48.579	47.349	45.065	58
59	52.568	51.266	50.025	47.717	59
60	55.452	54.141	52.891	50.558	60
61	58.539	57.220	55.960	53.602	61
62	61.844	60.518	59.248	56.868	62
63	65.385	64.050	62.772	60.369	63
64	69.180	67.838	66.549	64.124	64
65	73.248	71.898	70.600	68.152	65
66	77.607	76.249	74.942	72.471	66
67	82.279	80.913	79.596	77.100	67
68	87.286	85.911	84.583	82.062	68
69	92.649	91.263	89.924	87.375	69
70	98.393	96.996	95.643	93.065	70

Net Annual Premiums—Actuaries'—Various Rates of Interest.

Age.	Four per cent.	Four and a half per cent.	Five per cent.	Six per cent.	Age.
20	$12.948	$12.221	$11.583	$10.536	20
21	13.273	12.528	11.875	10.799	21
22	13 610	12.850	12.182	11.077	22
23	13.963	13.188	12.502	11.370	23
24	14.334	13.543	12.843	11.678	24
25	14.722	13.915	13.200	12.004	25
26	15.129	14.307	13 576	12.349	26
27	15.557	14.718	13.971	12.712	27
28	16.005	15.151	14.387	13.096	28
29	16.477	15.606	14.826	13.502	29
30	16.972	16.085	15.289	13.932	30
31	17.492	16.589	15.776	14.386	31
32	18.040	17.121	16.291	14.867	32
33	18.616	17.681	16.835	15.376	33
34	19.225	18.273	17.409	15.916	34
35	19.866	18.898	18.018	16.490	35
36	20.544	19.559	18.662	17.099	36
37	21.260	20.260	19.345	17.747	37
38	22.018	21.003	20.072	18.439	38
39	22.823	21.791	20.844	19.176	39
40	23.677	22.630	21.667	19.965	40
41	24.586	23.524	22.545	20.810	41
42	25.554	24.478	23.484	21.716	42
43	26.585	25.490	24.487	22.688	43
44	27.682	26.580	25.558	23.728	44
45	28.845	27.732	26.696	24.837	45
46	30 080	28.954	27.905	26.017	46
47	31.385	30.248	29.186	27.270	47
48	32.767	31.618	30.543	28.597	48
49	34.227	33.068	31.982	30.009	49
50	35.775	34.605	33.507	31.508	50
51	37.415	36.235	35.124	33.099	51
52	39.151	37.963	36.842	34.790	52
53	40.996	39.796	38.664	36.586	53
54	42.950	41.741	40.598	38.495	54
55	45.025	43.807	42.654	40.527	55
56	47.230	46.003	44.839	42.688	56
57	49.571	48.337	47.163	44.989	57
58	52.067	50.823	49.640	47.444	58
59	54.724	53.473	52.281	50.062	59
60	57.556	56.299	55.098	52.858	60
61	60.572	59.307	58 098	55.838	61
62	63.782	62.511	61.294	59.014	62
63	67.199	65.923	64.698	62.397	63
64	70.841	69.558	68.324	66.004	64
65	74.718	73.427	72.186	69.845	65
66	78.846	77.546	76.297	73.936	66
67	83.237	81.933	80.675	78.293	67
68	87.913	86.601	85.333	82.928	68
69	92.892	91.572	90.295	87.866	69
70	98.202	96.872	95.585	93.131	70

CHAPTER II.

COMMUTATION TABLES.

Method by which the Values placed in the Columns headed respectively C. M. R. D. N. and S. are computed.

Nearly one hundred years ago, it was noticed that, by commencing the calculations at the oldest age given in the tables of mortality, and then taking an age one year younger, and so on decreasing the age successively one year to the youngest age, the construction of the commutation-tables would be greatly facilitated, *provided* the numerator and the denominator of the fraction which gives the amount that will, at each age, insure \$1, is multiplied by a quantity obtained by raising the amount that will produce \$1 in one year to a power, the exponent of which is the age for which the calculation is being made. For instance, the greatest age given in the American Experience Table of Mortality is 95. Interest being 4½ per cent per annum, the amount that will at age 95 insure \$1 for one year is equal to $\frac{1}{1.045}$ multiplied by the fraction which at age 95 represents the chance that the insured will die during the first year. By this table, the whole number living at age 95 is 3, and the number of deaths during the year is 3; therefore, we may express the amount that will, at age 95, insure \$1 for life by the fraction $\frac{\frac{1}{1.045}\times 3}{3}$. Multiply the numerator and denominator by $(\frac{1}{1.045})^{95}$, which will not change the value of the fraction, and it becomes $\frac{(\frac{1}{1.045})^{96}\times 3}{(\frac{1}{1.045})^{95}\times 3}$. This is the expression used to designate the amount that will at age 95 insure \$1 for whole life.

The value of $(\frac{1}{1.045})^{96}$ is shown in the appended table opposite 96 years. This value is \$0.014616; multiply this by 3, which is the number of deaths between age 95 and age 96, and we have for the numerator of the above expression \$0.043849. This is called C_{95}, and is placed in the commutation-table in the column headed C, and opposite to age 95. (See pages 180, 182.) It is also placed in that column of the same table which is headed M, and opposite age 95. The denominator of the above expression is obtained by taking the value of $(\frac{1}{1.045})^{95}$, which is \$0.015274, and multiplying it by the number of persons living at age 95, which is 3. The result of this multiplication gives \$0.045822. This is called D_{95}, and is placed in that column of the table which is headed D, and opposite to age 95.

Next, take an age one year younger—namely, age 94. The amount that will, at age 94, insure \$1 for the first year is expressed by $\frac{1}{1.045}$ multiplied by the fraction which at age 94 represents the chance that the insured will die before he is 95. From the table, we find that the number living at age 94 is 21; of this number, the table shows that 18 will die before age 95; therefore, the fraction, which, at age 94, represents the chance that the insured will die during the first year, is $\frac{18}{21}$; from which we see that at age 94 the amount that will insure \$1 for the first year is expressed by $\frac{\frac{1}{1.045}\times 18}{21}$. The amount that will at age 94 insure \$1 for the second year is equal to $(\frac{1}{1.045})^2$ multiplied by the fraction which at age 94 represents the chance that the insured will die between age 95 and age 96. By the table, the number of deaths during this year is 3; the number living at age 94 being 21, it follows that the fraction which, at age 94, represents the chance that the insured will die between age 95 and age 96 is $\frac{3}{21}$. Therefore, the fraction $\frac{(\frac{1}{1.045})^2\times 3}{21}$ expresses the amount that will, if paid at age 94, insure \$1 for the second year. This carries us to the limit of the mortality table. Therefore, $\frac{\frac{1}{1.045}\times 18+(\frac{1}{1.045})^2\times 3}{21}$ expresses the amount that will, if paid in hand at age 94, insure \$1 for whole life. Multiply the numerator and denominator of this fraction by $(\frac{1}{1.045})^{94}$, and it becomes $\frac{(\frac{1}{1.045})^{95}\times 18+(\frac{1}{1.045})^{96}\times 3}{(\frac{1}{1.045})^{94}\times 21}$. The second term of the numerator at age 94 is identical with the numerator previously found at age 95; therefore we have only to calculate the first term of the numerator at age 94 and add it to the numerator at age 95, in order to obtain the whole numerator at age 94.

In order to obtain the first term of the numerator at age 94, we multiply the decimal value already found for $(\frac{1}{1.045})^{95}$ by 18. This is called C_{94}. It is placed in the column headed C and opposite to age 94. Add this to the numerator at age 95, call the result M_{94}, and place it in the table opposite age 94 in the column headed M. The denominator at age 94 is obtained by multiplying the decimal value of $(\frac{1}{1.045})^{94}$ by 21, the number living at age 94. The result is \$0.335188. This is called D_{94}, and it is placed in the column headed D, opposite age 94.

M_{94} divided by D_{94} is the net single premium that will at age 94 insure $1 for life.

The expression which gives the amount that will at age 93 insure $1 for the first year is $\frac{\frac{1}{1.045} \times 58}{79}$. The amount that will, if paid at age 93, insure $1 for the second year is expressed by $\frac{(\frac{1}{1.045})^2 \times 18}{79}$ The amount that will, if paid at age 93, insure $1 for the third year is expressed by $\frac{(\frac{1}{1.045})^3 \times 3}{79}$. We have reached the table limit; hence, adding together the above respective yearly amounts, we find that $\frac{\frac{1}{1.045} \times 58 + (\frac{1}{1.045})^2 \times 18 + (\frac{1}{1.045})^3 \times 3}{79}$ expresses the amount that will, if paid in hand at age 93, insure $1 for whole life. Multiply the numerator and denominator of this fraction by $(\frac{1}{1.045})^{93}$, and it becomes:

$$\frac{(\frac{1}{1.045})^{94} \times 58 + (\frac{1}{1.045})^{95} \times 18 + (\frac{1}{1.045})^{96} \times 3.}{(\frac{1}{1.045})^{93} \times 79}$$

The second and third terms of the numerator of this fraction are together equal to the numerator at age 94; therefore, we have only to calculate the value of the first term of the numerator at age 93, and add it to the numerator at age 94, in order to obtain the numerator at age 93. In making this calculation, take the decimal value of $(\frac{1}{1.045})^{94}$ from the table, it is $0.015961; multiply it by 58; call the result C_{93}, and place it in the column headed C, and opposite age 93. Add C_{93} to C_{94} and C_{95}, and call the sum M_{93}, and place it in the table opposite age 93 in the column headed M. To calculate the value of the denominator at this age, take the decimal value of $(\frac{1}{1.045})^{93}$ from the table and multiply it by 79; call the result D_{93}, and place it in the table opposite age 93 in the column headed D.

In like manner, at each successive younger age, calculate the numerator and denominator, multiply both by $\frac{1}{1.045}$ raised to a power, the exponent of which is the age for which the calculation is being made, and it will be found at each age that it will only be necessary to calculate the first term of the numerator of the general expression, and add to it the numerator of an age one year greater, in order to obtain the numerator at the age in question. The denominator at each age is calculated by raising $\frac{1}{1.045}$ to a power, the exponent of which is the age, and multiplying the result by the number living at that age. The values of M and D at each age having been calculated, to obtain the net single premium at any age, we have only to divide M at that age by D at the same age.

THE N COLUMN.—It will be remembered that, in order to convert the net single premium that will insure \$1 for life into an equivalent annual premium, it was stated to be convenient first to obtain at each age the value in hand of a life series of annual payments of \$1 each, the first being paid in advance, and \$1 paid at the beginning of each following year, as long as the person lives to make the payment. The method of calculating the commutation-tables for determining the value at each age of such a life series of annual payments will now be explained.

We again assume that the table of mortality used is the American Experience, and that the rate of interest is $4\frac{1}{2}$ per cent per annum. The first payment is \$1 in hand. At age 95, there are by the table 3 persons living. The value of the first payment is \$1. This may be expressed by $\frac{3}{3}$. Multiplying both numerator and denominator of this fraction by $(\frac{1}{1.045})^{95}$, the expression becomes $\frac{(\frac{1}{1.045})^{95}\times 3}{(\frac{1}{1.045})^{95}\times 3} = \$1$. There can in this case be no second payment, since, by the table, all living at age 95 die before they reach 96. The denominator of the preceding fraction is identical with the denominator previously called D_{95}. The numerator of the same fraction is also identical with D_{95}. This numerator is called N_{95}, and is placed in the table in the column headed N, and opposite age 95. In this case, no calculations are required to be made, because D_{95} has been previously determined, and we have $\frac{N_{95}}{D_{95}} = \frac{D_{95}}{D_{95}} = \$1$.

To find the value at age 94 *of a life series of annual payments of* \$1 *each.*—The number living at age 94 is 21; the value of the first payment may be represented by $\frac{21}{21}$. The value at age 94 of a payment of \$1 to be made at age 95, in case the person is alive to make the payment, is expressed by $\frac{1}{1.045}$ multiplied by the fraction which at age 94 represents the chance that the person will be alive at age 95. The table shows that, of 21 persons alive at age 94, 3 will be alive at age 95; therefore, the value at age 94 of the payment of \$1 to be made at age 95, is expressed by $\frac{\frac{1}{1.045}\times 3}{21}$. Add this to the value of the first payment as expressed above, and we have the value of the life series at age 94 expressed by $\frac{21+(\frac{1}{1.045})\times 3}{21}$. Multiply both the numerator and denominator of this fraction by $(\frac{1}{1.045})^{94}$, and we have $\frac{(\frac{1}{1.045})^{94}\times 21+(\frac{1}{1.045})^{95}\times 3}{(\frac{1}{1.045})^{94}\times 21}$. This is the value at age 94 of a life series of annual payments of \$1 each. The denominator is identical with the quantity we have previously called D_{94}, and which has been calculated and placed in the D column opposite age 94. Call N_{94} the numerator at age 94. It is seen that the first term of the numerator of the above expression is identical with the denominator. The second term of the numerator is identical with D_{95}; therefore, the expression may be written : $\frac{N_{94}}{D_{94}}=\frac{D_{94}+D_{95}}{D_{94}}$. The value of D_{94} and of D_{95} being already known, we have in this case no other calculation to make than to add together the two terms of the numerator and place the sum opposite age 94 in the column headed N.

In like manner, at age 93, to obtain the value of a life series of annual payments of \$1 each, represent the first payment by the number living at age 93, divided by the number living at the same age; represent the second by $\frac{1}{1.045}$ multiplied by the fraction which at age 93 expresses the chance that the second payment will be made; the third by $(\frac{1}{1.045})^2$ multiplied by the fraction which at age 93 expresses the chance that the third payment will be made. Add the three yearly values together. Their sum is the value in hand at age 93 of a life series of annual payments of \$1. Multiply both numerator and denominator of the fraction which expresses this value by $(\frac{1}{1.045})^{93}$ and we obtain an expression the denominator of which is identical with D_{93} previously calculated. We find, too, that the first term of the numerator is identical with D_{93}, that the second term of the numerator is D_{94}, the third term D_{95}. Therefore, at age 93, calling the numerator N_{93}, we have : $\frac{N_{93}}{D_{93}}=\frac{D_{93}+D_{94}+D_{95}}{D_{93}}$.

In like manner, at age 92, we find $\frac{N_{92}}{D_{92}}=\frac{D_{92}+D_{93}+D_{94}+D_{95}}{D_{92}}$; and so on for each successive younger age to the table limit, where we find: $\frac{N_{10}}{D_{10}}=\frac{D_{10}+D_{11}+D_{12}+***+D_{94}+D_{95}}{D_{10}}$.

THE R COLUMN.—In the table there is a column headed R. This is formed by adding to M at any age the sum of the Ms at all older ages. R at any age divided by D at the same age is the net single premium that will insure \$1 the first year, \$2 the second year, \$3 the third year, and so on, increasing the insurance \$1 each year to the table limit.

THE S COLUMN.—In the table there is a column headed S. This is formed by adding to N at any age the sum of the Ns at all older ages. S, at any age, divided by D at the same age, is equivalent in value to a life series of annual payments of \$1 in hand, \$2 at the beginning of the second year, \$3 at the beginning of the third year, and so on increasing the payments by one dollar each year to the table limit.

NOTE.—It is very important that the foregoing method of constructing the C. M. R. D. N. and S. columns be well understood. No person can comprehend the formulas and rules now generally used in making calculations of life insurance net values without first forming definite ideas in regard to the real meaning of these columns, and the manner of computing the quantities therein represented.

In illustration of the manner of using the Commutation Columns.—Suppose the age of the insured is 30 at the time he pays his net single premium, and that the insurance is not to commence until he is 40, and is then to continue for life: the amount that will at age 30 insure \$1, to be paid to the heirs of the insured in 11 years, provided he dies between age 40 and age 41, is expressed by $(\frac{1}{1.045})^{11}$ multiplied by the fraction which at age 30 represents the chance that the insured will die between age 40 and age 41. The amount that will at age 30 insure \$1 between age 41 and age 42 is expressed by $(\frac{1}{1.045})^{12}$ multiplied by the fraction which at age 30 expresses the chance that the insured will die between age 41 and age 42. In like manner, the amount is expressed for each year to the table limit. If we multiply the numerator and denominator by $(\frac{1}{1.045})^{30}$ the numerator becomes equal to M_{40} and the denominator to D_{30}. Therefore, the amount that will at age 30 purchase an insurance of \$1, beginning at age 40 and continuing from that time to the table limit, is expressed by $\frac{M_{40}}{D_{30}}$.

The net single premium that will at age 30 insure \$1 for whole life is expressed by $\frac{M_{30}}{D_{30}}$. Therefore, the net single premium that will at age 30 insure \$1 for 10 years is $\frac{M_{30}-M_{40}}{D_{30}}$.

If the insurance is effected at age 30, to begin at age 40, and continue until age 70; the net single premium in this case will be expressed by $\frac{M_{40}-M_{70}}{D_{30}}$.

The value at age 30 of a series of annual payments of \$1 each for 20 years, provided the person lives so long, is expressed by $\frac{N_{30}-N_{50}}{D_{30}}$. Because $\frac{N_{30}}{D_{30}}$ is the value at age 30 of the whole-life series, and $\frac{N_{50}}{D_{30}}$ is the value at age 30 of that portion of the series that is beyond the 20 years.

If the annual payments beginning at age 50 are only to continue until age 70, the expression becomes $\frac{N_{50}-N_{70}}{D_{30}}$.

The net annual premium that will at any age insure $1 for a designated term of years is obtained by dividing the difference between M at the beginning and M at the end of the term, by the difference between N at the beginning and N at the end of the term. For instance, to insure at age 30, $1 for twenty years. The amount $\frac{N_{30}-N_{50}}{D_{30}}$ in hand at age 30 is the equivalent of a series of annual payments of $1 for twenty years. The net single premium is, $\frac{M_{30}-M_{50}}{D_{30}}$. Therefore we have the proportion,

$$\frac{N_{30}-N_{50}}{D_{30}} : \frac{M_{30}-M_{50}}{D_{30}} :: \$1 : \frac{M_{30}-M_{50}}{N_{30}-N_{50}}.$$

Endowment combined with Term Insurance.—Suppose the age is 30, and the endowment is payable, if the insured is alive, at age 60: the amount that will at 4½ per cent produce $1 in thirty years is expressed by $(\frac{1}{1.045})^{30}$. The fraction which at age 30 expresses the chance that the insured will be alive at age 60 is the number living as shown by the mortality table at age 60, divided by the number living at age 30. By the American Experience table, this fraction is $\frac{57917}{85441}$. Therefore $\frac{(\frac{1}{1.045})^{30} \times 57917}{85441}$ is the net single premium that will effect the endowment. Multiply both numerator and denominator of this fraction by $(\frac{1}{1.045})^{30}$ and we have, $\frac{(\frac{1}{1.045})^{60} \times 57917}{(\frac{1}{1.045})^{30} \times 85441} = \frac{D_{60}}{D_{30}}$. A similar expression is obtained in case the endowment is effected at any age and is payable in any given number of years.

Therefore to obtain the net single premium at any age for an endowment payable at any greater age, divide D at the age when the endowment is payable by D at the age when the insurance is effected. For instance, at age 20, the net single premium that will, if paid at that time, insure an endowment of $1 at age 45 is expressed by $\frac{D_{45}}{D_{20}}$. The net single premium that will at age 20 insure $1 for 25 years is expressed by $\frac{M_{20}-M_{45}}{D_{20}}$. Add this to the net single premium that will effect the above endowment, and we have $\frac{D_{45}}{D_{20}} + \frac{M_{20}-M_{45}}{D_{20}}$. This is an expression for the amount that will, if paid at age 20, insure $1 to be paid to the heirs of the insured, at the end of any year in which he may die, provided he dies within 25 years, and insure $1 to be paid to himself if alive at the end of the 25 years.

The net annual premium that will effect this endowment and term insurance is obtained from the proportion:

$$\frac{N_{20}-N_{45}}{D_{20}} : \frac{D_{45}+M_{20}-M_{45}}{D_{20}} :: \$1 : \frac{D_{45}+M_{20}-M_{45}}{N_{20}-N_{45}}.$$

The net single premium that will at age 30 insure $1 the first year, $2 the second year, $3 the third year, and so on, increasing the insurance $1 each successive year for life, is expressed by $\frac{R_{30}}{D_{30}}$. The net single premium that will at age 30 insure $1, beginning at age 40, $2 at age 41, $3 at age 42, and so on, increasing the insurance $1 each successive year for life, is expressed by $\frac{R_{40}}{D_{30}}$.

Therefore $\frac{R_{30}}{D_{30}} - \frac{R_{40}}{D_{30}}$ is the amount that will at age 30 insure $1 the first year, $2 the second, $3 the third, and so on until age 40, and continue to insure $10 for life.

The net single premium that will at age 30 insure $10 to begin at age 40, and then continue for life, is expressed by $\frac{10 \times M_{40}}{D_{30}}$. Therefore $\frac{R_{30}}{D_{30}} - \frac{R_{40}}{D_{30}} - \frac{10 \times M_{40}}{D_{30}}$ is the net single premium that will at age 30 insure $1 the first year, $2 the second, $3 the third, and so on, increasing the insurance $1 each year for ten years; the insurance to cease at the end of that time.

For further illustration of the use of the commutation columns, see algebraic discussion and formulas.

CHAPTER III.

TRUST FUND DEPOSIT, OR "RESERVE," AS IT IS USUALLY CALLED.

This fund has by high authority been well styled "the great sheet-anchor of life insurance." By referring to the table of net single premiums (page 25), it will be seen that by the American Experience Table of Mortality, and $4\frac{1}{2}$ per cent interest, the net single premium that will insure $1000 for whole life, at age 20, is $217.448. At age 21, the net single premium is $221.155. The latter sum is the net amount that must be charged by the company in order to insure a person who is 21 years old. This is the sum that the company must hold at the end of the first year, upon the policy issued at 20, after paying the net cost of insurance for the year. The net single premium $217.448 paid at age 20 will, when increased by net interest for one year, furnish the required contribution of this policy to pay death claims, and leave in the hands of the company the net single premium necessary to effect the insurance for whole life at age 21, in case death did not occur before.

At the end of the second policy year, when the policy-holder will be 22 years old, the net single premium that will then insure $1000 for whole life is $225.019, and this is the amount that must then be held by the company to the credit of this policy, if the insured is still alive. In like manner, each successive year, if the policy-holder survives, the company must have, in order to comply with its contract, an amount on hand to the credit of this policy equal to the net single premium that will at the age the policy-holder has attained be sufficient to effect the insurance.

Deposit or "Reserve," in case a Policy is paid for by equal Annual Premiums.—From the table (page 33) it is seen that at age 42 the net annual premium that will insure $1000 for whole life (Actuaries' 4 per cent) is $25.554. This premium is to be paid at the beginning of each year, as long as the person is alive to make the payment. At the end of the first year, or beginning of the second—supposing the insured to be alive—he pays the net annual premium, $25.554, and is insured for another year; but he is now 43 years old, and $26.585 is the net annual premium required to insure $1000 for life at age 43.

Why is it that the man who was insured at age 42, and who has been insured one year, and has paid for that insurance, can, at 43 years of age, be insured by the company for a less premium than is required to insure a man of the same age, 43, but who now takes out a policy for the first time in that company? Taking, for further illustration, a still greater age, we find that at age 65 the net annual premium that will insure $1000 for life is $74.718; and yet the person who took out his policy at age 42, supposing he is still alive, can be safely insured at age 65 by the company for a net annual premium of $25.554.

How is this? Why is it that a man 65 years of age can be insured safely by a company for a net annual premium of $25.554, and another man of the same age, probably in better health, because he has just passed a medical examination, can not be safely insured by the company for a less net annual premium than $74.718?

The net annual premium is calculated to provide against all the probabilities and risks of the insured dying in any year, and of his policy becoming due; and also the risk of his being alive, from year to year, to pay his annual premium. At the end of each year, after the net annual premium has paid its proportion of the losses by death for the year, there must be in the hands of the company, on account of *and to the credit of* each and every outstanding policy, an amount in money or securely invested funds, that will be in present value the equivalent of a life series of annual premiums, each of which is equal to the difference between the net annual premium the insured paid on taking out his policy and the net annual premium he would now have to pay if he were taking out a new policy at his present advanced age. This amount that must be in the hands of the company at the end of each year's business, to the credit of the respective policies, is variously styled, by life insurance writers, "reserve," "reserve for reinsurance," "net premium reserve," "net value," "true value," "self-insurance," etc., etc.

As before stated, the net annual premium to insure $1000 at age 42 is $25.554, and the net annual premium to insure the same amount at age 43 is $26.585. The difference between these two premiums is $1.031. The value at age 43 of a life series of annual payments of $1 is from the table (page 31) found to be $15.374. We can find the value at the same age of a whole-life series of annual payments, each of which is equal to $1.031, by the proportion: $1 : $1.031 : : $15.374 is to the answer. Solving this proportion, we find that the value at age 43, of a life series of annual premiums of $1.031, is equal to $15.851.

If the company has the \$15.851 on hand in deposit, which is the cash equivalent of this difference in the future net annual premiums; this amount of cash in hand, together with the smaller net annual premium due to the age 42, is just the same value as the net annual premium due to age 43. This \$15.851 is the amount that must be held on deposit in trust for the policy of \$1000 taken out at age 42, at the end of the first year of the policy.

The net annual premium at age 44 to insure \$1000 for whole life is found from the same table to be \$27.682. The difference between the net annual premium due to age 44, and that which the person insured at age 42 will pay when he is 44 years of age, is obtained by subtracting \$25.554 from \$27.682; this difference is \$2.128, and there must be in the hands of the company a deposit at the end of the second year of this policy equal to the value at that time of a whole-life series of annual premiums, each of which is equal to \$2.128, which is the difference between the net annual premium due to age 44 and that which the insured will pay. From the table, we find that the value at age 44 of a whole-life series of net annual premiums of \$1 each is \$15.119. We find the value at same age of a whole-life series of annual premiums, each of which is \$2.128, by the proportion: \$1 : \$2.128 : : \$15.119 is to the answer.

Solving this proportion, we find the value sought is \$32.172. This is the fund on deposit, or the "reserve," for this policy at the end of the second year. In a manner entirely similar, we find the amount that must be on deposit at the end of each policy year; and if the company has it on hand, and keeps it securely invested at the net rate of interest, and regularly compounds the interest yearly, this "trust fund deposit," together with the present value of the future net annual premiums, will always keep the policy that is paying the smaller net annual premiums due to the younger age at which the holder entered the company, just on a par with those policies that come in later, or at a more advanced age of entry, and pay the larger annual premium due to this advanced age.

The amount of this deposit may be calculated by a somewhat different process, as follows: At the time the contract is entered into, the value at that time of the whole-life series of net annual premiums to be paid for the policy is exactly equal to the net single premium at that age. Remember that the net single premium is obtained by direct calculation for insurance each separate year, and we convert the net single premium into an equivalent net annual premium. At the end of any policy year, find the net single premium due to that age, then find the value at that age of the series of net annual premiums the insured is to pay; this will be less than the net single premium that at that age will effect the insurance, and this difference is the amount that must be held by the company in deposit to the credit of the policy. For instance, at age 42, the net single premium to insure $1000 for whole-life, actuaries' 4 per cent, is $399.184, and this is the value at that age of the whole-life series of net annual premiums, $25.554, due to the age. At the end of the twentieth policy year, the insured, if alive, will be 62 years old. The net single premium required to insure $1000 for whole-life at 62 is $623.826. Now the value at age 62 of a life series of annual payments of $1 each is $9.781; multiply this by the net annual premium the insured is paying, that is, $25.554, and we have the value at age 62 of the series of net annual premiums the insured is to pay. This amounts to $249.931; but direct calculation shows, as stated above, that the insurance on the assumed table of mortality and rate of interest can not be effected at that age for less than $623.826 net single premium. The difference between this sum and the value of the series at age 62 which the insured is to pay must be held by the company in deposit to the credit of the policy; therefore, subtracting $249.931 from $623.826, we have $373.895, which is the sum that must be in deposit at the end of the twentieth policy year belonging to a policy taken out at age 42 for $1000.

It is necessary to have the value of the net single premium at each age, and all that portion of this value not in the present value of the future net annual premiums must be on hand in deposit. Therefore, a company that charges a less net annual premium than that called for by the table of mortality and rate of interest designated by law, must be required to add to what would be the legal deposit, in case the future net premiums are equal to those required by the law, an amount equal to the value at that time of a series of annual premiums each of which is equal to the difference between the net annual premium called for by the legal data and the net annual premium the company has agreed to receive.

Illustration.—To illustrate the manner in which the "deposit" must accumulate in the earlier years of a life insurance company, in order to enable it to meet its obligations when the death-claims exceed the premiums, let us suppose that a company insures twenty thousand policy-holders for five thousand dollars each, at age thirty. The net annual premium required for each person is $84.85. This, on 20,000 policies, would make the first payment of annual premiums amount to $1,697,000. The net interest is assumed to be four per cent, and, for the first year, it amounts to $67,880. The company has, therefore, at the end of the first year, $1,764,880. By the table of mortality, 168 of the insured will die during the first year; to the heirs of each, the company must pay five thousand dollars. The losses by death are, therefore, $840,000; leaving on hand with the company, after all the death-claims are paid, $924,880; which would be a handsome "*surplus*" at the end of the first year's business, but for the fact that every dollar of this sum belongs to the trust fund deposit, and is an already *accrued liability—a debt.*

At the end of the thirty-fourth year, the deposit for each outstanding policy must be $2464.25. The table of mortality shows that 11,297 of the policy-holders will be living at the end of the thirty-fourth year; the company must, therefore, have on hand a trust fund deposit amounting to $27,838,632.25. We find that 11,742 policy-holders were living at the beginning of the thirty-fourth year, and their net annual premiums amounted, in the aggregate, to $996,308.70. There were 445 deaths during the year, and the aggregate losses by death amounted to $2,225,000. Thus, in this year, the death-claims exceed the annual premiums by more than one and one quarter millions of dollars. But the company has on hand, in deposit, at the end of the year, $27,838,632.25, after having paid the death-claims. The company, however, is not rich, nor more than able to pay its liabilities, because it will surely take the last cent of this amount, with all the future net annual premiums, and interest compounded regularly all the time, to enable it to meet and pay its now rapidly increasing death-claims.

Let us look into the accounts of the company at the end of the fiftieth year. The "deposit" on account of each policy at the end of this year is $3708.20; and there are living 3080 policy-holders. The aggregate "deposit" for the outstanding policies at this time is $11,421,256. There were 461 deaths during the year, and the aggregate of policies that matured during the year amounted to $2,305,000. There were 3541 policy-holders living at the beginning of the year, and the aggregate of the net annual premiums paid by them amounted to $300,453.85. We see from this, that the losses by death during the year exceeded the net annual premiums by more than $2,000,000. The "deposit" is reduced to $11,421,256, which is less than one-half the amount in "deposit" at the end of the thirty-fourth year. But the company has not lost money, it has only been paying its debts. At the end of the thirty-fourth year it had more, but it owed more. It had enough then, and only enough, to pay what it owed; it is in the same condition now.

At the end of the sixty-fifth year, we find the "deposit" that must be in the hands of the company to the credit of each policy is $4560.87 ; and there are twenty of the original policy-holders living. The aggregate "deposit" for these twenty outstanding policies is $91,217.40. The $27,838,632.25 that the company had on hand at the end of the thirty-fourth year is now reduced to less than $100,000. But the company has only been paying its debts to policy-holders—not losing money. In fact, it had none to lose *of its own.*

At the end of the sixty-ninth year, the "deposit" amounts to $4722.84 ; and there is *one* policy-holder living. He pays his regular net annual premium the day he is ninety-nine years old. The premium is $84.85. This, added to the "deposit" on hand at the end of the preceding year, makes $4807.69 of this policy-holder's money in the hands of the company the day the policy-holder is ninety-nine years old. At net interest, which is four per cent, the interest for the year will amount to $192.31 ; and this, added to the amount, $4807.69, on hand at the beginning of the year, makes $5000, with which to pay the policy of the last policy-holder in this company.

We see that the $27,838,632.25, which the company had in its possession at the end of the thirty-fourth year, belonging to policy-holders, has been paid to them. The policies were all paid at maturity ; the company has nothing left. In fact, it never had a cent of its own during the whole time, although we have seen it the custodian, at one time, of nearly twenty-eight millions of dollars of other people's money. It owed every cent, and it paid every cent it owed.

It is a marked peculiarity of life insurance business, as seen in this illustration, that the annual premiums exceed the death-claims for the first thirty or forty years; after which time, the losses by death largely exceed the annual premiums. The trust fund deposit, after a table of mortality and rate of interest have been designated, is a fixed mathematical amount; it increases for each policy at the end of every succeeding year of the existence of the policy.

Deposit at the end of each Year on a Whole-Life Policy for $1000, *taken out at Age* 45—*American Experience—Various Rates of Interest.*

Age.	Four per cent.	Four and a half per cent.	Five per cent.	Six per cent.	Age.
45	$17.24	$16.17	$15.18	$13.42	45
46	34.98	32.87	30.91	27.41	46
47	53.22	50.11	47.21	41.98	47
48	71.95	67 86	64.04	57.25	48
49	91.18	86.09	81.38	72.84	49
50	110.72	104.78	99.21	89.09	50
51	130.72	123.91	117.52	105.86	51
52	151.09	143.47	136.28	123.15	52
53	171.81	163.41	155.48	140.93	53
54	192.85	183.72	175.08	159.19	54
55	214.18	204.37	195.07	177.90	55
56	235.75	225.32	215.40	197.04	56
57	257.55	246.54	236.05	216.58	57
58	279.53	268.00	256.98	236.49	58
59	301.66	289.65	278.17	256.73	59
60	323.88	311.46	299 56	277.27	60
61	346.16	333.38	220.27	298.07	61
62	368.46	355.37	342.78	319.07	62
63	390.72	377.38	364.53	340.25	63
64	412.91	399.37	386.30	361.56	64
65	434.96	421.28	408.04	382.91	65
66	456.82	443.05	429.70	404.28	66
67	478.45	464.63	451.21	425.60	67
68	499.78	485.96	472.52	446.80	68
69	520.78	507.00	493.58	467.82	69
70	541.39	527.69	514.33	488.62	70
71	561.58	548.01	534.74	509.15	71
72	581.39	567.97	554.83	529.43	72
73	600.85	587.62	574.65	549.51	73
74	620.02	607.02	594.25	569.44	74
75	638.95	626.22	613.68	589.27	75
76	657.70	645.26	633.00	609.06	76
77	676.26	664.15	652.20	629.18	77
78	694.62	682.88	671.27	648.50	78
79	712.77	701.43	690.20	668.11	79
80	730.56	719.65	708.82	787.48	80
81	748.03	737.56	727.17	706.63	81
82	765.24	755.25	745.31	725.64	82
83	782.37	772.89	763.44	744.70	83
84	799.49	790.55	781.64	763.91	84
85	816.43	808.07	799.73	783.08	85
86	832.90	825.13	817.37	801.85	86
87	848.53	841.34	834.16	819.78	87
88	863.28	856 67	850.07	836.83	88
89	877.54	871.51	865.52	853.46	89
90	891.55	886.12	880.57	870.02	90
91	904.65	899.80	894.91	885.88	91
92	915.35	910.99	906.58	897.68	92
93	925.41	921.51	917.58	909.62	93
94	934.42	930.95	927 45	920.35	94
95	1000.00	1000.00	1000.00	1000.00	95

Deposit at the end of each Year on a Whole-Life Policy for $1000, *taken out at age* 45—*Actuaries'—Various Rates of Interest.*

Age.	Four per cent.	Four and a half per cent.	Five per cent.	Six per cent.	Age.
45	$18.01	$16.97	$16.01	$14.28	45
46	36.36	34.32	32.42	29.00	46
47	55.04	52.03	49.22	44.15	47
48	74.03	70.09	66.40	59.72	48
49	93.34	88.50	83.96	75.90	49
50	112.94	107.23	101.87	92.11	50
51	132.80	126.27	120.12	108.90	51
52	152.91	145.60	128.70	126.08	52
53	173.24	165.19	157.59	143.62	53
54	193.79	185.05	176.77	161.53	54
55	214.53	205.14	196.23	179.78	55
56	235.43	225.44	215.94	198.36	56
57	256.50	245.95	235.91	217.27	57
58	277.70	266.65	256.11	236.49	58
59	299.01	287.51	276.51	255.99	59
60	320.35	308.44	297.04	275.70	60
61	341.69	329.44	317.67	295.60	61
62	362.99	350.43	338.35	315.63	62
63	384.21	371.39	359.04	335.76	63
64	405.30	392.27	379.56	355.94	64
65	426.23	413.03	400.28	376.12	65
66	446.93	433.63	420.74	396.27	66
67	467.39	454.02	441.04	416.33	67
68	487.58	474.18	461.14	436.28	68
69	507.49	494.10	481.05	456.10	69
70	527.09	513.74	500.72	475.75	70
71	546.45	533.08	520.12	495.21	71
72	565.24	552.09	539.22	514.44	72
73	583.77	570.76	558.02	533.43	73
74	601.90	589.07	576.49	552.14	74
75	619.63	607.01	594.61	570.56	75
76	636.95	624.56	612.37	588 68	76
77	653.85	641.71	631.67	606.46	77
78	670.29	658.42	646.72	623.88	78
79	686.30	674.72	663.29	640.93	79
80	701.89	690.63	679.48	657.65	80
81	717.13	706.19	695.36	674.08	81
82	732.20	721.50	710.99	690.31	82
83	746.85	736.61	726.45	706.41	83
84	761.48	751.63	741.84	722.49	84
85	776 00	766.56	757.15	738.54	85
86	790.42	781.39	772.40	754.58	86
87	804.73	796 16	787.61	770.61	87
88	818.87	810.77	802 67	786.56	88
89	832.72	825.09	817.47	802.26	89
90	846.24	839.12	831.98	817.71	90
91	859.31	852.68	846.03	832.72	91
92	871.68	865.54	859.37	847.00	92
93	883.10	877.42	871.71	860.26	93
94	893.36	888.12	882.84	872.23	94
95	901.61	896.72	891.79	881.88	95
96	907.99	903.37	898.72	889.34	96
97	916.51	912.27	907.99	899.35	97
98	932.69	929.21	925.68	918.56	98
99	1000.00	1000.00	1000.00	1000.00	99

NOTE.—For further illustration of the manner of calculating the deposit, see Algebraic Discussion.

CHAPTER IV.

AMOUNT AT RISK—VALUATION OF POLICIES.

Having obtained the amount that must be in deposit at the end of any year, subtract this from the amount called for by the policy, and we have the amount the company has at risk during that year. The deposit increases from year to year; therefore on any given policy, the amount the company has at risk diminishes each year. During the last year of a policy that continues to the limit of the term of insurance, the amount the company has at risk is zero; because the deposit on hand at the beginning of the year, added to the net annual premium paid at that time, will, when increased by net interest for one year, produce the amount of the policy.

In case of insurance for one year only, no provision is made in the net premium for a deposit at the end of the year. The amount at risk in this case is expressed by the face of the policy. At the younger ages, the net premium that will effect insurance for one year is quite small in comparison with the policy it will pay for. For instance, at age 20, the amount that will, if paid at the beginning of the year, insure \$1, to be paid to the heirs of the insured, at the end of the year, in case he dies during the year (Actuaries' 4 per cent), is equal to $\frac{1}{1 \cdot 04} \times \frac{680}{93268} =$ \$0.0070104. For a policy of \$1000, the amount required is \$7.01. At age 99, the amount requisite to insure \$1 for one year is $\frac{1}{1 \cdot 04} \times \frac{1}{1} = \frac{1}{1 \cdot 04} =$ \$0.961538. Therefore the amount that will at age 99 insure \$1000 for one year is \$961.54. In case the insured pays at the beginning of any year, a net amount greater than that necessary to effect the insurance during the year, the company, after setting aside the amount that will pay for the insurance, will have in its hands a certain portion of the policy-holder's money, and the amount the company actually has at risk during the year is not the full amount called for by the policy; because the company will, in part payment of the policy, in case the insured dies during the year, use the money it holds belonging to the policy-holder. For instance, at age 20, a whole-life policy of \$1000 is paid for by a net single premium, \$251.907 (Actuaries' 4 per cent, see table, page 26). This will effect the insurance during the first year, and leave in the hands of the company at the end of the year, if the insured is living, an amount sufficient at that time, age 21, to pay for insurance for whole life; but we know from direct calculation (see same table) that the net single premium that will, at age 21, insure $1000 for whole life is $256.564. Therefore, when the insured paid $251.907 at age 20, he not only paid for insurance during the first year, but his own money supplied in addition $256.-564 at the end of the year. The amount the company has at risk during the year is $1000 less $256.564 = $743.436. The amount that will, at age 20, insure $1000 for one year is $7.0104 (see table, page 19). The amount required at same age to insure $743.436 for one year is found from the proportion $1000 : $743.436 : : $7.0104 : $5.211. Therefore $5.211 is the amount that will, if paid at the beginning of the year, effect insurance during the year on the $743.-436 that the company has at risk that year. As a test of this, notice that the net single premium paid at age 20, namely, $251.907, will, when increased by interest during the year at 4 per cent, amount to $261.983; but $5.211 of the net premium paid at the beginning of the year was for the purpose of insuring the amount at risk during the year. This, increased by 4 per cent, gives at the end of the year $5.419, to pay net cost of insurance at the end of the year on $743.436, at risk during the year. If we subtract $5.419 from $261.983, the remainder ought to give the net single premium at age 21. We have $261.983 — $5.419 = $256.564. The latter amount is, as previously shown by direct calculation for each separate year, the net single premium for age 21. In like manner, when the deposit for the end of the second year has been calculated, by subtracting this from the amount of the policy, we obtain the amount at risk during the second year. The net single premium that will at age 22 insure $1000 for whole life, as previously obtained by direct calculation for that age, is $261.378 (see table). This is the amount that must be on deposit to the credit of this policy, in case the insured is alive at age 22.

The amount at risk during the second year is, therefore, $1000 — $261.378 = $738.622. We have previously determined by direct calculation (see table, page 19), that at age 21 the amount that will, if paid at that age, insure $1000 for one year is $7.093. Therefore we obtain the amount that will, if paid at age 21, insure the amount the company has at risk the second year by the proportion $1000 : $738.-622 : : $7.093 : $5.239. Therefore, $5.239 is the amount that will, if paid at the beginning of the second year, insure the amount the company has at risk during that year. Increase this by 4 per cent for one year, and we have \$5.449, which will pay at the end of the second year the cost of insurance on the amount at risk during that year. The amount in deposit at the beginning of the second year is \$256.565. This, increased by interest at 4 per cent for one year, gives \$266.827, with which, at the end of the year, to pay cost of insurance on amount at risk during the second year, and leave in the hands of the company, in deposit, an amount that will, at age 22, effect the insurance of the policy for life. Therefore, after cost of insurance the second year is paid, we have \$266.827 — \$5.449 = 261.379 in deposit at the end of the second year. This is the amount that will, at age 22, insure \$1000 for life, as determined by direct calculation, for each separate year to the table limit.

In a manner similar to the above, the account of this policy can be carried year by year to the end of the table, and it will be found that after cost of insurance on the amount at risk each year has been paid, there will be on deposit at age 99 an amount which, at 4 per cent, will produce \$1000 in one year.

We will now assume that a policy for \$1000 is issued at age 42, and paid for by net annual premiums. It has already been shown that the net annual premium (Actuaries' 4 per cent) which will insure this policy is \$25.554 (see table, page 33). When the first premium is paid, it not only effects the insurance during the first year, but it provides a deposit for this policy at the end of the year. The amount that must be in deposit for this policy at age 43 is (see page 44) \$15.851. Therefore the amount the company has at risk during the year is \$1000—\$15.851=\$984.149. By direct calculation, it is found that the amount that will, if paid at age 42, insure \$1000 for one year is \$10.476 (see page 19). We obtain the amount that will, if paid at the same age, insure \$984.149 by the proportion \$1000 : \$984.149 : : \$10.476 : \$10.31. Increase \$10.31 at 4 per cent for one year, and we have \$10.72 at the end of the year to pay cost of insurance on \$984.149, the amount the company had at risk during the year. The net annual premium \$25.554, paid at the beginning of the year, will, when increased by 4 per cent, amount to \$26.57 at the end of the year. Subtract from this the cost of insurance on the amount at risk during the year which, as found above, is \$10.72, and the remainder \$15.85 is equal to the exact amount that by an independent calculation is known to be the deposit that must be in the hands of the company, to the credit of this policy at age 43.

It has been previously seen (page 44) that for the second year of this policy, the amount that must be on deposit at the end of this year is \$32.17236. The amount the company has at risk during the second year is therefore equal to \$1000—\$32.17236=\$967.82764, and this is the amount of insurance the policy-holder gets from the company during the second year. The amount that will, if paid at age 43, insure \$1000 for one year is \$10.818 (see table, page 19). To obtain the amount that will, if paid at the same age, insure the amount at risk during the year, we use the proportion \$1000 : \$967.82764 :: \$10.818 : \$10.47.

Therefore \$10.47 is the amount that will, if paid at age 43, insure the amount the company has at risk during the second year of this policy. Increase this by 4 per cent for one year, and we have \$10.889, which is the amount in the hands of the company at the end of the second year to pay the cost of all the insurance the policy-holder has had from the company during that year. The deposit on hand at the end of the first policy year was \$15.85. The net annual premium paid at the beginning of the second year was \$25.55. Therefore the company had in its possession at the beginning of the second year, \$41.40 of this policy-holder's money to the credit of this policy. This increased by 4 per cent amounts at the end of the year to \$43.06, out of which must be paid \$10.889, the cost of insurance during the year, which leaves on hand \$32.17, the deposit for the end of this year, as shown by previous direct calculation.

We have just seen that \$10.47 will, if paid at age 43, insure the amount at risk on this policy during the year between age 43 and age 44. This amount at that time pays for insurance for one year on \$967.828. The first question is, what is the value of this payment at age 42, when this policy was issued? \$10.47 to be paid certain in one year, interest being at the rate of 4 per cent per annum, is equal to $\frac{1}{1.04} \times \$10.47$; but it is only to be paid if the insured is alive at age 43. From the table of mortality (Actuaries') we find that the fraction which at age 42 represents the chance that the insured will be alive at age 43 is $\frac{76173}{77012}$. Therefore, $\frac{1}{1.04} \times \$10.47 \times \frac{76173}{77012}$ expresses the value at age 42 of the cost of insurance on the amount at risk during the year between age 43 and age 44.

In like manner, at the beginning of each year of the term of the policy, find the amount at risk during that year; find the amount that will, at the beginning of the year, pay, at the end of the year, the cost of insuring the amount at risk that year ; find the amount that will, if paid at age 42, produce at the beginning of the year in question the amount that must then be paid to provide for cost of insurance during that year, and multiply the result by the fraction which at age 42 represents the chance that the insured will be alive at the beginning of the year for which the calculation is made ; add together all these respective yearly amounts, and we have the amount that will, if paid at age 42, effect insurance on the amount the company has at risk on this policy of $1000.

From the foregoing remarks, it is seen that the net premium is composed of two parts, one of which, with net interest thereon, goes to pay each year the cost of insurance on the amount the company has at risk during that year ; the other, with net interest thereon, goes to form the deposit or reserve that must be held at the end of each year to the credit of the policy. After a number of years, it sometimes happens that the whole of the net annual premium, with net interest thereon, is not sufficient to pay cost of insurance on the amount at risk during the year ; but in all such cases, the deposit at the beginning of the year, with net interest thereon, will be sufficient to provide the requisite deposit at the end of the year, and make up whatever deficiency there may be in the net annual premium at net interest, in paying cost of insurance on the amount at risk during the year.

ILLUSTRATIVE TABLE.

Whole-Life Policy for $1000 *issued at Age* 20, *paid for by equal Annual Premiums of* $11.966 *each—American Experience, four and a half per cent.*

Age.	Net value at the beginning of the year.	Net value increased by four and a half per cent during the year.	Amount at risk.	Cost of insurance on amount at risk.	Deposit or reserve at the end of the year.	Age.
20	$11.966	$12.504	$995.264	$7.768	$4.736	20
21	16.702	17.454	990.325	7.779	9.675	21
22	21.641	22.615	985.175	7.790	14.825	22
23	26.791	27.997	979.801	7.798	20.199	23
24	32.164	33.612	974.193	7.804	25.807	24
25	37.773	39.473	968.336	7.809	31.664	25
26	43.630	45.593	962.230	7.823	37.770	26
27	49.736	51.974	955.861	7.835	44.139	27
28	56.105	58.629	949.216	7.845	50.784	28
29	62.750	65.574	942.290	7.864	57.710	29
30	69.676	72.811	935.068	7.879	64.932	30
31	76.898	80.358	927.356	7.894	72.464	31
32	84.430	88.229	919.687	7.916	80.313	32
33	92.279	96.431	911.515	7.946	88.485	33
34	100.451	104.971	903.003	7.974	96.997	34
35	108.963	113.866	894.133	7.999	105.867	35
36	117.833	123.135	884.907	8.042	115.093	36
37	127.059	132.776	875.307	8.083	124.693	37
38	136.659	142.809	865.333	8.142	134.667	38
39	146.633	153.231	854.965	8.196	145.035	39
40	157.001	164.066	844.203	8.269	155.797	40
41	167.763	175.313	833.024	8.337	166.976	41
42	178.942	186.994	821.428	8.422	178.572	42
43	190.538	199.112	809.400	8.512	190.600	43
44	202.566	211.682	796.949	8.631	203.051	44
45	215.017	224.692	784.060	8.752	215.940	45
46	227.906	238.161	770.750	8.911	229.250	46

Age.	Net value at the beginning of the year.	Net value increased by four and a half per cent during the year.	Amount at risk.	Cost of insurance on amount at risk.	Deposit or reserve at the end of the year.	Age.
47	$241.216	$252.071	$757.014	$9.085	$242.986	47
48	254.952	266.425	742.868	9.293	257.132	48
49	269.098	281.207	728.339	9.546	271.661	49
50	283.627	296.390	713.442	9.832	286.558	50
51	298.524	311.957	698.195	10.152	301.805	51
52	313.771	327.891	682.613	10.504	317.387	52
53	329.353	344.173	666.717	10.890	333.283	53
54	345.249	360.785	650.531	11.316	349.469	54
55	361.434	377.698	634.077	11.775	365.923	55
56	377.889	394.894	617.383	12.277	382.617	56
57	394.583	412.339	600.472	12.811	399.528	57
58	411.494	430.011	583.369	13.380	416.631	58
59	428.597	447.884	566.110	13.994	433.890	59
60	445.856	465.918	548.729	14.647	451.271	60
61	463.237	484.083	531.260	15.343	468.740	61
62	480.706	502.337	513.739	16.076	486.261	62
63	498.227	520.647	496.195	16.842	503.805	63
64	515.771	538.980	478.670	17.650	521.330	64
65	533.296	557.294	461.214	18.508	538.786	65
66	550.752	575.536	443.864	19.400	556.136	66
67	568.102	593.666	426.663	20.329	573.337	67
68	585.303	611.641	409.662	21.303	590.338	68
69	602.304	629.407	392.894	22.301	607.106	69
70	619.072	646.930	376.404	23.334	623.596	70
71	635.561	664.161	360.213	24.374	639.787	71
72	651.753	681.082	344.304	25.386	655.696	72
73	667.662	697.706	328.644	26.350	671.356	73
74	683.322	714.071	313.184	27.255	686.816	74
75	698.782	730.237	297.885	28.112	702.115	75
76	714.081	746.215	282.710	28.925	717.290	76
77	729.256	762.072	267.655	29.727	732.345	77
78	744.311	777.805	252.732	30.537	747.268	78
79	759.234	793.400	237.946	31.346	762.054	79
80	774.020	808.851	223.427	32.278	776.573	80
81	788.539	824.023	209.149	33.172	790.851	81
82	802.817	838.944	195.053	33.997	804.947	82
83	816.913	853.674	180.999	34.673	819.001	83
84	830.967	868.361	166.919	35.280	833.081	84
85	845.047	883.074	152.955	36.029	847.045	85
86	859.011	897.666	139.359	37.025	860.641	86
87	872.607	911.874	126.440	38.314	872.560	87
88	885.526	925.374	114.227	39.601	885.773	88
89	897.739	938.137	102.299	40.536	897.601	89
90	909.567	950.497	90.755	41.252	909.245	90
91	921.210	962.665	79.856	42.521	920.144	91
92	932.110	974.055	70.940	44.995	929.060	92
93	941.026	983.372	62.550	45.922	937.450	93
94	949.416	992.139	55.028	47.167	944.972	94
95	956.938	1000.000	00.000	00.000	1000.000	95

Valuation of Policies.—At the time the first premium is paid, which is at the beginning of the first policy year, the net value of the policy is the net annual premium. At the end of the first policy year, the net cost of insurance will have been paid, and there must be left in the hands of the company, in trust for the policy-holder, the requisite "deposit." This deposit (or "*reserve*," as it is often called) is the net value of the policy at the end of the first policy year. At the beginning of the second policy year, the net annual premium is paid, and the net value of the policy is then the "deposit" at the end of the preceding year, plus the net annual premium just paid. The net value of the policy at the end of the second policy year is the deposit (or "*reserve*") for the end of that year, and the net value of the policy at the beginning of the third policy year is equal to the deposit at the end of the second year, plus the net annual premium paid at the beginning of the third year. The rule is general, and applies to every year the policy is in force, because the net annual premium is sufficient, and only sufficient, when added to the "deposit" at the end of the preceding year, to pay the net cost of insurance during the year, and provide the requisite deposit for the end of the year. Of course it is understood that net or table interest is realized for the year.

On the supposition that a policy was taken out on the 1st day of January, 1875, the net value of the policy on that day is equal to the net annual premium just paid. On the 31st December, 1875, the net value is equal to the " deposit" at the end of the first policy year. On the 1st day of January, 1876, the net value of the policy, just after the net annual premium is paid, is equal to the deposit at the end of the preceding year, plus the net annual premium ; and the net value on the 31st of December, 1876, will be equal to the deposit at the end of the second policy year.

Having in this way determined the value of this policy at the beginning and at the end of any policy year, subtract one from the other, and by this means obtain the difference between the net value on the 1st day of January, and the net value on the 31st day of December of that year. Divide this difference by twelve: we will obtain the monthly difference in the net value. Assuming that the net value of a policy is greater at the beginning than it is at the end of the policy year in question; having found the monthly difference as above, we will subtract this monthly difference from the net value at the beginning of the year, in order to find the net value of this policy on the 1st day of February of that policy year. To find the net value of the policy on the 1st day of March, we will subtract the monthly difference from the net value on the 1st day of February; and in like manner we obtain the net value of the policy at the beginning of any month of the policy year, by subtracting from the net value at the beginning of the policy year this monthly difference multiplied by the number of months of the policy year that have expired.

On the 1st day of November, for instance, we obtain the net value by multiplying the monthly difference by ten, and subtracting the result from the net value of the policy on the 1st day of January, which day we have assumed to be, in this case, the first day of the policy year.

To obtain the net value on any day during a month, divide the monthly difference by thirty, in order to obtain the daily difference; and then use the daily difference in a manner entirely similar to that indicated above for finding the value of the policy at the beginning of any month.

Policies are taken out any day of the year, and it is usual in life insurance companies to have the net valuation of all policies computed on some one day every year. The day fixed for these valuations is generally the 31st of December.

The question will then arise every year, What is the net value, on the 31st of December, of each policy in force on that day?

First, determine what policy year the given policy is in at the time. Obtain its net value at the beginning of that policy year, and its net value at the end of that policy year. Take the difference between these two net values: divide this difference by twelve, in order to obtain the monthly difference in the net value; divide the monthly difference by thirty, in order to obtain the daily difference in net value. Then fix the month and day of the calendar year on which the policy was issued. The number of months and days that have, on the 31st of December, elapsed since the beginning of the policy year, will become known, and the net value of the policy on the 31st day of December can be determined by the general method above indicated.

We might make this calculation without reference to monthly differences by dividing the yearly difference by 365, in order to obtain the daily difference, and then multiplying this by the number of days from the beginning of the policy year in question, to the 31st day of December of that year. A table has been constructed showing the decimals of a year from each day to the 31st December inclusive, which will facilitate the calculation. Using this table, we have only to multiply the yearly difference by the decimal of a year opposite the month and day on which the policy was issued. This gives the difference in net value between the beginning of the policy year and the 31st December following.

If the net premium the company has agreed to receive is less than that called for by the designated data, then, since the deposit at the end of any policy year must be such an amount as will, when added to the value at that time of the net premiums still receivable, be equal to the net single premium at that time, it follows that whenever a company makes contracts of life insurance at a rate of net premium less than that called for by the legal standard of safety, it must have at the end of a policy year, in deposit, in addition to the net value above determined, an amount equal to the value at that time of a series of net premiums each of which is equal to the difference between the net premium called for by the standard and the net price the company has agreed to receive.

Owing to some peculiarity in the rate of mortality for the year, and the accumulation of interest arising from the funds on deposit, it happens at times, especially in whole-life policies paid for by equal annual premiums, that the net value of a policy, at the beginning of a year, will, at net interest, produce, at the end of the year, an amount sufficient to pay the cost of insurance during the year, and provide for a "deposit" at the end of the policy year, greater than the net value at the beginning of the year. In this case, the monthly and daily differences must be added to the net value at the beginning of the year, instead of being subtracted from it. This peculiar case does not happen in the earlier years of a policy; it is only after there is marked accumulation in the "deposit" or net value at the end of a year, that the net value at the beginning of a year will, at net interest, produce an amount sufficient to pay the cost of insurance during the year, and leave on hand at the end of the year a "deposit," or net value, greater than that at the beginning of the year.

These "*perturbations*" in the relative net values at the beginning and end of different years are indicated in the formula by unmistakable signs; they in no degree complicate the calculations, but require close observation on the part of computers to prevent mistakes.

The net value, at any time during a policy year, can be obtained with equal certainty by basing the calculations upon the deposit or net value of the policy at the end of the policy year, instead of, as above, upon the net value at the beginning of the policy year.

Having calculated the deposit that must be on hand at the end of the policy year, the value of the policy at the end of the first month of the policy year may be obtained by adding to the deposit that must be on hand at the end of the year eleven twelfths of the cost of insurance during the year. At the end of the second month the net value may be obtained by adding to the deposit that must be on hand at the end of the year ten twelfths of the cost of insurance during the year. At the end of the eleventh month, one twelfth is added. At the end of the twelfth month, or end of the policy year, there is nothing to be added. The net value and the deposit at the end of the year are equal.

What is said above in reference to the particular case in which the deposit or net value at the end of a policy year is greater than the net value at the beginning of the year, applies here; and, therefore, when the case occurs, the eleven twelfths of the difference between the net value at the beginning and that at the end of the year must be subtracted from the net value or deposit at the end of the year, in order to obtain the net value at the end of the first month of the policy year; and in like manner for other months.

It is assumed in both of the methods for calculating the net value of a policy during the policy year, that the variation in value is proportional to the time, and that each month has thirty days.

The net values of many of the different kinds of policies on the 31st of December, in each policy year, have been calculated and arranged in VALUATION TABLES convenient for use. Without the aid of these "Valuation Tables," the work of computing the net value of every policy in all the companies would be an almost impracticable labor. Even with the aid of "Valuation Tables," the work is enormous, as may be readily comprehended from the fact that one single company has more than ninety thousand policies in force.

CHAPTER V.

JOINT LIVES.

NOTE 1. If there be *a* chances of the happening of any event, that must either happen or fail to happen, and *b* chances for its not happening, then will the probability of such event taking place be represented by $\frac{a}{a+b}$. The probability of the event not happening will be expressed by $\frac{b}{a+b}$. The sum of these two fractions representing the probabilities of the happening and the failing is equal to unity, because $\frac{a}{a+b} + \frac{b}{a+b} = \frac{a+b}{a+b} = 1$. From this it follows that, one of the two fractions being given, by subtracting this from unity, we will obtain the other fraction.—(*Doctrine of Chances.*)

NOTE 2. In case we have to determine the fraction which represents the chance that two events will happen, it is necessary first to find the fraction that represents the chance in each separate case, and then multiply one of these fractions by the other. Suppose that there are two boxes, each containing 100 balls, 99 of which are black and one is white; the chance of the white ball being drawn from the first box is one out of 100 and is expressed by the fraction $\frac{1}{100}$. The person who drew the white ball from the first box now draws from the second box; again, his chance of drawing the white ball is only one out of one hundred, expressed by $\frac{1}{100}$. The chance of his getting both white balls is equal to the one hundredth part of $\frac{1}{100}$, or equal to $\frac{1}{100} \times \frac{1}{100} = \frac{1}{10000}$. The same method of reasoning may be applied to the happening of three or any other number of events.—(*Doctrine of Chances.*)

Net Single Premium—Joint Lives.—By the terms of an insurance contract upon two joint lives, the condition usually is that the policy is to be paid to the survivor at the end of any year during which either of the two joint lives may fail. There is marked similarity between the method of calculating the net single premium for insurance on joint lives and that already explained for calculating the net single premium in case one life only is insured.

Two Joint Lives each aged 40.—The fraction which represents the chance that a person aged 40 will live until he is 41 is expressed by 77341 divided by 78106; as shown by the American Experience Table of Mortality. When we add the condition that another person aged 40 will live until he is 41, the fraction which expresses the chance that the two lives will continue in being together during the first year is expressed by $\frac{77341}{78106} \times \frac{77341}{78106}$. Consequently the fraction which represents the chance that these two joint lives will *not* continue in being together through the first year is expressed by $1 - \frac{77341}{78106} \times \frac{77341}{78106}$. The amount that will at $4\frac{1}{2}$ per cent produce $1 certain in one year is expressed by $\frac{1}{1.045}$. Multiply this by $1 - \frac{77341}{78106} \times \frac{77341}{78106}$, and the result will give the amount that will insure these two joint lives for the first year.

The amount that will at age 40 insure these two joint lives during the second year is equal to $(\frac{1}{1.045})^2$, multiplied by the fraction which at age 40 represents the chance that the joint continuance of the two lives will cease during that year. At the beginning of the second year—that is, at age 41—the fraction which expresses at that time the chance that these two lives will continue in being together until age 42 is expressed by $\frac{76567}{77341} \times \frac{76567}{77341}$. Therefore the chance at age 41 that these two lives will not continue in being together until age 42 is expressed by $1 - \frac{76567}{77341} \times \frac{76567}{77341}$. Multiply this by the chance at age 40, that the two lives *will* continue in being together until age 41, and we have :

$$\left(1 - \frac{76567}{77341} \times \frac{76567}{77341}\right) \times \left(\frac{77341}{78106} \times \frac{77341}{78106}\right) = 1 - \frac{76567 \times 76567}{78106 \times 78106}.$$

The last expression gives the chance that the continuance of the two joint lives will be interrupted during the second year. Therefore the amount that will at age 40 insure these two joint lives during the second year is expressed by :

$$\left(\frac{1}{1045}\right)^2 \times \left(1 - \frac{76567 \times 76567}{78106 \times 78106}\right).$$

In like manner, obtain the fraction which at age 40 represents the chance that the continuance of the two joint lives will be interrupted during the third year, by first finding the fraction which at age 42 represents the probability that the two lives will continue in being together until age 43. Subtract this fraction from unity. This gives the probability, at age 42, that the two lives will not continue in being together during the third year. Multiply this by the fraction which at age 40 represents the chance that the two lives will continue in being together until age 42, and we have an expression for the fraction which at age 40 represents the probability that these two insured lives will not continue in being together during the third year. Multiply $(\frac{1}{1.045})^3$ by this fraction, and we have the amount that will at age 40 insure these two joint lives for the third year.

This being done for each year to the table limit, the sum of all these yearly amounts gives the net single premium that will at age 40 insure these two joint lives.

The same principles apply to joint lives of unequal ages, and to any number of joint lives.

The Value of a series of Annual Payments of \$1 *each, on condition that two Joint Lives continue in being together.*—This is calculated as follows : The first payment is made in hand, and it is \$1.

The second is to be made at the beginning of the second year, provided the two joint lives are in being at that time. In case of two joint lives aged 30 and 35 respectively, the fraction which represents the chance, at the time the insurance is effected, that the two joint lives will be in being together at the beginning of the second year, is expressed by $\frac{84721}{85441} \times \frac{81090}{81822}$. Multiply $\frac{1}{1.045}$ by the last expression, and we obtain the value in hand of the second payment of this series. In a similar manner, the value of each payment of the series may be calculated. The sum of the values of all these respective yearly payments will be the value of the whole series.

The net annual premium that will insure $1 on joint lives is obtained by dividing the net single premium that will effect the insurance by the value of a series of annual payments of $1 each as above.

Construction of Commutation Columns—Joint Lives—American Experience, 4½ per cent.—Begin at age 95. First, take the case of two joint lives, and assume that they are of equal age. By the table, all living at age 95 die before age 96; consequently there is no chance, according to this table, that the two joint lives will continue in being together during the year; therefore, the chance that they will not continue in being together during the year is equal to unity minus zero. There being, by the table, none living at age 96, the fraction which at age 95 represents the chance that the insured will be alive at age 96 may be expressed by $\frac{0}{3}$. The net single premium that will at age 95 insure $1, to be paid at the end of the year, provided either of the two joint lives fails during the year, is therefore expressed by $\frac{1}{1.045} \times (1 - \frac{0}{3} \times \frac{0}{3}) = \frac{1}{1.045}$. Assuming that the number of these joint-life insurances is equal to the number living in the table at age 95, which is 3, they will all be insured by an amount expressed by $3 \times \frac{1}{1.045}$, and each set of joint lives will be insured by an amount equal to

$$\frac{3}{3} \times \frac{1}{1045} = \frac{3}{3} \times \frac{3}{3} \times \frac{1}{1.045} = \frac{3 \times 3 \times \frac{1}{1.045}}{3 \times 3}.$$

Multiply the numerator and denominator of this fraction by $(\frac{1}{1.045})^{95}$. This gives $\frac{3 \times 3 \times (\frac{1}{1.045})^{96}}{3 \times 3 \times (\frac{1}{1.045})^{95}}$. Call the numerator of this fraction $C_{95.95}$, and the denominator $D_{95.95}$, and we have the net single premium at age 95 for these two joint lives expressed by $\frac{C_{9595}}{D_{9595}} = \frac{M_{9595}}{D_{9595}}$.

At age 94, the amount that will insure for one year two joint lives of this age is expressed by $\frac{1}{1.045}$ multiplied by the fraction which expresses at age 94 the chance that the two lives will not continue in being together during the year. Therefore we have $\frac{1}{1.045} \times (1 - \frac{3}{21} \times \frac{3}{21})$ = the amount that will at age 94 insure \$1, to be paid at the end of the year in case either of these joint lives fail during the year. The expression may be written:

$$\frac{21 \times \frac{1}{1.045} \times (1 - \frac{3}{21} \times \frac{3}{21})}{21}.$$

Multiply the numerator and denominator by $(\frac{1}{1.045})^{94}$, and it becomes $\frac{21 \times (\frac{1}{1.045})^{95} \times (1 - \frac{3}{21} \times \frac{3}{21})}{21 \times (\frac{1}{1.045})^{94}} = \frac{C_{94 \cdot 94}}{D_{94 \cdot 94}}$

The amount that will at age 94 insure these two joint lives during the second year is obtained by multiplying $(\frac{1}{1.045})^2$ by the fraction which at age 94 expresses the chance that the two joint lives will not continue in being together between age 95 and age 96. The fraction which at age 95 expresses the chance that the two joint lives will not continue in being together until age 96 has just been found to be unity. Multiply this by $\frac{3}{21} \times \frac{3}{21}$, which is the fraction at age 94 that represents the chance that the two lives will continue in being together until age 95, and we have $\frac{3}{21} \times \frac{3}{21}$. This is the expression which at age 94 represents the chance that the joint continuance of the two lives will cease during the year between age 95 and age 96. Therefore $(\frac{1}{1.045})^2 \times \frac{3}{21} \times \frac{3}{21} = \frac{3 \times 3 \times (\frac{1}{1.045})^2}{21 \times 21}$ = the amount that will at age 94 insure these joint lives during the second year. Multiply the numerator and denominator of the fraction by $(\frac{1}{1.045})^{94}$, and we have

$$\frac{3 \times 3 \times (\frac{1}{1.045})^{96}}{21 \times 21 \times (\frac{1}{1.045})^{94}} = \frac{C_{95 \cdot 95}}{D_{94 \cdot 94}}.$$

Therefore $\frac{C_{94 \cdot 94} + C_{95 \cdot 95}}{D_{94 \cdot 94}} = \frac{M_{94 \cdot 94}}{D_{94 \cdot 94}}$ = net single premium that will at at age 94 insure \$1 for whole life on two joint lives, each aged 94.

In a similar manner find the net single premium that will at age 93 insure two joint lives of equal ages. The numerator in this case having been calculated, it will be found that the second term is identical with $C_{94 \cdot 94}$, and the third term with $C_{95 \cdot 95}$. Therefore we have only to compute $C_{93 \cdot 93}$ and $D_{93 \cdot 93}$ in order to obtain the net single premium for these two joint lives at age 93. Continue in this way at each successive younger age to the table limit, and we have the C, M, and D commutation columns for two joint lives of equal ages, from which the R, N, and S columns for joint lives of these ages can be easily made.

When the difference of ages of two joint lives is one year, a set of commutation columns is constructed in a manner similar to the above. Assuming that the older of the two lives has reached the age of 95, the factor $\frac{1}{1.045}$, introduced into the numerator and denominator, is raised to the 95th power; at age 94 to the 94th power, and so on each successive year, until the younger life is aged 10.

When the difference of ages is two years, a set of columns is constructed for this case, and so on increasing the difference of ages one year, until the columns are completed for every combination of two ages up to and including a difference in age of 85 years.

When there is a difference in the ages of the two joint lives, the D column may be constructed by multiplying the D, for single lives, of the older, by the number living at the age of the younger —for instance, the two joint lives having a difference in age of 10 years, commencing the calculation at age 95, $D_{95 \cdot 85}$ will be formed by taking D_{95} for single lives, and multiplying it by the number living at age 85.

When three or more lives are associated in joint insurance, the same general principles apply. The commutation columns for joint lives are too voluminous for general publication.

PART I.—CONTINUED.

ALGEBRAIC DISCUSSION.

CHAPTER VI.

NET PREMIUMS.

THE arithmetical discussion of the method of calculating net values in life insurance was commenced by giving the rule for determining the amount of money that will, if invested at a given rate of interest per annum, compounded annually, produce \$1 in any designated number of years.

As this is a subject of vital importance in these calculations, the algebraic discussion will be preceded by further remarks on compound interest.

We will suppose that the amount to be placed at interest is unity, it may be 1 cent, 1 dollar, or any unit of value. We will assume that it is one dollar. The rate of interest is represented by r for any unit of time, 1 day, 1 month, 1 year, or any *one* defined length of time. Then in the given unit of time the \$1 will produce an amount of interest equal to r; and at the end of the first unit of time there will be on hand, adding interest to principal, an amount equal to \$$1 + r$. This amount is to be placed at interest during the second unit of time.

We have just seen that \$1 will, in a unit of time, at a rate of interest r, produce the amount $1 + r$. Any other sum placed at interest at the same rate and for the same length of time must produce a proportional amount. Hence, we have, \$$1 : 1 + r :: 1 + r$ is to the amount that will be produced by $1 + r$ in one unit of time. Therefore, $1 + r$ multiplied by $1 + r$, or $\overline{1+r}^2$, is the amount that will be produced in a unit of time by an amount $1 + r$ at the rate r. Then, since \$1 will, in the same length of time, and at the same rate of interest, produce $1 + r$, it follows that $\overline{1+r}^2$ is the amount that will be produced by \$1 in two units of time when interest is compounded at the rate r.

At the beginning of the third unit of time, the amount to be placed at a rate of interest r during that time is $\overline{1+r}^2$; from the proportion, $1 : 1 + r :: \overline{1+r}^2$ is to the amount at the end of the third unit of time, it follows that $\overline{1+r}^3$ is the amount that will at the rate r be produced by \$1 in three units of time, at compound interest. In like manner it may be shown that at the end of four units of time the amount produced is expressed by $\overline{1+r}^4$. In short, the rule is general: "First add the rate of interest to unity, and then raise this quantity to a power, the exponent of which is the number of units of time."

In illustration, suppose the unit of value is $1, the rate of interest is 4 per cent per annum, the two added together make $1.04. For the end of the second year it is $\overline{1.04}^2$, for the third $\overline{1.04}^3$, for the end of 1000 years it is $\overline{1.04}^{1000}$, and so on for any named period.

To find what $1 will amount to if placed at compound interest at 4 per cent per annum, for 1000 years, we have by simple arithmetic to multiply 1.04 by itself 999 times. A much shorter and easier process would be to find the logarithm of the number 1.04, multiply this by 1000, and find the number corresponding to the logarithm obtained by this multiplication. The latter computation can be easily made in round numbers in a few minutes' time, and the result shows that $1 placed at compound interest, at the rate of 4 per cent per annum, will, in 1000 years, amount to $107,978,999,539,174,369.

Now, let us suppose the question is, How much money will, if invested at the rate r, produce 1 unit of value in 1 unit of time? We will again assume that the unit of value is $1. We have seen that $1 invested at the rate r will in 1 unit of time produce an amount $1+r$; now if $1+r$ is produced by $1, the following proportion shows that $1 will be produced in the same time at the same rate of interest by an amount equal to $\frac{1}{1+r}$. That is, $1+r : 1 :: 1 : \frac{1}{1+r}$. Now the question is, how much money will it require to produce the amount $\frac{1}{1+r}$ in a unit of time at the rate r? This is easily determined, because if $1 is produced in a unit of time by an amount $\frac{1}{1+r}$, the amount $\frac{1}{1+r}$ will be produced by a proportional sum. From which we have the following : $1 : \frac{1}{1+r} :: \frac{1}{1+r} : (\frac{1}{1+r})^2$. We have before seen that $\frac{1}{1+r}$ will, in a unit of time, at a rate of interest r, produce $1; therefore $(\frac{1}{1+r})^2$ is the amount that will, if invested at compound interest, at the rate r, for two units of time, produce $1.

In like manner, it may be shown that the expression for the amount that will produce $1 in three units of time is $(\frac{1}{1+r})^3$; and the rule is general: *First divide unity by unity plus the rate of interest, and then raise this quantity to a power, the exponent of which is the number of units of time."*

In illustration, suppose that the time is three months, the rate of interest is 1 per cent per month, interest compounded monthly, and the amount to be paid is $1000. In the first place, make the calculation on the supposition that the amount to be paid at the end of three months is $1. The expression then becomes $(\frac{1}{1.01})^3 =$

\$0.97059015. Multiply this by 1000, and we have \$970.59, which is the amount that will produce \$1000 in three months, at compound interest, at the rate of one per cent per month.

In further illustration, suppose the question is, how much money will produce \$1000 in fifty years, if invested at compound interest, at 4 per cent per annum? First, calculate the amount that will produce \$1. The expression in this case becomes $(\frac{1}{1.04})^{50}$. Divide 1 by 1.04, the result is 0.96153846; multiply this by itself forty-nine times, or else find the logarithm corresponding to this number, multiply it by 50, and find from the table the number corresponding to this logarithm. By either process, the result is \$0.14071262. This is the amount that will produce \$1 in fifty years, if invested at 4 per cent per annum, compound interest; multiply it by 1000, and we have \$140.71, which is the amount that will produce \$1000 in fifty years, at 4 per cent compound interest.

In further illustration of the subject of compound interest, suppose we represent by v the amount that will, if invested at a rate of interest r, per annum, produce \$1 in one year. Then r times v divided by 100 will represent the interest on v at the rate r for one year—that is, $\frac{r\ v}{100}$ is the interest. Add this to the principal, which is v, and the two together must, from the condition imposed, be equal to one dollar. Therefore, we have the equation $v+\frac{r\ v}{100}=\$1$. Multiply both members of this equation by 100, in order to clear it of fractions, and we have $100\,v+rv=100$, or $v\,(100+r)=100$; hence $v=\frac{100}{100+r}$.

To find the amount that will produce \$1 in two years, the rate of interest per annum being represented by r, and the interest compounded yearly. Designate this amount by $v.''$

Now, if we multiply v'' by the rate of interest r, and divide the product by 100, we will obtain an expression which represents the interest on v'' at the rate r for the first year. The interest for the first year is therefore represented by $\frac{r\ v''}{100}$. Add this interest to the principal v'' and we have $v''+\frac{r\ v''}{100}$, which is the sum to be placed at interest at the beginning of the second year. This sum $v''+\frac{r\ v''}{100}$, multiplied by r, and the product divided by 100, will give us

$\frac{r}{100}\left(v''+\frac{r\,v''}{100}\right)$, which is the interest during the second year. The original sum v'', with the interest for the first year and the interest for the second year added to it, is equal to one dollar; therefore we have $v''+\frac{r\,v''}{100}+\frac{r}{100}\left(v''+\frac{r\,v''}{100}\right)=\$1$. Multiplying both members of this equation by 10,000, in order to clear it of denominators, we have $10{,}000v'' + 200rv'' + r^2 v'' = 10{,}000$, or $v''\ (10{,}000 + 200r + r^2)=10{,}000$. Hence, $v''=\frac{10{,}000}{10{,}000+200r+r^2}$.

The algebraic expression for v, in terms of r, namely, $v=\frac{100}{100+r}$ will, when multiplied by itself, or raised to the second power, become $v^2=\frac{10{,}000}{10{,}000+200r+r^2}$; and this is the precise expression found above for the value of v''. Therefore, $v''=v^2$, that is to say, the present value of one dollar, payable certain at the end of two years, at any rate of interest r, compounded annually, is equal to the present value of one dollar, payable certain at the end of one year, at the same rate of interest, raised to the second power.

Calling the present value of one dollar, to be paid certain at the end of three years, v''', and placing this at a rate of interest r, we find in a similar manner an algebraic expression for the value of v'''. Having found this value, an inspection of the algebraic expression will show that v''' is equal to v raised to the third power.

In all cases the present value of one dollar (computed at any given rate of interest), to be paid *certain* at the end of one year, will, when raised to a power, the exponent of which is n, be equal to the present value of one dollar, to be paid certain at the end of n years, interest being compounded annually.

NOTATION.—Let $l=$ the number of persons living at any age according to the mortality table used; then $l_{30}=$ number of persons living at age 30; and in general, $l_x=$ number living at any designated age, x.

Let $n=$ the number of years that a policy has been in force. Then $l_{x+n}=$ the number of persons, as shown by the table, living n years after the policy was taken out at age x. Suppose the policy was taken out at age 40 and had been in force 10 years, then l_{x+n} becomes l_{40+10}, or l_{50}.

Let $d=$ number of deaths during any year, and $d_x=$ number of deaths in the year between age x and age $x+1$. If the age is 40, d_x becomes d_{40}, which represents the number of deaths given in the table opposite age 40, which is the number of deaths between age 40 and age 41; d_{x+n} = the number of deaths during the year between age $x+n$ and age $x+n+1$. Suppose the policy was taken at age 30 and had been in force 6 years, then $x=30$, $n=6$, and $d_{x+n}=d_{30+6}=d_{36}$, and is given in the table opposite age 36, and is the number of deaths between age 36 and age 37.

Let v = the value in hand, or amount of money that will at a given rate of interest per annum produce $1 in one year.

Net Single Premium.—The foregoing notation being understood, we are ready to write out the expression for the value of the net single premium that will, at any age, insure $1 to be paid to the heirs of the insured at the end of the year in which he may die.

The amount that will insure $1 the first year is equal to the amount that will produce $1 in one year multiplied by the fraction which represents, at the age the policy is issued, the chance that the insured will die during the first year. v is the amount that will, when increased by interest, produce $1 certain in one year; $\frac{d_x}{l_x}$ is the fraction which at age x represents the chance that the insured will die before he reaches age $x+1$. Therefore the amount that will at age x insure $1 for the first year is expressed by $v \times \frac{d_x}{l_x}$.

The amount that will at compound interest produce $1 in two years is v^2; the fraction which at age x represents the chance that the insured will die during the second year is $\frac{d_{x+1}}{l_x}$;* the amount that will at age x insure $1 for the second year is expressed by $v^2 \times \frac{d_{x+1}}{l_x}$. The amount that will at age x insure $1 for the third year is $v^3 \times \frac{d_{x+2}}{l_x}$. In like manner we obtain the amount that will if paid in hand at age x insure $1 for each separate year to the table limit. Add together all these respective yearly values, call the sum sP_x, which is the symbol we will use to represent the net single premium that will at age x insure $1 for whole life, and we have—

* The fraction which at the beginning of the second year represents the chance that the insured will die during that year is expressed by $\frac{d_{x+1}}{l_{x+1}}$; but in order that there may be at age x any chance that the insured will die *in* the second year, he must be alive at the beginning of that year. The chance at age x of the insured living to age $x+1$ is expressed by $\frac{l_{x+1}}{l_x}$. Therefore $\frac{d_{x+1}}{l_{x+1}} \times \frac{l_{x+1}}{l_x} = \frac{d_{x+1}}{l_x}$ = the fraction which at age x represents the chance that the insured will die between age $x+1$ and age $x+2$.

$$sP_x = v\frac{d_x}{l_x} + v^2\frac{d_{x+1}}{l_x} + v^3\frac{d_{x+2}}{l_x} +, \text{ etc., to the table limit;}$$

$$\text{or, } sP_x = \frac{vd_x + v^2d_{x+1} + v^3d_{x+2} +, \text{ etc., to the table limit.}}{l_x}$$

Multiplying both numerator and denominator of the second member of this equation by v^x, and we have—

$$sP_x = \frac{v^{x+1}d_x + v^{x+2}d_{x+1} + v^{x+3}d_{x+2} +, \text{ etc., to the table limit.}}{v^x l_x}$$

Call the sum of the terms of the numerator of the second member of the equation M_x, and the denominator D_x, and the equation becomes $sP_x = \frac{M_x}{D_x}$. In like manner, $sP_{x+1} = \frac{M_{x+1}}{D_{x+1}}$, $sP_{x+2} = \frac{M_{x+2}}{D_{x+2}}$, and $sP_{x+n} = \frac{M_{x+n}}{D_{x+n}}$.

The numerical values of M and D at each age have been calculated and placed in tables, as previously explained.

The value at age x of the net single premium that will, if paid at age $x+1$, insure \$1 from that age to the table limit is, $v \times \frac{M_{x+1}}{D_{x+1}} = \frac{vM_{x+1}}{v^{x+1}l_{x+1}}$; because $D_{x+1} = v^{x+1}l_{x+1}$. The fraction which at age x represents the chance that the insured will be alive at age $x+1$, is expressed by $\frac{l_{x+1}}{l_x}$; therefore the value in hand at age x of the net single premium that will effect the insurance of \$1 for whole life, commencing at age $x+1$, is expressed by $\frac{vM_{x+1}}{v^{x+1}l_{x+1}} \times \frac{l_{x+1}}{l_x}$; which may be written $\frac{M_{x+1}}{v^x l_x} = \frac{M_{x+1}}{D_x}$. The same reasoning will apply to age $x+2$, age $x+3$, and to any age, $x+n$. Therefore the amount that will if paid at age x insure \$1 at age $x+n$ and continue the insurance from that time for whole life is expressed by $\frac{M_{x+n}}{D_x}$.

Value at age x of a life series of payments of \$1 each, the first being paid in hand and one at the beginning of each year during life.—The first payment is \$1. The amount that will, if paid in hand and increased by interest, produce \$1 in one year is v. The fraction which at age x represents the chance that the person will be alive at age $x+1$ is $\frac{l_{x+1}}{l_x}$; therefore the value at age x of the payment that is to be made at the beginning of the second year is $v\frac{l_{x+1}}{l_x}$. In like manner the value at age x of the payment to be made at the beginning of the third year is $v^2\frac{l_{x+2}}{l_x}$. For the fourth year it is $v^3\frac{l_{x+3}}{l_x}$. And so on to the table limit of life. Add together all these yearly values, call their sum A_x, and we have the equation: $A_x = \$1 + \frac{vl_{x+1}}{l_x} + \frac{v^2 l_{x+2}}{l_x} +$, etc., to table limit. Or,

$$A_x = \frac{l_x + vl_{x+1} + v^2 l_{x+2} +, \text{ etc., to table limit.}}{l_x}$$

Multiplying both numerator and denominator of the second member of this equation by v^x, and we have—

$$A_x = \frac{v^x l_x + v^{x+1} l_{x+1} + v^{x+2} l_{x+2} +, \text{ etc., to table limit.}}{v^x l_x}$$

We have previously represented $v^x l_x$ by D_x; call the sum of the terms of the numerator of the second member of the equation N_x, and we have $A_x = \frac{N_x}{D_x}$.

Net Annual Premium that will at age x insure \$1 *for whole life.*—We have found that the net *single* premium that will at age x insure \$1 for whole life is $\frac{M_x}{D_x}$. The value at the same age of a whole life series of annual payments of \$1 each is $\frac{N_x}{D_x}$. Therefore calling the net *annual* premium that will at age x insure \$1 for whole life aP_x, we have the proportion, $\frac{N_x}{D_x} : \frac{M_x}{D_x} :: \$1 : aP_x$, from which $aP_x = \frac{M_x}{N_x}$.

If the insurance is for n years only, the expression for the net single premium becomes, $\frac{M_x - M_{x+n}}{D_x}$; because $\frac{M_x}{D_x}$ will effect the insurance for whole life; and $\frac{M_{x+n}}{D_x}$ will, if paid in hand at age x, insure \$1 from age $x+n$ to the table limit. Therefore, the difference between the two is the net single premium that will effect the insurance during the first n years. The net annual premium for n years that will effect the insurance of \$1 for this term is expressed by $\frac{M_x - M_{x+n}}{N_x - N_{x+n}}$; because the value at age x of n annual premiums of \$1 each, to be paid if the insured is alive at the time, is expressed by $\frac{N_x - N_{x+n}}{D_x}$; and since we have previously found the net single premium that will at age x insure \$1 for n years is $\frac{M_x - M_{x+n}}{D_x}$, we have:

$$\frac{N_x - N_{x+n}}{D_x} : \frac{M_x - M_{x+n}}{D_x} :: \$1 : \frac{M_x - M_{x+n}}{N_x - N_{x+n}}.$$

The net annual premium for n years that will at age x insure \$1 for whole life is $\frac{M_x}{N_x - N_{x+n}}$; because the net single premium is $\frac{M_x}{D_x}$, and the value at age x of n annual payments of \$1, each, to be paid if the insured is alive, is $\frac{N_x - N_{x+n}}{D_x}$. We therefore have the proportion:

$$\frac{N_x - N_{x+n}}{D_x} : \frac{M_x}{D_x} :: \$1 : \frac{M_x}{N_x - N_{x+n}}.$$

To insure at age x an Endowment of \$1 to be paid to the insured at age $x+n$, in case he is alive at the latter age.—The amount that will if invested at age x produce \$1 in n years is v^n. The fraction that at age x represents the chance that the insured will be alive at age $x+n$ is $\frac{l_{x+n}}{l_x}$; therefore the amount that will at age x insure \$1, to be paid to the insured in case he is alive at age $x+n$, is $\frac{v^n l_{x+n}}{l_x}$. Multitiplying both terms of this fraction by v^x, it becomes $\frac{v^{x+n} l_{x+n}}{v^x l_x}$; but $v^{x+n} l_{x+n} = D_{x+n}$, therefore $\frac{D_{x+n}}{D_x}$ is the amount that will if paid at age x effect the endowment of \$1 at age $x+n$. The net annual premium for n years that will be the equivalent of this net single premium is $\frac{D_{x+n}}{N_x - N_{x+n}}$. This is obtained from the proportion:

$$\frac{N_x - N_{x+n}}{D_x} : \frac{D_{x+n}}{D_x} :: \$1 : \frac{D_{x+n}}{N_x - N_{x+n}}.$$

Term Insurance combined with Endowment at the end of the Insurance.—There being in this case two different contracts, the simpler if not the shorter method will be to find as above the net premium for each, and then add the two premiums together.

The Columns R and S. $\frac{M_x}{D_x}$ will at age x insure \$1 for whole life; $\frac{M_{x+1}}{D_x}$ will at age x insure \$1, commencing at age $x+1$, and then continue the insurance for whole life; and in general $\frac{M_{x+n}}{D_x}$ will at age

x insure \$1, commencing at age $x+n$, and continue the insurance for whole life.

The quantity in the column headed R opposite any age, x, is equal to the sum arising from adding to M at that age all the Ms at older ages. The sum of these Ms divided by D_x gives the net single premium that will at age x insure \$1 the first year, \$2 the second, \$3 the third, and so on, increasing the insurance \$1 each year to the table limit, and is expressed by $\frac{R_x}{D_x}$.

The amount that will, if paid in hand at age x, insure \$1, commencing at age $x+n$, \$2 at age $x+n+1$, \$3 at age $x+n+2$, and so on, increasing the insurance \$1 each year, is expressed by $\frac{R_{x+n}}{D_x}$. Therefore the amount that will at age x insure \$1 the first year, \$2 the second, \$3 the third, and so on for n years, and then continue to insure n times \$1 to the table limit, is expressed by $\frac{R_x}{D_x}-\frac{R_{x+n}}{D_x}$ $=\frac{R_x-R_{x+n}}{D_x}$.

The amount that will at age x insure \$1, commencing at age $x+n$, and then continue the insurance for whole life, has been previously shown to be $\frac{M_{x+n}}{D_x}$; therefore, the amount that will at age x insure n times \$1 at age $x+n$, and continue the insurance for whole life, is expressed by $\frac{n\times M_{x+n}}{D_x}$. From which it is seen that the amount that will, if paid at age x, insure \$1 the first year, \$2 the second, \$3 the third, and so on, increasing the amount insured \$1 each year for n years, and then ceasing to insure, is expressed by $\frac{R_x-R_{x+n}-nM_{x+n}}{D_x}$

The S column of the commutation tables is formed by adding to N at any age all the Ns of greater ages; and as N at any age divided by D at the same age is the amount at that age that is equivalent to a life series of annual payments of \$1 each; S at any age, divided by D at the same age, is the amount at that age that is equivalent to a life series of annual payments of \$1 the first year, \$2 the second, \$3 the third, and so on, increasing the annual payment by \$1 each successive year.

The relation between sPx, Ax, and aPx.—The general expression for the amount that will, if paid at age x, insure \$1 for whole life, is (see page 72) $sPx = \frac{v^{x+1}d_x + v^{x+2}d_{x+1} + v^{x+3}d_{x+2} + \text{etc., to table limit.}}{v^x l_x}$

Noting that $d_x = l_x - l_{x+1}$; $d_{x+1} = l_{x+1} - l_{x+2}$; $d_{x+2} = l_{x+2} - l_{x+3}$, etc., the above expression may be written:

$$sPx = \frac{v^{x+1}(l_x - l_{x+1}) + v^{x+2}(l_{x+1} - l_{x+2}) + v^{x+3}(l_{x+2} - l_{x+3}) + \text{etc.}}{v^x l_x}.$$

By separating the negative from the positive portion of each term, writing v as a common factor of all the positive terms, and placing all the negative terms in parentheses, with minus sign prefixed, we have:

$$sPx = \frac{v(v^x l_x + v^{x+1}l_{x+1} + v^{x+2}l_{x+2} + \text{etc})}{v^x l_x} - \frac{(v^{x+1}l_{x+1} + v^{x+2}l_{x+2} + v^{x+3}l_{x+3} + \text{etc.})}{v^x l_x}.$$

Referring to the general expression for A_x (page 73) it will be seen that the first term of the second member of the foregoing equation may be written vAx, and the second term will be identical with Ax, provided we prefix to it the expression $\frac{v^x l_x}{v^x l_x} = 1$; this term may, therefore, be written, $A_x - 1$. From which we have $sP_x = vA_x - (A_x - 1) = vA_x - A_x + 1 = 1 - A_x + vA_x = 1 - (A_x - vA_x) = 1 - (1 - v)A_x = 1 - (1 - v)\frac{N_x}{D_x}$.

The net annual premium is obtained from the proportion, $A_x : 1 - (1 - v)A_x :: \$1 : aP_x$. From which we have $aP_x = \frac{1}{A_x} - (1 - v) = \frac{D_x}{N_x} - (1 - v)$.

Net Single Return Premium.—To determine the amount that will, if paid in hand, insure $1 for whole life, to be paid at the end of any year in which the insured may die, and at the same time return the premium without interest, designate this net single premium by Z_x. The amount insured for whole life is therefore $\$1 + Z_x$. Since $\frac{M_x}{D_x}$ is the net single premium that will insure $1, the net single premium that will insure $\$1 + Z_x$ is expressed by $(1 + Z_x)\frac{M_x}{D_x}$. Therefore we have $Z_x = \frac{M_x}{D_x} + Z_x\frac{M_x}{D_x}$; or, $Z_x D_x = M_x + Z_x M_x$, or $Z_x(D_x - M_x) = M_x$, or $Z_x = \frac{M_x}{D_x - M_x}$.

Net Annual Return Premium.—In case the premiums on the return plan are paid annually, we will designate the net annual premium by Z'_x. In this case the amount insured the first year is $\$1 + Z'_x$; the second year it is $\$1 + 2Z'_x$; the third, $\$1 + 3Z'_x$, and so on, increasing each year the amount insured by one net annual premium.

The amount in hand that will insure \$1 the first year, \$2 the second, \$3 the third, and so on, is expressed by $\frac{R_x}{D_x}$, therefore the amount that will insure Z'_x the first year, $2Z'_x$ the second, $3Z'_x$ the third, and so on, is expressed by $\frac{Z'_x R_x}{D_x}$. This is the net single premium that will insure the return of the net annual Z'_x premiums. Add to this the net single premium, $\frac{M_x}{D_x}$, that will insure \$1, and we have $\frac{M_x}{D_x} + \frac{Z'_x R_x}{D_x}$, which expresses the net single premium that will insure \$1 and return the net annual premiums. But the value in hand of this series of annual Z'_x premiums is $Z'_x \frac{N_x}{D_x}$, therefore we have the equation: $Z'_x \frac{N_x}{D_x} = \frac{M_x}{D_x} + Z'_x \frac{R_x}{D_x}$, or $Z'_x (N_x - R_x) = M_x$, or $Z'_x = \frac{M_x}{N_x - R_x}$. This is the net annual premium that will insure \$1 and the return of all the net annual premiums at the end of the year in which the insured dies.

Suppose the amount to be returned is the net annual premiums plus m per cent thereof. Designate the net annual premium in this case by Z''_x. The amount insured the first year will be $\$1 + (1+m) Z''_x$, the second $\$1 + 2(1+m) Z''_x$, the third $\$1 + 3(1+m) Z''_x$, and so on. From this we form the equation:

$$Z''_x \times \frac{N_x}{D_x} = \frac{M_x}{D_x} + (1+m) Z''_x \times \frac{R_x}{D_x}, \text{ or } Z''_x = \frac{M_x}{N_x - \overline{1+m}\, R_x}.$$

When Payments of Annual Premiums continue for n years only.—Call the net annual premium in this case Z'''_x. The net single premium that will at age x insure \$1 and return all the Z'''_x net annual premiums that are paid in n years is expressed by $\frac{M_x}{D_x} + Z'''_x \times \frac{R_x - R_{x+n}}{D_x}$. But the annual premium Z'''_x for n years is equivalent to $Z'''_x \times \frac{N_x - N_{x+n}}{D_x}$ paid in hand; therefore we have the equation, $Z'''_x \times \frac{N_x - N_{x+n}}{D_x} = \frac{M_x}{D_x} + Z'''_x \times \frac{R_x - R_{x+n}}{D_x}$. Multiplying by the common denominator, and transposing, we have:

$$Z'''_x \left\{ (N_x - N_{x+n}) - (R_x - R_{x+n}) \right\} = M_x, \text{ from which}$$

$$Z'''_x = \frac{M_x}{(N_x - N_{x+n}) - (R_x - R_{x+n})}$$

To determine the net annual premium for n years that will provide for the return of the premium and m per cent thereof in addition. Call this net premium Z^{iv}_x. The amount insured the first year is $\$1+\overline{1+m}\,Z^{iv}_x$, the second $\$1+2\times\overline{1+m}\,Z^{iv}_x$, the third $\$1+3\times\overline{1+m}\,Z^{iv}_x$, and so on for n years.

In this case we find:

$$Z^{iv}_x=\frac{M_x}{(N_x-N_{x+n})-\overline{1+m}\,(R_x-R_{x+n})}.$$

This is the amount that will, if paid annually for n years, insure \$1 for life, and return all the net premiums, with m per cent thereof in addition.

Decreasing Net Annual Premiums to Insure \$1 *for Life.*—First find the value in hand of a life series of annual premiums, the first of which is \$1, and each succeeding premium is m per cent less than the one that precedes it. The first payment being \$1, its value in hand may be represented by $\frac{l_x}{l_x}$. The second payment is $\$1-\frac{m}{100}=\frac{100-m}{100}$. The amount that will, at a rate of interest represented by r produce \$1 in one year is expressed by v; therefore the amount that will, at the same rate of interest, produce $\frac{100-m}{100}$ of a dollar is expressed by $\frac{100-m}{100}\times v$. But the second payment is only to be made in case the person is alive at the beginning of the second year; therefore the value in hand of the second payment is expressed by $\frac{100-m}{100}\times v\times\frac{l_{x+1}}{l_x}$. The third payment, to be made at the beginning of the third year, in case the person is alive, is m per cent less than the second. Its amount is then expressed by

$$\frac{100-m}{100}-\frac{m}{100}\left(\frac{100-m}{100}\right)=\frac{10000-100m-100m+m^2}{10000}=$$
$$\frac{10000-200m+m^2}{10000}=\left(\frac{100-m}{100}\right)^2.$$

Therefore the value in hand of the third payment of this decreasing series is expressed by $\left(\frac{100-m}{100}\right)^2\times v^2\times\frac{l_{x+2}}{l_x}$. Taking m per cent from $\left(\frac{100-m}{100}\right)^2$, we find the amount of the fourth payment to be

$\left(\frac{100-m}{100}\right)^3$; therefore the value in hand of this payment is $\left(\frac{100-m}{100}\right)^3 \times v^3 \times \frac{l_{x+3}}{l_x}$. In like manner the amount of each succeeding yearly payment is obtained. Designating $\frac{100-m}{100} \times v$ by the symbol v^1, adding together the respective values in hand of the several decreasing annual premiums, and multiplying both numerator and denominator of the fraction by v^1 raised to the x power, we shall have an expression for the value in hand of a life series of decreasing annual premiums, each of which is m per cent less than the next preceding. Representing the numerator by N^1, and the denominator by D^1, we have the equation:

$$\frac{N^1_x}{D^1_x} = \frac{v^{1x} l_x + v^{1x+1} l_{x+1} + v^{1x+2} l_{x+2} + v^{1x+3} l_{x+3}}{v^{1x} l_x} + \text{etc., to table limit.}$$

Before calculating the D^1 and N^1 columns of the commutation table for decreasing premiums, the rate per cent of decrease must be designated. A set of D^1 and N^1 columns will have to be computed for each different rate of decrease. Suppose, for instance, the rate of decrease is ten per cent; the first payment being \$1, the second \$0.90, the third \$0.81, and so on, making each payment ten per cent less than the next preceding; and so for any other designated rate of decrease.

Having determined the rate per cent of decrease and constructed the corresponding D^1 and N^1 columns, represent the value of the first net annual premium of this decreasing series by the symbol p_x. Then since $\frac{N^1_x}{D^1_x}$ represents the value, at age x, of a life series of annual premiums, the first of which is \$1, and each succeeding one a certain per cent less than that which immediately precedes it, the value in hand, at age x, of a similar series of decreasing premiums, the first of which is p_x, is expressed by $p_x \times \frac{N^1_x}{D^1_x}$. But the quantity p_x must be such that the value, at age x, of the life series of decreasing annual premiums will insure \$1 for life. The net single premium that will, at age x, insure \$1 for whole life, as previously shown, is $\frac{M_x}{D_x}$. Therefore we have the equation:

$p_x \times \frac{N^1_x}{D^1_x} = \frac{M_x}{D_x}$, or $p_x = \frac{M_x D^1_x}{D_x N^1_x} = \frac{M_x}{D_x} \times \frac{D^1_x}{N^1_x}$ = the first net annual premium of this decreasing series for whole life.

If the decreasing annual premiums are to be paid for n years only, call the first of this series p^1. Then, since the value in hand of a life series of similar decreasing premiums for n years, the first of which is \$1, is expressed by $\frac{N^1_x - N^1_{x+n}}{D^1_x}$, the value of this series, the first term of which is p^1_x, will be expressed by $p^1_x \times \frac{N^1_x - N^1_{x-n}}{D_x}$. But the value in hand of this series of n annual decreasing premiums must, in order to effect the insurance of \$1, be equal to $\frac{M_x}{D_x}$. Therefore, the equation:

$$p^1_x \times \frac{N^1_x - N^1_{x+n}}{D^1_x} = \frac{M_x}{D_x}, \text{ or, } p^1_x = \frac{M_x D^1_x}{(N^1_x - N^1_{x+n}) D_x} = \frac{M_x}{D_x} \times \frac{D^1_x}{N^1_x - N^1_{x+n}}.$$

JOINT LIVES.

NOTE.—"The probability of the happening of any event is to be understood as the ratio of the chances by which the event may happen, to all the chances by which it may either happen or fail; and it may be expressed by a fraction whose numerator is the number of chances whereby the event may happen, and whose denominator is the number of chances whereby it may either happen or fail. Thus, if there be a chances for the happening of an event, and b chances for it not happening, then will the probability of such an event taking place be represented by $\frac{a}{a+b}$. In like manner, the probability of any event failing (or of not happening) may be expressed by a fraction whose numerator is the number of chances whereby it may fail, and whose denominator is, as before, the whole number of chances whereby it may either happen or fail. Thus, the probability of the above event failing will be truly expressed by $\frac{b}{a+b}$. Since the sum of the two fractions, representing the probabilities of the happening and of the failing of any event, is equal to unity, it follows that, one of them being given, the other may be found by subtraction. Thus, the probability of an event happening being denoted by $\frac{a}{a+b}$, the probability of the same event failing will be truly represented by $1 - \frac{a}{a+b} = \frac{b}{a+b}$, and *vice versa*. The probability of the happening of several events that are independent of each other is equal to the product of the probabilities of the happening of each event considered separately; and the probability of the failing of any number of independent events is equal to the product of the probability of the failing of each event considered separately."—(*Doctrine of Chances.*)

Suppose that the two joint lives are aged respectively x and y. Then the chance, at the time the contract is made, that the person aged x will live till he is aged $x + 1$ is expressed by the fraction $\frac{l_{x+1}}{l_x}$, and the value in hand of \$1, payable at the beginning of the second year on condition that the person is alive at the age $x+1$, will be $v\frac{l_{x+1}}{l_x}$. The chance at the time the contract is made that the person aged y will live to age $y + 1$ is expressed by $\frac{l_{y+1}}{l_y}$. Therefore

$\frac{l_{x+1}}{l_x}\times\frac{l_{y+1}}{l_y}$ is the fraction that expresses the probability, at the time the contract is made, that both the joint lives will be in existence at the beginning of the second year. Consequently $1-\frac{l_{x+1}}{l_x}\times\frac{l_{y+1}}{l_y}$ is the expression which represents, at the time the contract is made, the probability that both of the joint lives will *not* be in existence at the beginning of the second year. In other words, it expresses the chance that either one or the other of the two joint lives may die during the first year. Therefore $v\times\left(1-\frac{l_{x+1}}{l_x}\times\frac{l_{y+1}}{l_y}\right)$ will insure \$1 on these two joint lives the first year. The expression may be written, $v\left(\frac{l_xl_y}{l_xl_y}-\frac{l_{x+1}l_{y+1}}{l_xl_y}\right)=v\left(\frac{l_xl_y-l_{x+1}l_{y+1}}{l_xl_y}\right)$.

The fraction which represents at the beginning of the second year the probability at that time that these two joint lives will continue in being together during that year is expressed by $\frac{l_{x+2}}{l_{x+1}}\times\frac{l_{y+2}}{l_{y+1}}$, and the probability at the beginning of the second year that the two lives will *not* continue in being together during the second year is expressed by $1-\frac{l_{x+2}}{l_{x+1}}\times\frac{l_{y+2}}{l_{y+1}}$.

At the beginning of the first year, there can be *no chance* that the insurance will become due at the end of the second year, unless both of the insured persons live until the beginning of that year; therefore we must in the previous expression impose this additional condition. The expression which represents, at the time the contract is made, the chance that the two lives will continue in being until the beginning of the second year is $\frac{l_{x+1}}{l_x}\times\frac{l_{y+1}}{l_y}$. Therefore $\left(1-\frac{l_{x+2}}{l_{x+1}}\times\frac{l_{y+2}}{l_{y+1}}\right)\times\frac{l_{x+1}}{l_x}\times\frac{l_{y+1}}{l_y}$ expresses the chance at the time the contract is made that either one or the other of the two joint lives will fail during the second year. The above expression may be written $\left(\frac{l_{x+1}l_{y+1}}{l_{x+1}l_{y+1}}-\frac{l_{x+2}l_{y+2}}{l_{x+1}l_{y+1}}\right)\times\frac{l_{x+1}l_{y+1}}{l_xl_y}$. By striking out the factor $l_{x+1}l_{y+1}$, which is common to the numerator and denominator, it becomes $\frac{l_{x+1}l_{y+1}-l_{x+2}l_{y+2}}{l_xl_y}$. Multiply this by v^2, and we have the amount that will, if paid at age x y, insure \$1 on these two joint lives during the second year.

By a process entirely similar, we find for the third year,

$v^3\frac{l_{x+2}l_{y+2} - l_{x+3}l_{y+3}}{l_xl_y}$, and in like manner for each successive year to the limit of the mortality table. Add together all these respective yearly values, and we have the net single premium that will at age $x\ y$ insure these two joint lives for whole life.

Representing this net single premium by sP_{xy}, we have $sP_{xy} =$ $v\frac{(l_xl_y - l_{x+1}l_{y+1})}{l_xl_y} + v^2\frac{(l_{x+1}l_{y+1} - l_{x+2}l_{y+2})}{l_xl_y} + v^3\frac{(l_{x+2}l_{y+2} - l_{x+3}l_{y+3})}{l_xl_y}$ + etc., to the table limit.

By separating the negative from the positive terms and writing v as the common factor of all the positive terms, the equation becomes:

$$sP_{xy} = v\frac{(l_xl_y + vl_{x+1}l_{y+1} + v^2l_{x+2}l_{y+2} + \text{etc.})}{l_xl_y} - \frac{(vl_{x+1}l_{y+1} + v^2l_{x+2}l_{y+2} + v^3l_{x+3}l_{y+3} + \text{etc.})}{l_xl_y}.$$

Multiply both numerator and denominator of these fractions by v^x, and we have:

$$sP_{xy} = v\frac{(v^xl_xl_y + v^{x+1}l_{x+1}l_{y+1} + v^{x+2}l_{x+2}l_{y+2} + \text{etc.})}{v^xl_xl_y} - \frac{(v^{x+1}l_{x+1}l_{y+1} + v^{x+2}l_{x+2}l_{y+2} + v^{x+3}l_{x+3}l_{y+3} + \text{etc.})}{v^xl_xl_y}.$$

Represent the second factor of the first term of the second member of this equation by $\frac{N_{xy}}{D_{xy}}$, and the equation becomes $sP_{xy} = v\frac{N_{xy}}{D_{xy}} - \left(\frac{N_{xy}}{D_{xy}} - 1\right) = vA_{xy} - (A_{xy} - 1)$, or $sP_{xy} = 1 + v\frac{N_{xy}}{D_{xy}} - \frac{N_{xy}}{D_{xy}} = 1 + \frac{N_{xy}}{D_{xy}}(v - 1) = 1 - (1 - v)\frac{N_{xy}}{D_{xy}} = \frac{D_{xy} - (1 - v)N_{xy}}{D_{xy}}$; this is equal to $1 - (1 - v)A_{xy}$.

The net annual premium that will insure \$1 on the two joint lives is obtained by the proportion:
$\frac{N_{xy}}{D_{xy}} : \frac{D_{xy} - (1 - v)N_{xy}}{D_{xy}} :: \$1 : \frac{D_{xy} - (1 - v)N_{xy}}{N_{xy}} = \frac{D_{xy}}{N_{xy}} - (1 - v)$ $= \frac{1}{A_{xy}} - (1 - v)$.

When a third life aged z is associated in joint insurance with the two lives aged x and y, the fraction which expresses the chance that the three lives will continue in being together during the first year of the insurance is $\frac{l_{x+1}l_{y+1}l_{z+1}}{l_xl_yl_z}$. And the chance at the time the insurance is effected that the three lives will *not* continue in being together during the first year is $1 - \frac{l_{x+1}l_{y+1}l_{z+1}}{l_x l_y l_z}$. The amount that will if paid at the time the policy is issued insure these three joint lives for one year is $v\left(1 - \frac{l_{x+1}l_{y+1}l_{z+1}}{l_x l_y l_z}\right)$. The principles already explained apply to any number of joint lives.

The formulas used in calculating net values in the insurance of joint lives are similar to those for single lives, using, however, joint-life commutation columns in place of corresponding columns for single lives.

CHAPTER VII.

THE DEPOSIT, USUALLY CALLED RESERVE.

Full-paid Insurance.—In case a policy has been fully paid for, the deposit that must be held by the insurer to the credit of the policy is the net amount in hand that will at that time effect the insurance for the unexpired term of the policy; this amount is computed on the basis of a designated table of mortality and rate of interest, both of which are, in most States, specified by law, and form the standard of legal net values in life insurance. The net single premium at age x, that will insure $1 for whole life, the value of which is expressed by $\frac{M_x}{D_x}$, having been paid at that age, the law requires that the insurer, in whose hands these trust funds have been placed, shall have in possession to the credit of the insured, at the time the policy-holder has reached the age $x+n$, an amount equal to $\frac{M_{x+n}}{D_{x+n}}$; because this is the net single premium that will at age $x+n$ effect the insurance on the designated legal data.

In general, whatever may be the kind of policy, an original net single premium paid at age x is the amount that will, on the designated data, pay for insurance each successive year, and leave in the hands of the company, at the end of each year, an amount sufficient to effect at that time all the insurance still called for by the terms of the contract.

Whole-Life Insurance, by Net Annual Premiums.—In case a whole-life policy is paid for by net annual premiums, the yearly payments being equal to each other; we have previously seen that the amount of the annual premium is determined by the condition imposed that the value in hand of the life series of annual premiums shall be equal to the net single premium. The latter at age x is equal to $\frac{M_x}{D_x}$. At the same age the equivalent net annual premium is $\frac{M_x}{N_x}$. The value in hand at age x of a life series of annual payments of $1 each is expressed by $\frac{N_x}{D_x}$; therefore the value at the same age of a life series of annual payments each equal to $\frac{M_x}{N_x}$ is expressed by $\frac{M_x}{N_x} \times \frac{N_x}{D_x} = \frac{M_x}{D_x}$; which satisfies the conditions imposed—namely, that the value in hand at age x of the life series of net annual premiums shall be equal to the net single premium that will on the designated data effect the insurance at age x.

At age $x+n$, the net single premium that will insure $1 for whole life is $\frac{M_{x+n}}{D_{x+n}}$. The net annual premium that will at age $x+n$ effect the insurance is $\frac{M_{x+n}}{N_{x+n}}$. But at age $x+n$ the insured does not pay the net annual premium $\frac{M_{x+n}}{N_{x+n}}$ due to this age, but has only to pay the net annual premium $\frac{M_x}{N_x}$ due to the age x, which is less than that due to age $x+n$.

The difference in value at age $x+n$ between a life series of annual payments each equal to $\frac{M_{x+n}}{D_{x+n}}$ and a similar series each equal to $\frac{M_x}{D_x}$ is by law required to be held by the insurer to the credit of the policy at age $x+n$. This amount may be calculated either by subtracting from the net single premium at age $x+n$ the value in hand at that age of a life series of net annual premiums each equal to $\frac{M_x}{N_x}$, which gives $\frac{M_{x+n}}{D_{x+n}} - \frac{M_x}{N_x} \times \frac{N_{x+n}}{D_{x+n}}$; or by subtracting the net annual premium $\frac{M_x}{N_x}$ from the net annual premium $\frac{M_{x+n}}{N_{x+n}}$, and then finding the value at age $x+n$ of a life series of annual premiums each equal to $\frac{M_{x+n}}{N_{x+n}} - \frac{M_x}{N_x}$, which gives $\left(\frac{M_{x+n}}{N_{x+n}} - \frac{M_x}{N_x}\right) \times \frac{N_{x+n}}{D_{x+n}}$, and may be written $\frac{M_{x+n}}{N_{x+n}} \times \frac{N_{x+n}}{D_{x+n}} - \frac{M_x}{N_x} \times \frac{N_{x+n}}{D_{x+n}} = \frac{M_{x+n}}{D_{x+n}} - \frac{M_x}{N_x} \times \frac{N_{x+n}}{D_{x+n}}$.

In still further illustration of the method of computing the amount that must be held in deposit at the end of any year for a whole-life policy of $1 paid for by equal net annual premiums; take the expressions previously obtained for the net single premium in terms of A_x and of N_x and D_x, namely, $sP_x = 1-(1-v)\ A_x = 1-(1-v)\ \frac{N_x}{D_x}$; and that for the net annual premium, namely, $aP_x = \frac{1}{A_x} - (1-v) = \frac{D_x}{N_x} - (1-v)$. At age $x+n$ these formulas become

$sP_{x+n} = 1-(1-v)\,A_{x+n} = 1-(1-v)\frac{N_{x+n}}{D_{x+n}}$, and $aP_{x+n} = \frac{1}{A_{x+n}} - (1-v) = \frac{D_{x+n}}{N_{x+n}} - (1-v)$.

The difference between the net annual premium at age x and that at age $x+n$ is $aP_{x+n} - aP_x$. The value at age $x+n$ of a series of annual premiums, each equal to this difference, is obtained from the proportion, \$1 : $(aP_{x+n} - aP_x)$: : A_{x+n} : $A_{x+n}\,(aP_{x+n} - aP_x)$.

The fourth term of this proportion gives the deposit or "reserve" for this policy at age $x+n$.

Another expression for the deposit is obtained by taking the net single premium, at age $x+n$, and subtracting from it the value at that age of the future life series of aP_x annual premiums. This is the amount that must be on hand in deposit, to cause the future aP_x annual premiums and the deposit to be equivalent to the future aP_{x+n} annual premiums. From this we have the equation, $sP_{x+n} - (aP_x \times A_{x+n})$ = the *deposit* at the end of n years from the date of the policy. Substituting for sP_{x+n} its value, $1-(1-v)\,A_{x+n}$, and for aP_x its value, $\frac{1}{A_x}-(1-v)$, and we have $1-(1-v)\,A_{x+n} - \left[\frac{1}{A_x}-(1-v)\right]A_{x+n}$ = the deposit at the end of n years. And as the two expressions $(1-v)\,A_{x+n}$ have different signs, they cancel each other, and we have $1-\frac{A_{x+n}}{A_x}$ = "deposit" at the end of n years.

Joint Lives.—In case the N and D columns for joint lives are constructed and the M column is not, the deposit is calculated by the formulas involving the terms N_x and D_x, or A_x. For two joint lives paid for by net annual premiums, the formula is $1-\frac{A_{x+n.y+n}}{A_{x.y.}}$. A similar formula is used when there are more than two joint lives.

Decreasing Premiums.—The first net annual premium of the decreasing series as previously shown is expressed by $\frac{M_x}{D_x} \times \frac{D'_x}{N'_x}$. The second premium is m per cent less than the first. The value of a series of decreasing annual premiums, the first of which is \$1, and each premium thereafter is m per cent less than that immediately preceding, is expressed by A'_x. The value at age $x+1$ of a series of regularly decreasing net annual premiums, the first of which is $p-\frac{mp}{100}$, is expressed by $A'_{x+1}\times(p-\frac{mp}{100})$. Therefore the deposit required at the end of the first year is $\frac{M_{x+1}}{D_{x+1}} - A'_{x+1}\,(p-\frac{mp}{100})$. The premium at age $x+2$ is $(p-\frac{mp}{100})^2$. The deposit at the end of the second year is therefore $\frac{M_{x+2}}{D_{x+2}} - A'_{x+2}\,(p-\frac{mp}{100})^2$. At age $x+n$ the expression for the deposit becomes $\frac{M_{x+n}}{D_{x+n}} - A'_{x+n}\,(p-\frac{mp}{100})^n$.

NOTE.—The quantity represented by A′ in the above expression must not be based on a rate of interest greater than that designated as the basis of valuation.

Annual Payments for a Years.—In case a whole-life policy for \$1 is to be paid for by equal annual premiums in a years, each annual premium is expressed by $\frac{M_x}{N_x - N_{x+a}}$. The deposit at the end of n years, but before a years have elapsed, is, $\frac{M_{x+n}}{D_{x+n}} - \frac{M_x}{N_x - N_{x+a}} \times \frac{N_{x+n} - N_{x+a}}{D_{x+n}}$. After a years have elapsed, the policy is full paid, and the deposit at the end of any year must be equal to the net single premium that will at that age effect the insurance.

NOTE.—The general reader not specially interested in return premium policies is advised to pass at once to page 93.

Return Premium.—The net single premium that will, at age x, insure \$1 for whole life, and return this net single premium plus m per cent thereof, is $\frac{M_x}{D_x-(1+m)\,M_x}$. Assuming that the premium actually paid, and which is to be returned, is m per cent greater than this net single premium, the amount insured will then be $\$1 + \frac{(1+m)M_x}{D^x-(1+m)M_x}$. The net single premium that will, at age $x+n$, insure \$1 for whole life, is $\frac{M_{x+n}}{D_{x+n}}$, and the net single premium that will, at age $x+n$, insure $\frac{(1+m)M_x}{D_x-(1+m)\,M_x}$ is $\frac{M_{x+n}}{D_{x+n}} \times \frac{(1+m)M_x}{D_x-(1+m)\,M_x}$. Therefore the reserve is in this case expressed by $\frac{M_{x+n}}{D_{x+n}} + \frac{M_{x+n}}{D_{x+n}} \times \frac{(1+m)M_x}{D_x-(1+m)\,M_x} = \frac{M_{x+n}}{D_{x+n}} \times (1 + \frac{(1+m)M_x}{D_x-(1+m)\,M_x}) = \frac{M_{x+n}}{D_{x+n}} \times \left(\frac{D_x-(1+m)M_x+(1+m)M_x}{D_x-(1+m)M_x}\right) = \frac{M_{x+n}D_x}{D_{x+n}(D_x-(1+m)M_x)} =$ deposit for this policy n years after issue.

The net annual premium that will insure \$1 for whole life, and return all the net annual premiums paid plus m per cent thereof, is expressed by $\frac{M_x}{N_x-(1+m)R_x}$. Assuming that the annual premiums actually paid are each m per cent greater than this net, it will then become $\frac{(1+m)M_x}{N_x-(1+m)R_x}$. The annual premiums paid in n years amount to $n\times\frac{(1+m)M_x}{N_x-(1+m)R_x}$. The net single premium that will, at age $x+n$, insure this amount for whole life, is $\frac{M_{x+n}}{D_{x+n}}\times n\times\frac{(1+m)M_x}{N_x-(1+m)R_x}$.

The net single premium that will, at age $x+n$, insure \$1 the first year, \$2 the second, \$3 the third, and so on to the table limit, is $\frac{R_{x+n}}{D_{x+n}}$; therefore the net single premium that will, at age $x+n$, insure the return of the annual premiums yet to be paid, is $\frac{R_{x+n}}{D_{x+n}}\times\frac{(1+m)M_x}{N_x-(1+m)R_x}$.

The value in hand at age $x+n$ of the net annual premiums yet to be paid is $\frac{N_{x+n}}{D_{x+n}}\times\frac{M_x}{N_x-(1+m)R_x}$.

Therefore we have the deposit at the end of n years expressed by:

$$\frac{M_{x+n}}{D_{x+n}}+\frac{M_{x+n}}{D_{x+n}}\times n\times\frac{(1+m)M_x}{N_x-(1+m)R_x}+\frac{R_{x+n}}{D_{x+n}}\times\frac{(1+m)M_x}{N_x-(1+m)R_x}-\frac{N_{x+n}}{D_{x+n}}\times\frac{M_x}{N_x-(1+m)R_x}.$$

Noticing that $\frac{M_{x+n}}{D_{x+n}}\times n\times\frac{(1+m)M_x}{N_x-(1+m)R_x}=\frac{M_x}{N_x-(1+m)R_x}\times n\times\frac{(1+m)M_{x+n}}{D_{x+n}}$,

and that $\frac{R_{x+n}}{D_{x+n}}\times\frac{(1+m)M_x}{N_x-(1\ \ m)R_x}=\frac{M_x}{N_x-(1+m)R_x}\times\frac{(1+m)R_{x+n}}{D_{x+n}}$

we have $\frac{M_{x+n}}{D_{x+n}}-\frac{M_x}{N_x-(1+m)R_x}\left\{\frac{N_{x+n}-(1+m)(R_{x+n}+n\times M_{x+n})}{D_{x+n}}\right\}=$ reserve for this policy n years after issue.

The net single premium that will, at age x, insure \$1, to be paid at age $x+z$, in case the insured is alive, and return this net premium plus m per cent thereof, if the insured dies before age $x+z$, is expressed by $\frac{D_{x+z}}{D_x-(1+m)(M_x-M_{x+z})}$. In case the insured pays m per cent in addition to this net single premium, the premium actually paid, and which has to be returned, is $\frac{(1+m)D_{x+z}}{D_x-(1+m)(M_x-M_{x+z})}$.

At age $x+n$ the net single premium that will insure \$1 until age $x+z$ is expressed by $\frac{M_{x+n}-M_{x+z}}{D_{x+n}}$; therefore $\frac{M_{x+n}-M_{x+z}}{D_{x+n}} \times$

$$\frac{(1+m)D_{x+z}}{D_x-(1+m)(M_x-M_{x+z})} = \frac{D_{x+z}}{D_{x+n}} \times \frac{(1+m)(M_{x+n}-M_{x+z})}{D_x-(1+m)(M_x-M_{x+z})} = \text{the net}$$

single premium that will, at age $x+n$, insure $\frac{(1+m)D_{x+z}}{D_x-(1\times m)(M_x-M_{x+z})}$.

The net single premium that will, at age $x+n$, insure \$1, to be paid to the insured, in case he is alive at age $x+z$, is $\frac{D_{x+z}}{D_{x+n}}$. From the above, we have

$$\frac{D_{x+z}}{D_{x+n}} + \frac{D_{x+z}}{D_{x+n}} \left\{ \frac{(1+m)(M_{x+n}-M_{x+z})}{D_x-(1+m)(M_x-M_{x+z})} \right\} =$$

$$\frac{D_{x+z}}{D_{x+n}} \left\{ 1 + \frac{(1+m)(M_{x+n}-M_{x+z})}{D_x-(1+m)(M_x-M_{x+z})} \right\} = \frac{D_{x+z}}{D_{x+n}} \times$$

$$\left\{ \frac{D_x-(1+m)(M_x-M_{x+z})+(1+m)(M_{x+n}-M_{x+z})}{D_x-(1+m)(M_x-M_{x+z})} \right\} =$$

$$\frac{D_{x+z}}{D_x-(1+m)(M_x-M_{x+z})} \times \frac{D_x-(1+m)(M_x-M_{x+n})}{D_{x+n}} = \text{the deposit}$$

for this policy n years after issue.

To obtain the net annual premium that will at age x insure \$1, to be paid at age $x+z$ in case the insured is alive, and if he dies before age $x+z$, the net annual premiums to be returned; call this net annual premium W. Then since at age x the net single premium that will insure \$1 the first year, \$2 the second, \$3 the third, and so on to the table limit, is expressed by $\frac{R_x}{D_x}$, the net single premium that will at age x insure W the first year, 2W the second year, 3W the third year, and so on to table limit, is expressed by $\frac{R_x}{D_x}\times W$.

The net single premium that will at age x insure W at age $x+z$, 2W at age $x+z+1$, 3W at age $x+z+2$, and so on to the table limit, is expressed by $\frac{R_{x+z}}{D_x}\times W$.

The net single premium that will at age x insure W the first year, 2W the second, 3W the third, and so on, increasing by W each year for z years, and then insure $z \times W$ for whole life, is expressed by $\frac{R_x - R_{x+z}}{D_x} \times W$. But the insurance of $z \times W$ from age $x+z$ to the table limit is not included in the policy now under consideration, and it must therefore be deducted. The net single premium that will at age x insure \$1 for life, to commence, however, from age $x+z$, is expressed by $\frac{M_{x+z}}{D_x}$. Therefore $\frac{M_{x+z}}{D_x} \times z \times W$ is the net single premium that will at age x insure the amount $z \times W$ from age $x+z$ to table limit. Hence, the net single premium that will at age x insure W the first year, 2W the second, 3W the third, and so on for z years, at which time this insurance ceases, is expressed by,

$$\frac{R_x - R_{x+z} - z \times M_{x+z}}{D_x} \times W.$$

The net single premium that will at age x insure \$1, to be paid at age $x+z$ if the insured is then alive, is expressed by $\frac{D_{x+z}}{D_x}$. Therefore the net single premium that will in this case effect all the insurance required is expressed by $\frac{D_{x+z}}{D_x} + \frac{R_x - R_{x+z} - z \times M_{x+z}}{D_x} \times W$.

The value at age x of annual life premiums for z years each equal to W is $\frac{N_x - N_{x+z}}{D_x} \times W$. From this we have the equation:

$$W \times \frac{N_x - N_{x+z}}{D_x} = \frac{D_{x+z}}{D_x} + W \times \frac{R_x - R_{x+z} - z \times M_{x+z}}{D_x}, \text{ or}$$

$$W \left\{ (N_x - N_{x+z}) - (R_x - R_{x+z} - z \times M_{x+z}) \right\} = D_{x+z}, \text{ or}$$

$$W = \frac{D_{x+z}}{(N_x - N_{x+z}) - (R_x - R_{x+z} - z \times M_{x+z})} = \text{the net annual premium}$$

that will insure \$1 to be paid at age $x+z$ if the insured is then alive, and return all the net premiums paid in case the insured dies before that time.

If the net annual premium is calculated to return itself plus m per cent thereof, the above expression is modified by introducing the factor $(1+m)$ in the last term of the denominator which involves R_x, R_{x+z}, and $z \times M_{x+z}$. It will then become:

$$\frac{D_{x+z}}{N_x - N_{x+z} - (1+m)(R_x - R_{x+z} - z \times M_{x+z})}.$$

The reserve on the above form of policy n years after issue is found as follows:

The amount that will at age $x+n$ insure $n \times W$ until age $x+z$ is,

$$\frac{M_{x+n} - M_{x+z}}{D_{x+n}} \times n \times W.$$

The amount that will at age $x+n$ insure W the first year, 2W the second, 3W the third, and so on until age $x+z$, is,

$$W \left\{ \frac{R_{x+n} - R_{x+z} - (z-n)\,M_{x+z}}{D_{x+n}} \right\}.$$

The amount that will at age $x+n$ insure an endowment of \$1 at age $x+z$ is $\frac{D_{x+z}}{D_{x+n}}$.

Therefore the net single premium that will at age $x+n$ effect the required insurance and endowment is expressed by,

$$n \times W \left(\frac{M_{x+n} - M_{x+z}}{D_{x+n}} \right) + W \left(\frac{R_{x+n} - R_{x+z} - (z-n)\,M_{x+z}}{D_{x+n}} \right) + \frac{D_{x+z}}{D_{x+n}}.$$

From this subtract the present value of the future net annual premiums, W, for a number of years equal to $z-n$, which value is $W\,\frac{N_{x+n} - N_{x+z}}{D_{x+n}}$, and we have the expression for the reserve for this policy at age $x+n$:

$$W \left\{ \frac{n(M_{x+n} - M_{x+z})}{D_{x+n}} + \frac{R_{x+n} - R_{x+z} - (z-n)M_{x+z}}{D_{x+n}} - \frac{N_{x+n} - N_{x+z}}{D_{x+n}} \right\} + \frac{D_{x+z}}{D_{x+n}},$$

or

$$W \left\{ \frac{n \times M_{x+n}}{D_{x+n}} + \frac{R_{x+n} - R_{x+z} - z \times M_{x+z}}{D_{x+n}} - \frac{N_{x+n} - N_{x+z}}{D_{x+n}} \right\} + \frac{D_{x+z}}{D_{x+n}}$$

Substituting for W its value, we have—

$$\frac{D_{x+z}}{D_{x+n}} \left\{ \frac{n \times M_{x+n} + R_{x+n} - R_{x+z} - z \times M_{x+z} - N_{x+n} + N_{x+z}}{N_x - N_{x+z} - (R_x - R_{x+z} - zM_{x+z})} + 1 \right\}, \text{ or}$$

$$\frac{D_{x+z}}{D_{x+n}} \left\{ \frac{n \times M_{x+n} + R_{x+n} - R_{x+z} - z \times M_{x+z} - N_{x+n} + N_{x+z} + N_x - N_{x+z} - (R_x - R_{x+z} - z \times M_{x+z})}{N_x - N_{x+z} - (R_x - R_{x+z} - z \times M_{x+z})} \right\}$$

$$= \frac{D_{x+z}}{D_{x+n}} \left\{ \frac{N_x - N_{x+n} - (R_x - R_{x+n} - n \times M_{x+n})}{N_x - N_{x+z} - (R_x - R_{x+z} - z \times M_{x+z})} \right\} = \text{reserve at age } x+n.$$

In case of premiums loaded m per cent, the expression is modified as follows:

$$\frac{D_{x+z}}{D_{x+n}} \left\{ \frac{N_x - N_{x+n} - (1 \times m)\,(R_x - R_{x+n} - nM_{x+n})}{N_x - N_{x+z} - (1 \times m)\,(R_x - R_{x+z} - zM_{x+z})} \right\}.$$

To obtain the reserve that must be held at the end of n years to the credit of a policy issued at age x to secure \$1 at age $x+z$ or at previous death: in either case, the actual premiums paid to be returned, together with the amount of insurance, the policy to be paid for by annual premiums.

The net annual premium that will at age x insure \$1 for z years, and an endowment of \$1 at age $x+z$, is $\frac{M_x - M_{x+z} + D_{x+z}}{N_x - N_{x+z}}$.

The net annual premium that will at age x insure \$1 the first year, \$2 the second, \$3 the third, and so on for z years, and insure the endowment of \$$z$ at age $x+z$, is,

$$\frac{R_x - R_{x+z} - z \times M_{x+z} + z \times D_{x+z}}{N_x - N_{x+z}}.$$

Represent the net annual premium, the value of which we wish to find in this case, by W′. We will then have—

$$W' \times \frac{R_x - R_{x+z} - z \times M_{x+z} + z \times D_{x+z}}{N_x - N_{x+z}} =$$

the net annual premium that will at age x insure W′ the first year, 2W′ the second, 3W′ the third, and so on for z years, and insure the endowment of $z \times W'$ at age $x+z$.

Add this to the net annual premium $\frac{M_x - M_{x+z} + D_{x+z}}{N_x - N_{x+z}}$ that will pay for the insurance and endowment of \$1 for z years, and we have—

$$W' = \frac{M_x - M_{x+z} + D_{x+z}}{N_x - N_{x+z}} + W' \times \frac{R_x - R_{x+z} - z \times M_{x+z} + z \times D_{x+z}}{N_x - N_{x+z}}, \text{ or}$$

$$W' \left\{ (N_x - N_{x+z}) - (R_x - R_{x+z} - z \times M_{x+z} + z \times D_{x+z}) \right\} = M_x - M_{x+z} + D_{x+z}.$$

$$\text{or } W' = \frac{M_x - M_{x+z} + D_{x+z}}{(N_x - N_{x+z}) - (R_x - R_{x+z} - z \times M_{x+z} + z \times D_{x+z})}.$$

When it is desired that the net annual premium shall insure \$1 as above, and provide for the return of the net annual premiums plus m per cent thereof; call this net annual premium W″, and we have,

$$W'' = \frac{M_x - M_{x+z} + D_{x+z}}{N_x - N_{x+z} - (1+m)(R_x - R_{x+z} - z \times M_{x+z} + z \times D_{x+z})}.$$

The reserve at the end of n years is found as follows:

The net single premium that will at age $x+n$ insure \$1 until age $x+z$, and an endowment of \$1 at age $x+z$, is expressed by—

$$\frac{M_{x+n}-M_{x+z}+D_{x+z}}{D_{x+n}}.$$

Suppose the annual premium actually paid is $(1+m)\,W''$. These annual premiums paid for n years will amount to $n\times(1+m)\,W''$; and at age $x+n$ the net single premium that will insure $n\times(1+m)\,W''$ until age $x+z$, and secure an endowment of the same amount at that age, is expressed by $n\times(1+m)W''\times\frac{M_{x+n}-M_{x+z}+D_{x+z}}{D_{x+n}}$.

The net single premium that will at age $x+n$ insure $(1+m)W''$ the first year, $2\times(1+m)W''$ the second, and so on until age $x+z$, and secure an endowment of $(z-n)\times(1+m)\,W''$ at that age, is,

$$(1+m)\,W''\,\frac{R_{x+n}-R_{x+z}-(z-n)M_{x+z}+(z-n)D_{x+z}}{D_{x+n}}.$$

From the sum of the above three net single premiums subtract the expression which gives at age $x+n$ the value of the net annual premiums to be paid between age $x+n$ and age $x+z$, namely,

$$W''\times\frac{N_{x+n}-N_{x+z}}{D_{x+n}},$$

and we have the required deposit.

A GENERAL FORMULA FOR CALCULATING THE DEPOSIT OR RESERVE.

The letter H is used to express this value. This symbol comes from the question, "How much must be in deposit?" The expression for the deposit at the end of the first policy year is H_{x+1}. The amount at risk during the first year will therefore be equal to $\$1-H_{x+1}$. The amount that will at age x insure \$1 for one year is $v\frac{d_x}{l_x}$. The amount that will at the same age insure $\$1-H_{x+1}$ for one year is therefore $v\frac{d_x}{l_x}(1-H_{x+1})$; subtract this amount from the net premium which is represented by P_x and we shall have, in case the insurance is paid for by a net single premium, $sP_x-v\frac{d_x}{l_x}(1-H_{x+1})$. This is the expression for that part of the net premium that goes to form the deposit or reserve that must be held at the end of the first year. This part of the premium paid at the beginning of the year will, when increased by net interest, be the amount that must be in deposit at the end of the first year.

Let the *ratio* of interest be represented by r'. Observe that this r' is *not the rate of interest;* it is a quantity which will, when the principal is multiplied by this quantity, produce what the principal will amount to when increased by net interest for one year. For instance, v being the principal and r' the ratio of interest, $r'v$ is equal to one dollar; *and of course r' is equal to one divided by v.*

From this we have the equation,

$$H_{x+1}=r'[sP_x-v\frac{d_x}{l_x}(1-H_{x+1})].$$

If the insurance is effected by the payment of annual premiums, each equal in amount and designated by aP_x, the equation becomes,

$$H_{x+1}=r'\ [aP_x-v\frac{d_x}{l_x}(1-H_{x+1})].$$

This equation contains but one unknown quantity, namely, H_{x+1}. Performing the operations indicated in the second member, we have,

$$H_{x+1}=r'aP_x-r'v\frac{d_x}{l_x}+r'v\frac{d_x}{l_x}H_{x+1}.$$

Representing $v\frac{d_x}{l_x}$ by c_x, the equation becomes,

$$H_{x+1}=r'aP_x-r'c_x+r'c_xH_{x+1}.$$

Transposing the third term of the second member, we have,

$$H_{x+1}-r'c_xH_{x+1}=r'aP_x-r'c_x,\ \text{and}$$
$$H_{x+1}\ (1-r'c_x)=r'(aP_x-c_x),\ \text{or}$$
$$H_{x+1}=\frac{r'}{1-r'c_x}(aP_x-c_x).$$

Call $\frac{r'}{1-r'c_x}$, u_x, and we have

$$H_{x+1}=u_x\ (aP_x-c_x).$$

Represent the amount that must be in deposit at the end of the second year by H_{x+2}. Then the amount at risk the second year will be expressed by $\$1-H_{x+2}$. The amount that will, if paid at the beginning of the second year, insure $1 during the year, is $v\frac{d_{x+1}}{l_{x+1}}$. Therefore $v\frac{d_{x+1}}{l_{x+1}}(1-H_{x+2})$ is the amount that will, if paid at the beginning of the second year, insure the amount at risk during that year. Subtract this from the net annual premium paid at the beginning of the second year, and that part of this premium which remains will go to form deposit at the end of the second year. But the deposit at the end of the first year also goes to form deposit at the end of the second year. The amount of net funds on hand at the beginning of the second year, just after the second net annual premium is paid, is represented by $H_{x+1}+aP_x$. Deduct $v\frac{d_{x+1}}{l_{x+1}}(1-H_{x+2})$, which is that portion of the second net annual premium that will be required to effect insurance on the amount at risk during the second year, and we have $H_{x+1}+aP_x-v\frac{d_{x+1}}{l_{x+1}}(1-H_{x+2})$. This is the amount on hand at the beginning of the second year that goes to form deposit at the end of the year. Increase this by net interest for one year by multiplying the whole expression by r', and the result gives the amount that must be on deposit at the end of the second year; hence we have the equation,

$$H_{x+2}=r'\left(H_{x+1}+aP_x-v\frac{d_{x+1}}{l_{x+1}}(1-H_{x+2})\right).$$

Call $v\frac{d_{x+1}}{l_{x+1}}$, c_{x+1}, and we have,

$$H_{x+2}=r'\left(H_{x+1}+aP_x-c_{x+1}\,(1-H_{x+2})\right), \text{ or}$$

$$H_{x+2}=r'\,(H_{x+1}+aP_x-c_{x+1}+c_{x+1}\times H_{x+2}).$$

Transposing to the first member that term of the second member which contains the unknown quantity H_{x+2}, and we have,

$$H_{x+2}-r'c_{x+1}\times H_{x+2}=r'\,(H_{x+1}+aP_x-c_{x+1}), \text{ or}$$

$$H_{x+2}\,(1-r'c_{x+1})=r'\,(H_{x+1}+aP_x-c_{x+1}), \text{ from which}$$

$$H_{x+2}=\frac{r'}{1-r'c_{x+1}}(H_{x+1}+aP_x-c_{x+1}).$$

Call $\frac{r'}{1-r'c_{x+1}}$, u_{x+1}, and we have,

$$H_{x+2}=u_{x+1}\,(H_{x+1}+aP_x-c_{x+1}).$$

From this equation, the amount that must be in deposit at the end of the second year can be obtained, provided we have previously calculated the deposit for the end of the first year.

The amount in deposit at the end of the third year is H_{x+3}. The amount at risk during the year is therefore \$1—H_{x+3}. The amount that will, if paid at the beginning of the third year, insure \$1 for that year is $v\frac{d_{x+2}}{l_{x+2}}$, therefore $v\frac{d_{x+2}}{l_{x+2}}(1-H_{x+3})$ is the amount that will, if paid at the beginning of the third year, insure the amount at risk during that year. Subtract this from the net annual premium, and we obtain that part of the third premium that goes to produce deposit at the end of the third year. Hence we have,

$$H_{x+3} = r'\left[H_{x+2} + aP_x - v\frac{d_{x+2}}{l_{x+2}}(1-H_{x+3})\right].$$

Call $v\frac{d_{x+2}}{l_{x+2}}$, c_{x+2}, and we have,

$$H_{x+3} = r'(H_{x+2} + aP_x - c_{x+2}) + r'c_{x+2} \times H_{x+3}$$

Transposing, we have,

$$H_{x+3} - r'c_{x+2} \times H_{x+3} = r'(H_{x+2} + aP_x - c_{x+2}), \text{ or}$$

$$H_{x+3}(1 - r'c_{x+2}) = r'(H_{x+2} + aP_x - c_{x+2}), \text{ or}$$

$$H_{x+3} = \frac{r'}{1-r'c_{x+2}}(H_{x+2} + aP_x - c_{x+2}).$$

Call $\frac{r'}{1-r'c_{x+2}}$, u_{x+2}, and we have

$$H_{x+3} = u_{x+2}(H_{x+2} + aP_x - c_{x+2}).$$

The deposit at the end of the third year can be calculated from this equation, after the deposit for the end of the second year has been found.

In a manner entirely similar, we find,

$$H_{x+4} = u_{x+3}(H_{x+3} + aP_x - c_{x+3}), \text{ and in general,}$$

(1) $$H_{x+n} = u_{x+n-1}(H_{x+n-1} + aP_x - c_{x+n-1}).$$

The above formula may be written :

$$H_{x+n} = u_{x+n-1}(H_{x+n-1} + aP_x) - u_{x+n-1} \times c_{x+n-1}.$$

We have previously represented $\frac{r'}{1-r'c_x}$ by u_x, and $v\frac{d_x}{l_x}$ by c_x; therefore $u_x = \frac{r'}{1-r'v\frac{d_x}{l_x}}$. Multiply both numerator and denominator by v (noting that $r'v$ is equal to 1), and we have

$$u_x = \frac{r'v}{v - r'v^2\frac{d_x}{l_x}} = \frac{1}{v - v\frac{d_x}{l_x}} = \frac{l_x}{vl_x - vd_x}.$$

Multiply the numerator and denominator of this fraction by r', and we have, $u_x = \frac{r'l_x}{r'vl_x - r'vd_x} = \frac{r'l_x}{l_x - d_x} = \frac{r'l_x}{l_{x+1}}$.

u_x being found equal to $\frac{r'l_x}{l_{x+1}}$, and c_x equal to $v\frac{d_x}{l_x}$, we have $u_x \times c_x = \frac{r'l_x}{l_{x+1}} \times v\frac{d_x}{l_x} = \frac{r'vd_xl_x}{l_{x+1}l_x} = \frac{d_x}{l_{x+1}}$. The expression $\frac{d_x}{l_{x+1}} = c_x \times u_x$ is designated by the symbol k_x.

Equation (1) then becomes,

$$(2) \qquad H_{x+n} = u_{x+n-1}(H_{x+n-1} + aP_x) - k_{x+n-1}.$$

The expression for k_x may assume various forms:

$$k_x = \frac{d_x}{l_{x+1}} = \frac{l_x - l_{x+1}}{l_{x+1}} = \frac{l_x}{l_{x+1}} - 1 = \frac{l_x}{l_x - d_x} - 1 = \frac{1}{1 - \frac{d_x}{l_x}} - 1 =$$

$$\frac{1}{1 - \frac{vr'd_x}{l_x}} - 1 = \frac{1}{1 - r'c_x} - 1 = \frac{vr'}{1 - r'c_x} - 1 = v\frac{r'}{1 - r'c_x} - 1 = vu_x - 1.$$

Referring again to $u_x = \frac{r'l_x}{l_{x+1}}$; if both numerator and denominator of this expression are multiplied by v^{x+1}, we have $u_x = \frac{v^{x+1}r'l_x}{v^{x+1}l_{x+1}} = \frac{v^x l_x}{v^{x+1}l_{x+1}} = \frac{D_x}{D_{x+1}}$.

The numerical values of u, c, and k at each age have been calculated and placed in columns, headed respectively u, c, and k.

The quantities represented by the symbols u and k, although always retaining their correct numerical value, may come up in the general discussions in a variety of shapes. Sometimes these transformations are very convenient in the practical work of computing net values, as seen above in case of the factor $u_x = \frac{r'}{1 - r'c_x}$ becoming equal to $\frac{D_x}{D_{x+1}}$; from which it is easy to obtain u, by using the D column which has already been constructed.

A THIRD GENERAL FORMULA FOR RESERVE.

The deposit at the beginning of the nth year being represented by H_{x+n-1}, the net annual premium by aP_x, and the number living at the beginning of the year by l_{x+n-1}. Assume that the number of insured persons is that given in the table. We will then have the net funds on hand at the beginning of the year represented by l_{x+n-1} $(H_{x+n-1}+aP_x)$. As before, call the ratio of interest r'. Then the amount that will be on hand at the end of the year will be expressed by,

$$r'l_{x+n-1}(H_{x+n-1}+aP_x).$$

Subtract from this the whole amount of death losses during the year, which is $l_{x+n-1}-(l_{x+n})$; because the amount insured in each case is $1, and the number of deaths during the year is equal to the number living at the beginning of the year minus the number living at the end of the year. The net fund remaining on hand at the end of the year, after the death losses are paid, is $r'l_{x+n-1}$ $(H_{x+n-1}+aP_x)-(l_{x+n-1}-l_{x+n})$. Divide this by the number living at the end of the year, and we will have the amount on deposit for each policy-holder at the end of the year. Therefore,

$$H_{x+n}=\frac{r'l_{x+n-1}(H_{x+n-1}+aP_x)-(l_{x+n-1}-l_{x+n})}{l_{x+n}}, \text{ or}$$

$$=\frac{l_{x+n}-[l_{x+n-1}-l_{x+n-1}\times r'(H_{x+n-1}+aP_x)]}{l_{x+n}}, \text{ or}$$

$$=1-\frac{l_{x+n-1}}{l_{x+n}}\left(1-r'(H_{x+n-1}+aP_x)\right), \text{ or}$$

$$=1-\frac{r'l_{x+n-1}}{l_{x+n}}\left(\frac{1}{r'}-(H_{x+n-1}+aP_x)\right).$$

But $\frac{r'l_x}{l_{x+1}}$ has previously been shown equal to u_x, and $\frac{r'l_{x+n-1}}{l_{x+n}}=u_{x+n-1}$ and since $r'v=1$, and $\frac{1}{r'}=v$, the equation becomes,

$$(3) \qquad H_{x+n}=1-u_{x+n-1}(v-aP_x-H_{x+n-1}).$$

NOTE.—It should be borne in mind that all the formulas and rules for determining the amount that should be in deposit at the end of any policy year are based upon the supposition that the net premiums the insurer has contracted to receive are those called for by the table of mortality and rate of interest designated. The amount insured has been assumed to be $1.

The return premium plan insures the premium in addition to the $1. This somewhat complicated arrangement requires care in the application of the general formulas for calculating the amount that must be held in deposit. For instance, formula (2) previously deduced shows that the net funds on hand at the beginning of any policy year, just after the net annual premium has been paid, must be multiplied by u_x, and k_x subtracted from the product, in order to get the deposit at the end of that year. This k_x is the amount that each policy-holder must contribute to pay losses by death during the year, on the supposition that the whole number of persons in the table were insured for \$1 each. The return premium plan changes the amount insured from \$1 to \$1 plus the premiums paid. Therefore, after having multiplied the net funds on hand at the beginning of the year by u_x, it is necessary in this case to subtract k_x times the amount actually insured, which, as stated before, is \$1, plus the premiums paid.

CHAPTER VIII.

ANNUITIES PAID OFTENER THAN ONCE A YEAR.

SUPPOSE that \$1 is to be paid quarterly in advance for life. The value at age x of the four quarterly payments of \$1 each, to be made the first year, is expressed by $\frac{D_x+D_{x+\frac14}+D_{x+\frac12}+D_{x+\frac34}}{D_x}$. On the supposition that the rate of mortality is uniform during the first year, we have :

$$D_{x+\frac14}=D_x-\tfrac14(D_x-D_{x+1})=\tfrac34 D_x+\tfrac14 D_{x+1}$$
$$D_{x+\frac12}=D_x-\tfrac12(D_x-D_{x+1})=\tfrac12 D_x+\tfrac12 D_{x+1}$$
$$D_{x+\frac34}=D_x-\tfrac34(D_x-D_{x+1})=\tfrac14 D_x+\tfrac34 D_{x+1}$$

Therefore the above expression for the value at age x of the four quarterly payments of \$1 each, to be made the first year, may be written :

$$\frac{\frac44 D_x+\frac34 D_x+\frac12 D_x+\frac14 D_x+\frac14 D_{x+1}+\frac12 D_{x+1}+\frac34 D_{x+1}}{D_x},$$

$$\text{or } \frac{(\frac44+\frac34+\frac12+\frac14)D_x+(\frac14+\frac12+\frac34)D_{x+1}}{D_x}, \text{ or } \frac{\frac{10}{4}D_x+\frac64 D_{x+1}}{D_x}.$$

For the second year's quarterly payments of \$1 each, the value at age x is expressed by : $\frac{D_{x+1}+D_{x+1\frac14}+D_{x+1\frac12}+D_{x+1\frac34}}{D_x}$.

But we have, on the supposition that the rate of mortality is uniform during the second year .

$$D_{x+1\frac14}=D_{x+1}-\tfrac14(D_{x+1}-D_{x+2})=\tfrac34 D_{x+1}+\tfrac14 D_{x+2}$$
$$D_{x+1\frac12}=D_{x+1}-\tfrac12(D_{x+1}-D_{x+2})=\tfrac12 D_{x+1}+\tfrac12 D_{x+2}$$
$$D_{x+1\frac34}=D_{x+1}-\tfrac34(D_{x+1}-D_{x+2})=\tfrac14 D_{x+1}+\tfrac34 D_{x+2}$$

Therefore the foregoing expression for the value at age x of the four quarterly payments of \$1 each, to be made during the second year, may be written:

$$\frac{\frac44 D_{x+1}+\frac34 D_{x+1}+\frac24 D_{x+1}+\frac14 D_{x+1}+\frac14 D_{x+2}+\frac24 D_{x+2}+\frac34 D_{x+2}}{D_x},$$

$$\text{or } \frac{(\frac44+\frac34+\frac24+\frac14)D_{x+1}+(\frac14+\frac24+\frac34)D_{x+2}}{D_x}, \text{ or } \frac{\frac{10}{4}D_{x+1}+\frac64 D_{x+2}}{D_x}.$$

In a similar manner we find that the value at age x of the four quarterly payments of $1 each, to be made during the third year, is expressed by $\frac{\frac{10}{4}D_{x+2}+\frac{6}{4}D_{x+3}}{D_x}$, and so on, for each successive year to the table limit. Adding together all these respective yearly values, we have the numerator of this life series of quarterly payments of $1 expressed by: $\frac{10}{4}D_x+\frac{16}{4}D_{x+1}+\frac{16}{4}D_{x+2}+\frac{16}{4}D_{x+3}+\text{etc.}$ By adding $\frac{6}{4}D_x$ to the numerator, it becomes $\frac{16}{4}N_x$, therefore the value of this series is expressed by: $\frac{\frac{16}{4}N_x-\frac{6}{4}D_x}{D_x}=\frac{\frac{16}{4}N_x}{D_x}-\frac{6}{4}$. If the quarterly payments are to be $\frac{1}{4}$ each, the foregoing expression is divided by 4 in order to give the value at age x. Thus we have: $\frac{\frac{16}{16}N_x}{D_x}-\frac{6}{16}=\frac{N_x}{D_x}-\frac{3}{8}$. If the first payment of $\frac{1}{4}$ is deferred one term, the value becomes: $\frac{N_x}{D_x}-(\frac{3}{8}+\frac{1}{4})=\frac{N_x}{D_x}-\frac{5}{8}$.

In general, if the payment of $1 is made t times a year, the first payment in advance, the second at the end of a term expressed by one year divided by t, the third at the end of two of these terms, and so on, we have for the value of these t payments of $1 each, for the first year:

$$D_x+D_{x+\frac{1}{t}}+D_{x+\frac{2}{t}}+\cdots\cdots+D_{x+\frac{t-1}{t}}.$$

It is assumed that the rate of mortality is uniform during any one year. The number of deaths will then be proportional to the time, and it follows that $D_{x+\frac{1}{t}}=D_x-\frac{1}{t}(D_x-D_{x+1})=\frac{tD_x-D_x+D_{x+1}}{t}$ $=\frac{t-1}{t}D_x+\frac{1}{t}D_{x+1}$; and $D_{x+\frac{2}{t}}=D_x-\frac{2}{t}(D_x-D_{x+1})=\frac{t-2}{t}D_x+\frac{2}{t}D_{x+1}$; finally $D_{x+\frac{t-1}{t}}=D_x-\frac{t-1}{t}(D_x-D_{x+1})=\frac{1}{t}D_x+\frac{t-1}{t}D_{x+1}$. The number of terms containing D_x is equal to t. The first term is one time D_x, which may be written $\frac{t}{t}D_x$, the second term is $\frac{t-1}{t}D_x$, the third term is $\frac{t-2}{t}D_x$, the last term is $\frac{1}{t}D_x$. The sum of this arithmetical series $\frac{t}{t}+\frac{t-1}{t}+\frac{t-2}{t}+\cdots\cdots+\frac{1}{t}$ is obtained by the ordinary rule for finding the sum of an arithmetical series of terms, namely, multiply the sum of the extremes by the number of terms, and divide the product by 2. The sum of the extremes in this series is $\frac{t}{t}+\frac{1}{t}=\frac{t+1}{t}$. Multiply by t, we have $\frac{t^2+t}{t}$; dividing this by 2, we have $\frac{t^2+t}{2t}=$ the number of times D_x occurs in the expression that gives the value at age x of \$1, paid t times the first year. But in the expression for the same year, we find D_{x+1} enters a number of times equal to $t-1$. This series is $\frac{1}{t}+\frac{2}{t}+\cdots\cdots\cdots+\frac{t-1}{t}$. The sum of this series is $\left(\frac{1}{t}+\frac{t-1}{t}\right)\times(t-1)\div 2=\frac{t^2-t}{2t}$. Therefore, $\frac{D_{x+1}\times\frac{t^2-t}{2t}}{D_x}$ represents that part of the value at age x of the t payments of \$1 each, made the first year, which is expressed in terms of D_{x+1}. Hence $\frac{\frac{t^2+t}{2t}D_x+\frac{t^2-t}{2t}D_{x+1}}{D_x}$ expresses the value at age x of t payments of \$1 each, made the first year.

For the second year, the quantity D_{x+1} enters into the expression in a manner entirely similar to that in which D_x enters into the expression for the first year. We therefore find that $\frac{\frac{t^2+t}{2t}D_{x+1}}{D_x}$ expresses the value at age x of that part of the t payments, made the second year, which is expressed in terms of D_{x+1}. That part of the first year's payments, expressed in terms of D_{x+1}, was previously found to be $\frac{t^2-t}{2t}D_{x+1}$. From which we have:

$$\frac{t^2-t}{2t}D_{x+1}+\frac{t^2+t}{2t}D_{x+1}=\frac{2t^2}{2t}D_{x+1}=tD_{x+1}.$$

This is the sum of all the terms of the general expression involving D_{x+1}, because none occur, except in the first and second years. In a manner entirely similar, the sum of the terms involving D_{x+2} are found to be expressed by tD_{x+2}, and so for D_{x+3} and all the Ds to the table limit.

Referring to the terms involving D_x, we find that these occur only in the first year, and that their sum has previously been found to be expressed by $\frac{t^2+t}{2t}D_x=\frac{t+1}{2}D_x$; therefore, the value at age x of this life series of payments of \$1 each, made t times per year, the first in advance, is expressed by:

$$\frac{\frac{t+1}{2}D_x+tD_{x+1}+tD_{x+2}+tD_{x+3}+\text{etc.}}{D_x}$$

By adding $\frac{t-1}{2}D_x$ to the numerator, the first term becomes tD_x, and the numerator will become tN_x. Therefore, we have,

$$\frac{tN_x-\frac{t-1}{2}D_x}{D_x}$$

the value at age x of this life series of payments of \$1 each made t times a year. Divide this by t, and we have, we have,

$$\frac{N_x}{D_x}-\frac{t-1}{2t}$$

which is equal to the value at age x of a similar life series, but each payment equal to $\$\frac{1}{t}$, amounting to \$1 per year, but paid in t installments at equal intervals, the first payment being made in advance. If the first payment of $\frac{1}{t}$ is not made in advance, but is deferred one term, or a time equal to one year divided by t, the value of the life series is less by $\$\frac{1}{t}$ than the above expression will give. The expression in this case is:

$$\frac{N_x}{D_x}-\left(\frac{t-1}{2t}+\frac{1}{t}\right)=\frac{N_x}{D_x}-\left(\frac{t-1}{2t}+\frac{2}{2t}\right)=\frac{N_x}{D_x}-\frac{t+1}{2t}.$$

PART II.

PRACTICAL LIFE INSURANCE.

"Consider for a moment the peculiar nature of Life Assurance. This is a business that presents the direct converse of ordinary commercial business. Ordinary commercial business, if legitimate, begins with a considerable investment of capital, and the profits follow, perhaps, at a considerable distance. But here, on the contrary, you begin with receiving largely, and your liabilities are postponed to a distant date. Now, I dare say there are not many members of this House who know to what an extraordinary extent this is true, and, therefore, to what an extraordinary extent the public are dependent on the prudence, the high honor, and the character of those concerned in the management of these institutions."—GLADSTONE, 1864.

"Correct *mortality tables and a safe rate of interest* as a basis for rates of insurance, *ample reserves* to cover all contingencies, and *sound and reliable assets, always available,* out of which to pay obligations as they mature, are the corner-stones upon which life insurance rests. Lacking either, a company will sooner or later fail."—F. S. WINSTON, 1871.

CHAPTER IX.

GENERAL MANAGEMENT.

In order to pay the expenses of conducting the business, it is necessary that additional means should be provided over and above the *net* premiums; the latter being enough, and only enough, on the data designated by the State, to pay the cost of insurance, and furnish the requisite deposit or "*reserve.*"

It is usual to add to the net premium from twenty to thirty per cent, or even more, for the purpose of defraying expenses. This addition to the net premium is technically called loading.

The loading may, and often does, more than pay expenses.

The interest actually received is nearly always more than the net interest assumed in the table calculations.

And the actual mortality, particularly in the earlier years of a company, is, in practice, generally less than that given in the table.

From each of the three above-named sources, surplus may be obtained. By surplus is here meant *money*, or its equivalent, in excess of what is required to pay losses by death during the year, to form the "*deposit*" for the policy at the end of the year, and pay all expenses. The surplus, in *purely* mutual companies, belongs to the policy-holders. In the *purely* stock companies, all the surplus goes to the share-holders. The *mixed* companies are those stock companies that give some portion of the surplus to the policy-holders.

In order to investigate the nature of practical Life Insurance business for one year, let us suppose that the cost of insurance, and all expenses of the previous year, have been paid, and that the company had on hand, at the close of the previous year, the requisite deposit for each and all of its outstanding policies. We will, for the present, suppose that the surplus of the previous year had been distributed to its respective owners.

At the beginning of the year, the business of which we are now investigating, each policy-holder pays his *full* annual premium. There is then in the hands of the company, on account and to the *credit* of each policy, the two amounts—namely, the deposit at the end of the preceding year, and the full annual premium.

These sums are both invested at the best, safe rate of interest; and out of these two amounts, thus increased by interest, actually received during the year, the "expenses" for the year, properly chargeable to each policy, must be paid; the cost of insurance, or proportion of losses by death during the year, properly chargeable to each policy, must be paid; and the requisite deposit at the end of the year for each policy must be securely invested for the policy-holder at the net or table rate of interest at least. If there is any thing left on account of each policy, it is surplus produced by the policy.

When the surplus arising from the funds of each policy is obtained as above, and is distributed in accordance with this principle, it is said to be divided upon the "*contribution plan.*"

Let us now consider the loading which has been added to the net annual premium, and the expense which this loading is intended to provide for. In the first place, it may be remarked that the "*expenses,*" properly chargeable to a policy, are not necessarily the same proportion of the annual premium in different cases. At the end of the year, although it may require some labor to adjust with precision the expense account for each separate policy, or each distinctive set of policies, this should be attempted, and substantial equity in this respect can always be attained. The amount charged any year to a policy on account of general expenses should be in proportion to the amount of insurance the company furnishes that year to the holder of the policy—that is, the amount called for by the policy less the deposit.

In favorable or even in ordinary years, the loading and the interest on the funds of the company (because of their realizing usually a higher rate than that called for by the table calculations) will produce a "surplus" on each policy at the end of the business of a year. This surplus arises from previous *over-payment* in advance, demanded by the company, in order to make the business safe in the worst year that may occur in a lifetime. The surplus distributed to policy-holders is merely a return to them of that part of the premium they paid at the beginning of the year, which, at the end of the year, is found not to have been required during the year, either in effecting the insurance, providing the means (the deposit) for paying the policy at maturity, or in paying "*expenses.*"

In Life Insurance, there are peculiar and mandatory arithmetical laws by which particular money values are computed—in addition, and after these values are accurately determined—practical Life Insurance becomes like all other business which involves the handling and control of vast amounts of money. Good judgment, great industry, the strictest integrity, and sound practical business sense are all absolutely essential to successful management.

No prudent man will ever attempt to control or conduct any important business without making some kind of estimate in advance. The mortality table furnishes the means for making certain estimates with an accuracy that is not usually found in ordinary business. But the "*expenses*" that will be incurred, or the rate of interest that will be realized on the investments, or the bad investments that may be made, or whether some of its officers may not prove to be dishonest, and a variety of highly important questions of this nature, can not be settled by estimates made beforehand by life insurance companies, any more definitely than similar estimates can be made in any other business. Nevertheless, these estimates of practical results ought always to be made in advance.

Some companies assume at the beginning of a year, that the business during the year will be such that they can safely deduct a certain per cent from the premium. This deduction is miscalled a dividend. Business men understand that dividends are paid only out of earned net profits. They would be shocked at the idea of dividends paid on an assumption in regard to future profits, and consider it a fraud for the shareholders of a company to declare a dividend upon the stock when the capital is impaired.

The subject of accounts in life insurance companies will never be definitely settled, until the book-keepers and accountants clearly understand the theory and principles upon which life insurance is founded. It is safe to say, that if any money account is kept with a policy at all, it ought to be correct.

Illustrative Example.—The following arithmetical example is given in illustration of the accounts of a policy for any year:

It is assumed that an ordinary whole-life policy for one thousand dollars, taken out at age forty-two, is in its tenth year. The net annual premium (Actuaries' 4 per cent), as previously calculated, is \$25.55; take the loading to be $33\frac{1}{3}$ per cent of this, then the *full* annual premium is \$34.05. To make out the account of this policy during the tenth year, we will assume that the expenses properly chargeable to it during the year are, twenty per cent of the full or gross annual premium; that every thing to the credit of this policy at the end of the preceding year, except the deposit, had been distributed to its owner: that the rate of interest actually realized by the company on its aggregate investments during the year was seven per cent ; and that the mortality amongst the insured during the year was that called for by the table.

The deposit for this policy at the end of the ninth or the beginning of the tenth year is $156.33. From the gross premium, $34.05 paid at the beginning of the tenth year, deduct twenty per cent for expenses, and we have left $27.24 ; add this to the deposit, and we have $183.57 at the beginning of the year to the credit of the policy, after having provided for expenses.

This increased by seven per cent during the year amounts at the end of the year to $196.42. The amount that must be on deposit at the end of the year is $175.16. The cost of insurance on the amount at risk during the year is $13.93. After this is paid, and the deposit at the end of the year is set apart, there will be $7.33 *surplus* on hand. This is about twenty-one per cent of the gross annual premium paid at the beginning of the year. If the company returns it to the policy-holder, this may prove that he paid at the beginning of the year more than was necessary ; but in a business sense, it can not be maintained that the policy-holder invested the $34.05 at twenty-one per cent per annum.

In case the expenses for the year and the mortality amongst the insured had been greater than that assumed in this example, and the interest had been less, this surplus would have been diminished. On the other hand, had the variation in expenses, mortality, and interest been the opposite of the above, the *surplus* would have been greater. We have seen, that with a loading of 33⅓ per cent on the net annual premium, there was, at the end of the year, a surplus of $7.33: *no great margin, when the question is that of the prompt and certain payment at maturity of a policy of one thousand dollars, more especially in case the surplus or over-payment made at the beginning of the year, in order to make the payment of the policy safe, is returned to the policy-holder at the end of the year.*

When the surplus belonging to the policy-holder is not distributed, but remains in the hands of the company to the credit of the policy that produced it, it ought to be invested for the holder of the policy. When the surplus has all been distributed, the true value of the policy at the end of any year, and before the payment of the next annual premium, is the *deposit ;* but when it has not been distributed, the true value of the policy is the *deposit, plus any surplus there may be in the hands of the company to the credit of the policy.*

When the surplus is distributed to the policy-holders, it may be used in part payment of the next annual premium, or it may be applied to the purchase of additional full-paid insurance. The latter would progressively increase the amount of the policy; the former would diminish the annual premium.

Reversionary Value.—When the amount of surplus to be returned has been determined, the amount of full-paid insurance that this surplus will purchase at that age is calculated by first finding the net single premium that will insure one dollar at that age.

For instance, suppose that at age 30 the surplus is $15.36 (besides a loading for expenses). The net single premium that will at that age insure one dollar for whole life is $0.306158; and the question simply is, if $0.306158 will insure one dollar for whole life, how much will $15.36 insure?

By solving this simple proportion, we find the amount is $50.17; and this is the addition to the policy that the surplus named will purchase. This additional insurance is full paid, and the $50.17, in this case, is called by insurance writers the *reversionary value* of the surplus, $15.36.

Any proceeds that may in the future arise from interest on this $15.36, in excess of the four per cent necessary to pay the cost of insurance, pay expenses, and provide the requisite deposit, will be additional surplus, and may be used as it accrues in purchasing additional full-paid insurance.

Premium Notes.—A life insurance company can, with safety to itself, accept the notes of a policy-holder in part payment of the "net annual premium," and the amount of these "notes" or "loans" bearing net or table interest, may equal, but must not exceed, the deposit. The deposit increases from year to year, and the notes or loans may be increased to the same extent, but no more. The notes or loans must be deducted from the face of the policy at maturity; therefore, *the amount actually insured* becomes less and less each year. The question is not, "*Can a life insurance company safely accept notes in part payment of the annual premiums?*" but rather, "*Can a policy-holder, for any great length of time, afford to accept the credit proffered by the company?*"

Suppose that we take this case to the limit of the table, ninety-nine years. The policy-holder will have paid, each year, his proportion of the losses by death, and the yearly expenses; and the deposit, consisting entirely of his own *notes*, will have amounted to within a very small fraction of the whole amount of the face of his policy. The man dies in the one hundredth year of his age, and the heirs receive his *notes* in part payment of the policy; and *these notes are, in this particular case, enough to fully pay the policy when the last annual payment only, in money, is added to these notes.*

This certainly is not a desirable kind of life insurance for those who live long. On the other hand, if the insured dies early, he will gain by the note or loan system.

The life insurance company is safe in this case, *provided* it has a large number of policy-holders, and *retains* them to the end of their lives.

It is true that note or loan companies seldom, if ever, in practice, push the credit system to the extreme limit given above; but they may do it with safety under the above *proviso*. The question is, can the policy-holder stand it if he does not die soon?

The complication in the accounts of a company arising from the note system, when carried into a large number of policies, results in great confusion and irregularities. The better opinion seems to be, that it will be to the ultimate advantage of companies and policy-holders if this system of credits in life insurance by notes, loans, or other devices is abandoned, or, at least, brought within very narrow limits.

This note or loan system of life insurance has strong advocates amongst well-informed insurance writers. But in the long run, policy-holders will find there is some delusion about the credit so generously proffered and urged upon their acceptance. It is true that if a man is certain that he will die soon, and he can get $100 worth of insurance for $50 in cash and his note for $50, he would do well to take out a policy in a note company, die during the year, and let his heirs receive the amount of the policy, less his note for $50; but there are strong reasons why the system of note or loan life insurance is not advantageous to those who continue to renew their policies in such companies for any great length of time.

Stock and Mutual Rates.—Purely stock companies are those in which all the surplus belongs to the shareholders. Such companies seldom, if ever, accept notes or give credit in part payment of premiums. As a general rule, they charge less than the purely mutual or mixed companies. Their theory is, that *they make dividends to policy-holders in advance* by charging less premiums. The fact is, that *dividends* to holders of life insurance policies are simply a return of that part of the annual premium which was paid to the company at the beginning of the year, and which, at the end of the business of the year, is found not to have been required in paying the expenses, paying the losses by death, and providing the requisite deposit at the end of the year.

Mutual companies often abate, say twenty or thirty per cent, more or less, from the annual premium called for by the policy. This practically reduces the premium for the year, but can not fairly be called a dividend in the sense of income from premiums invested in life insurance. In some cases, these deductions have been nearly uniform for a period of years.

Stability of Companies.—Notwithstanding the correctness of the theory upon which the business of life insurance is founded, assuming that the table of mortality is accurate, and that net interest is always realized, there are many contingencies that may prove fatal to companies in practice; and whilst strict compliance with certain fixed principles and definite rules will always enable a company to pay its policies at maturity, there are many things that will, if permitted to occur, bankrupt a life insurance company. These companies are not exempt from the effects produced by dishonesty, fraud, and defalcation. Moreover, continued lavish expenditures, the selection of bad risks by insuring impaired or unhealthy lives, or making unsafe investments, will result in disaster.

There can scarcely be any saying more groundless than the statement often heard, that "life insurance companies can not break." And, on the other hand, it is absurd to say, that, when well conducted in every particular, it is impossible for life insurance companies to comply with all their obligations, and pay all their policies at maturity. The plain fact is, that *life insurance companies can break, and will break, unless managed with skill and integrity. On the other hand, it is undoubtedly true that the business of life insurance can be made more secure than any other commercial business known amongst men;* and whilst it may be made the safest, it is a business in which, if it is not thoroughly comprehended and strictly guarded, designing fraud may raise a curtain, behind which the worst schemes can be carried on free from detection, until such time as the death claims exceed the annual premiums; that is to say, for thirty or forty years.

To fully appreciate this fact, it is only necessary to recall the illustration previously given, in which it was seen, that, at the end of the thirty-fourth year, nearly $28,000,000 was on hand in deposit, after paying all the death claims that had previously matured. This sum, and all the future net annual premiums, with compound interest on the whole, is required in order to enable the company to meet its liabilities. Suppose that this $28,000,000 had been appropriated to other purposes? This might have been done, and the company have paid all its losses up to that time, paid all expenses out of the loading, and, to external appearance, have seemed all right; and this, too, with a real defalcation of $28,000,000.

It is essential to the policy-holder that the life insurance company with which he may take out a policy, should be controlled by wise and stringent laws, rigidly enforced; because, from the nature of this business, the funds held in trust are peculiarly liable to misapplication. To insure safety in the business, every detail should be furnished, at least once in every year, to some competent State officer; and by the latter the accounts should all be carefully recomputed, and the results published. Sound and well-conducted companies desire this, and others should be forced to a full exhibit of all their affairs.

Conditions contained in the Policy.—If the officers are, in every respect, the right men for this most important and gigantic business, it is well to look further and inquire closely into the terms and conditions of the contract between the company and the policy-holder. These are expressed in the policy, and in some companies are liberal and just; in others they are harshly restrictive, not to say unjust. It is but a few years since it was the universal practice of life insurance companies to appropriate to themselves the whole accrued value of a policy in case the holder thereof failed on a given day to pay his annual premium.

There was no justification or excuse for this rule of forfeiture for non-payment of premiums except that this was a condition expressed in the contract. That it continued for so long a time to be the universal custom can only be accounted for by the fact that the principles upon which life insurance is founded were not thoroughly understood by business men. There can be no safety or certainty of the payment of policies at maturity, and, therefore, no real insurance, in case a company charges less than than the net annual premium, and a loading sufficient to cover expenses. Because, in spite of all we hear about large "*dividends*" to policy-holders, arising from the "*investment*," the net annual premium and net interest upon it must go to effect the insurance, and the expenses must be paid in addition. It appears, from this view of the case, that a life insurance company may charge too little.

Certainty of the Payment of his Policy at Maturity is what every Policy-holder wants.—To insure this, it is necessary that the company should charge enough to enable it to meet all its liabilities during the worst year that may reasonably be expected to occur during the continuance of the contract; and this is generally for a lifetime. Therefore, when the mortality is greatest, and the interest on investments lowest, and expenses heaviest, the company must have the means of meeting its liabilities. It follows that, in favorable years, there will be an over-payment. In case this over-payment is all returned to the policy-holder at the end of the business of the year, it is not a matter of vital importance whether the premium is a little more or a little less, provided it is enough to make the payment of the policy at maturity certain.

Numerical Bragging.—The expenses of life insurance companies are large. Agents' commissions, salaries of officers, traveling expenses, taxes, printing, rents, stationery—these and other expenses have to be paid *in cash.* The losses that occur during the year, by death, must be paid. The expenses and the losses by death are paid by the company; *but this is done with the money of the policy-holders.*

The deposit is a specific amount, determined by accurate arithmetical calculation; this amount must be in the hands of the company, and held securely invested at a certain rate of interest, and this interest regularly compounded every year, in order to enable the company to pay its policies at maturity. The company must retain the deposit for each and every one of its outstanding policies; must pay current expenses; must pay the losses that occur by death, each year, of a certain number of policy-holders; and as the company can only make seven or eight per cent by safe investments of the funds intrusted to it by the policy-holders, the "*enormous dividends*" so much talked of may well be styled "*numerical bragging.*"

Method of Calculating Net Values should be understood.—The mere fact that a man can compute interest on money will not make him a competent banker, neither will a knowledge of the formulas and rules be in itself sufficient to fit one for the important business of life insurance. But it would be far better to intrust banking to men who can not calculate interest on money, than to intrust life insurance to those who are not acquainted with the method upon which calculations of important money-values in this business are based.

There is danger to all in the doctrine, *often promulgated by companies and agents*, that life insurance business can be better conducted by men who do not understand the "method of calculating these values" than by those who do understand the simple principles upon which alone this business can be safely conducted. Those who talk in this way are, generally speaking, "*forty per cent dividend men*," who propose to lend one third or one half the premium to the policy-holder at six per cent, and promise him forty per cent *dividend* per annum upon the whole amount of the premium. The same persons generally style the money of the policy-holder that is held by the company in trust for the purpose of enabling it to pay the policy at maturity, "*cash capital*," or, at least, announce millions of *assets*, and are silent about these assets being a deposit debt, held by the company in trust for policy-holders.

Medical Examiners.—The general law governing the duration of human life will be of little or no avail in case a life insurance company accepts risks upon impaired or diseased lives; and companies that have only a small number of policy-holders will always be, to some extent, liable to a number of losses not in accordance with the general law of duration of human life; because this law only applies to a large number of selected lives, not to a single individual, or to a small number of individuals. Much of the success of life insurance companies depends upon the skill and integrity of the medical examiners.

It is worthy of notice, too, that if the number of deaths in any one year should prove to be remarkably small, it is not safe to assume that, because the losses by death in that year are greatly less than those called for by the Table of Mortality, the difference is clear gain, and can be disposed of as "*surplus*," and distributed at the end of the year; because the variation from the number of deaths called for by the Table of Mortality will probably soon vary on the other side. These losses have to be paid, and that promptly.

Besides variations from the table rate of mortality that may and do occur in practice, it should be noticed that in case a policy for $100,000 is grouped with ninety-nine others of $1000 each, the death of this single individual would be a greater loss to the company than that of the other ninety-nine policy-holders. These things and many others of a similar nature have to be closely watched.

Comparison between the Mortality experienced and that called for by the Table.—To compare, at the end of any calendar year, the mortality actually experienced by a company during that year, with that called for by the table of mortality used in computing net premiums, the following method may be and often is used. The results obtained, though not theoretically exact, seldom in practice involve appreciable error. Take all the insured in the company that attained, during the year, any named age. These are assumed to be exposed to the same risk. Those that were insured only for portions of the year are treated as so many fractions of a year. In illustration, take age 40; suppose that the number who reached this age during the year just passed is 120; and that of this number 100 have been insured during the whole year, five for three fourths of the year each, ten for half the year, three for one fourth of the year, and two for one twelfth of the year. We have $100+\frac{15}{4}+\frac{10}{2}+\frac{3}{4}+\frac{2}{12}=109\frac{2}{3}$=number of lives at risk for the whole year that reached forty years of age. The American Experience Table of Mortality shows that of 78,862 living at age 39, 756 of these will die before they reach age 40. Therefore the number of deaths to be expected in this case, as shown by the table of mortality we are now using, is expressed by $\frac{756\times109\frac{2}{3}}{78862}=1.051305$. If the actual mortality is less than the above, the result for this age is favorable; and if more it is unfavorable.

By a similar process, compare the deaths at each age with those called for by the mortality table, and the general result will show whether the actual number of deaths amongst all the insured in the company during the year just passed is greater or less than the number indicated by the table used.

It is not enough to know how the actual death rate compares with that of the table; because those who die in the year may be insured for more or less than the average policy in the company. To make an estimate of the whole amount of claims that should have accrued during the year for death losses on the original assumptions, it will be necessary to ascertain at each age the average amount at that age on which a year's risk of mortality has occurred, and multiply this amount by the table rate of mortality at the age.

The comparison of actual results with table assumptions, in regard both to number of deaths and amount of death claims, should be made in each company at least once a year. To facilitate these computations, tables have been constructed, that give in decimals the fraction of a year, from any day on which a policy may be issued to the end of the calendar year, and others giving the percentage of deaths to number living at each age in the mortality table.

Life Companies great Money Lenders.—It is often urged, that life insurance companies are absorbing a very large portion of the currency of the country; and many persons seem to apprehend that this will result in extraordinary scarcity of money. But it must be remembered that life insurance companies are compelled to keep their funds constantly invested; they are, therefore, forced to be lenders of money; and, as a general rule, they are more careful about the character of their securities than anxious to realize exorbitant rates of interest. Some of the States have passed laws requiring their companies to invest exclusively in securities in their own State or in United States bonds. These restrictive laws are unjust to the citizens of other States, policy-holders of these companies. A company should be allowed—if not peremptorily required—to invest in any State the net funds received from citizens of that State.

Campaign Literature.—The large per cent of the premiums paid to agents is an item of very heavy expense to life companies; and another great expense is the publishing of a large amount of what is called "campaign literature." It is perhaps impracticable for the companies to materially lessen these enormous expenses, so long as the present extraordinary competition is kept up, and *the public are not informed in regard to the true principles upon which the business ought to be conducted.*

If policy-holders had clear and distinct ideas of their own in regard to life insurance, and would seek for the best article at a fair price, as they already do in regard to their other purchases, the best companies would no doubt be but too glad to abate from their premiums that portion of the "loading" which now goes to pay these large commissions to agents and publish "campaign literature."

Re-insuring.—Existing laws in most of the States authorize insurance companies to re-insure any of their risks, or any part thereof. This was no doubt intended to apply to cases in which a company might have an opportunity to insure more upon one risk than it would, in the opinion of its officers, be justified in carrying. For instance, a person might desire to insure his life for $20,000. This risk, say, is taken by a company that can safely carry only $5000 on any one life. The company is by law authorized to place in other companies the remaining $15,000, or even the whole $20,000. This is done without consulting the policy-holder, or intimating to him that the company unaided does not feel safe in carrying the $20,000. The law in this respect, whilst very convenient for companies and advantageous to the agents who receive commissions on these large amounts, is hardly fair to policy-holders.

But when permission to reinsure any risk is used for the purpose of wholesale transfer of all the policy-holders of one company to another, without the knowledge or consent of the insured, and the interests of managers are alone consulted, reinsuring becomes in many cases a great evil, resulting in wholesale amalgamations, disaster, and ruin on a large scale.

To prevent this, it has been strongly urged that life insurance companies be prohibited from reinsuring any of their risks, or any part thereof, without the written consent of the policy-holder. Against this prohibition great outcry is made by many on the assumed ground that the interests of the policy-holders would often be sacrificed because companies are not allowed to transfer them by wholesale to the highest bidder. It has been well said that "the evil resulting from the power to reinsure given to life companies more than counterbalances the good possibly inherent in the exercise of that power." In admitting this, some over-zealous friends of policy-holders still insist that companies should be allowed to reinsure without consulting the insured. It required the consent of both parties to make the contract, and it is but fair that the consent of the insured should be obtained before he is traded off by the company that contracted with him.

On no account should any life insurance company be permitted to transfer its policy-holders or any portion of them to another company, and this company allowed to issue its own policies in lieu of those formerly issued by the first company, the new policy bearing the date of the transfer. This should not be permitted even with the written consent of the policy-holder, because it is a fraud for the purpose of escaping, on the part of the second company, liability for the accrued net value of the original policy.

Suppose, for instance, that a company has been doing business for ten years, it has 10,000 policies, the aggregate deposit or accrued net value of these policies being, say, $3,000,000. If all these policies are taken up by the second company, and new policies issued containing the same terms, *except* the date is that of the transfer instead of being that at which the policy was originally issued, the accrued liability is lost out of the accounts, and the manipulators of this transaction can at once appropriate the deposit of $3,000,000, leaving the future to take care of itself.

CHAPTER X.

VARIETY IN PLANS OF INSURANCE.

It has been recently stated on good authority, that "some companies in their prospectuses propose to issue as many as eight or nine hundred varieties of policies, each of which would require a distinct table of surrender values." This must be understood to apply to the length of time for which insurance is effected, as well as to differences of general plan.

The Superintendent of the Insurance Department of New-York, in his report, 1870, says: "It is believed to be a fact now causing quite general complaint, that there are too many complicated schemes or plans of insuring, as well as too many and too elaborate forms of contract or policy. It is difficult to perceive any excuse for the promulgation of so many theories and schemes, except upon the ground that they are intended to accomplish just what is accomplished, to wit, the entering into contracts by the insured, the true force and effect of which they do not understand."

It is suggested that life insurance companies and the actuaries should use their influence to lessen instead of increasing the number of plans and schemes, and endeavor to impart to the educated public correct and practical knowledge of the simple principles upon which true life insurance is founded.

Insurance for one year only.—The first question is the price to be paid at the beginning of the year for each $1 of insurance purchased by the policy-holder.

It is usual to assume that a person who applies for insurance is exactly a given number of years old. The mortality tables and the calculations are based upon whole years; and the age is taken to be the whole number of years nearest to the real age. For instance, if the real age of a person is thirty years and five months, he is considered thirty years old; but if the real age is thirty years and seven months, he is taken as thirty-one years old.

Although in theory the amount of a policy is not due until the end of the policy year within which the insured may die, it is usual for life insurance companies, in practice, to pay the policy within from thirty to ninety days after proof of the death of the insured.

In case of insurance for one year only, the *net* amount that must be paid at the beginning of the year to insure $1 to the heirs of the insured at the end of the year, *provided* he dies before that time, is calculated in the following manner.

Notice that if the insured does not die, the $1 is not to be paid to him or his heirs, and that the premium paid for this insurance is gone ; not lost, however, but paid out by the insured for insurance on his life for one year.

To obtain at any age the amount that will insure $1000, to be paid to the heirs of the insured at the end of one year, in case the insured dies during the year : a table showing the rate of mortality must be furnished, and a rate of interest fixed upon. Assume that the table is that which purports to give the rate of mortality among insured lives in this country, which is called, *American Experience Table of Mortality*. (See page 15.) Suppose the interest is assumed to be seven per cent, and that the person to be insured for one year is aged 50. The amount that will, if paid in advance, and invested at seven per cent, produce $1 certain in one year, when principal and interest at this rate for one year are added together, is obtained by dividing 100 by 107. This makes $0.934579. Then multiply this amount by the number of deaths given in the table opposite to age 50, which is 962, and divide the product by the number living at the same age, which is 69,804. The result is $0.012879. This is the amount that will insure $1 for one year, if paid in hand at age 50. One thousand times this amount, or $12.88, will insure $1000 for one year at the same age. In a precisely similar manner, the calculations are made for insurance for one year at any age, and for any amount, and at any rate of interest.

NOTE. The rate of interest that may be realized for one year must be judged of by the parties to the contract—namely, the insurer and the insured.

The mortality table is actuarial work—that is to say, the actuaries collect and arrange the statistics, and from observation of the death-rate deduce a table for practical use. In reference to tables of mortality, the distinguished Professor Edward Sang, of Edinburgh, says (in 1864), "The *smoothing*, as it is called, of a life-table is always to be deprecated; we can only judge of the propriety of smoothing by comparison with some table which we deem more trustworthy, but we ought to adopt that which is more deserving of confidence."

The differences in the tables now mostly used in this country are not so great as to be of much consequence in practice. None of them are supposed to express with perfect accuracy the law of duration of human life. Even if they did so express this law, there would be no certainty in advance that this law of duration would always apply to the insured lives in each company.

If the insurer can make only six per cent on the money during the year, the net amount that would have to be paid for the insurance in this case is greater than that in the foregoing example, in which the rate of interest is assumed to be seven per cent; because the amount of money necessary, at six per cent, to produce $1 in one year, is greater than the amount that will at seven per cent produce $1 in the same length of time. Whatever may be the rate of interest assumed, the insured can readily calculate as above the net price of his insurance for one year on the designated table of mortality, and at any named rate of interest. In this *net price* no allowance has been made for expenses or profits. Business men usually know something about expenses in general; and after getting at the above *net price*, they may form some idea of what the expense of this transaction ought to be to the company. In addition to expenses, there must be some margin for profit to the insurer, otherwise capital would not engage in the business.

From the above calculation, interest being seven per cent, we find that at age 50 it takes $128.79 *net price* to insure $10,000 for one year. Add to this say fifteen per cent for expenses and ten per cent for profits, and we have $160.99 full premium.

By comparing this with the premium charged by a company, an idea can be formed of the margin for contingencies and profits. On this plan, the policy-holder pays for insurance for one year only; if he does not die during the year, his premium goes to pay the policies of those that did die, and he has nothing. The objection to this plan is, that these yearly payments gradually increase until at the table limit, the *net price* of insurance for one year is the amount that will at net or table interest produce in one year the amount insured.

Another objection is, that the insured may not be able to pass the medical examination at the beginning of each following year. Medical examinations every year are expensive as well as vexatious. This kind of insurance at the younger ages is cheap, but not generally desirable for the reasons above given. Still there are many cases in which insurance for a short term may be advantageous.

Insurance for Whole Life paid for in Advance.—The *net* price in this case, as previously explained, is obtained from the commutation-tables by dividing M, at the age of the applicant for insurance, by D at the same age. The net single premium that will at age 50 insure $10,000 for whole life is $4300.37

We have just previously seen that, at age 50 the net price, interest being seven per cent, for insuring $10,000 for one year is $128.79. It is supposed that a man insures his life because he desires to leave money to his heirs in case of his death. There is no certainty that any individual will live for any named length of time, no matter how short that time may be. Suppose he insures his life for $10,000 for one year only, at age 50, as above, and dies during the year; his heirs get the $10,000. The net price is $128.79. But suppose he insures upon the net single premium plan for whole life and dies during the first year; his heirs would get the $10,000, but the net price is $4300.37. The *net* cost to the insurer is the same in each case, but the insured has paid $4300.37 for an amount that he might have secured to his heirs by the payment of $128.79. If he had not died before the end of the first year, the $128.79 he paid would have been gone, and he would not have been insured after the first year; whereas, the payment of $4300.37 effected his insurance for whole life. It is not easy to see why a person should desire to pay for whole-life insurance by a single premium in advance, if an arrangement can be made by which he can be certain that the insurance will continue for whole life, paid for by installments.

Insurance for Whole Life paid for by net Annual Premiums.—By reference to the table (page 32), it will be seen that, at age 50 (Am. Ex. 4½), the net annual premium that will insure $1000 for whole life is $32.490. Therefore, $324.90 is the net annual premium for a similar policy for $10,000. The net premium at age 50 for insuring $10,000 for one year only is $131.88 (Am. Ex. 4½. See page 19). Therefore, in case the insured pays $324.90 net annual premium at the beginning of the first year, he pays for more insurance than he gets from the company during that year; this overpayment is placed to his credit and forms the deposit at the end of the year for his policy. This plan is a medium between insurance for one year only and that for whole life by a net single premium.

Insurance for a long term of years, or for whole life, paid for in a limited number of years by equal annual premiums, partakes in a modified degree of the plan by which the whole insurance is effected by a single premium in advance. This plan may be advantageous in case the insured wants to pay fast and largely, in order to get through sooner than he would by paying less each year, but continuing to pay for a greater number of years.

The Decreasing Annual Premium Plan may be advantageous in case the insured desires to pay excessively the first year in order that his payment may be less the second year, but still pay excessively the second year in order that his payment for the third year may be less than it was the second; and so on, decreasing each year.

The Return Premium Plan.—A glance at the following table will show what these premiums must be at the different ages in order to carry out a contract to insure $1000 for whole life, and return all the premiums at death, *without interest*, and will show at the different ages the amount of *insurance* for each age that might be purchased with the same money under a contract with different conditions:

Age.	Net Annual Premium that will at different ages insure $1000 for whole life, and enable the Company to pay the policy at death, and return, in addition, the whole amount of premiums paid by the insured, *without interest.*	Amount of insurance for the first policy-year on the "Return Premium Plan."	Amount of insurance on the ordinary whole-life plan, purchased by a net annual premium, equal in amount to that charged on the Return Premium Plan. at same age.	Amount of insurance at different ages, for one year only, purchased by a net premium equal to net annual premium charged at the same age, on the Return Premium Plan.
10	13.584	1013.584	1362.078	1895.354
15	15.247	1015.247	1406.161	2087.201
20	17.472	1017.472	1460.137	2339.268
25	20.496	1020.496	1526.931	2655.954
30	24.687	1024.687	1609.742	3061.384
35	30.630	1030.630	1713.375	3577.853
40	39.284	1039.284	1844.233	4191.187
45	52.261	1052.261	2011.121	4892.436
50	72.313	1072.313	2225.700	5483.242
55	103.986	1103.986	2504.058	5851.443
60	155.365	1155.365	2869.637	6082.250
65	241.331	1241.331	3356.575	6284.498
70	389.633	1389.633	4017.001	6567.992
75	656.338	1656.338	4948.191	7267.853
80	1199.354	2199.354	6372.763	8675.569
85	2524.608	3524.608	8808 637	11200.170
90	6691.213	7691.213	13536.088	15383.089
95	22222.222	23222.222	23222.222	23222.222

Insurance for a Term of Years and Endowment at the end of the Term.—Strictly speaking, the ordinary life policies are, in fact, endowments at age 100 by the Actuaries' table, and at 96 by the American Experience. In the former, it is assumed that all living at age 99 will die before they reach 100, and in the latter that all living at age 95 will die before they are 96. It has been recommended with good reason that insurance upon lives in general should not extend beyond age 75, and suggested that endowment at that age be combined with insurance to that time. This suggestion, if adopted, would make the policy more costly, but would have the advantage of conferring upon the person who had paid the premiums means for his own use in case he survived the time at which men generally are not capable of much useful work, and when their dependents usually have no insurable pecuniary interest in their lives.

Insurance coupled with endowment, payable at age 75, or at death if prior, would have no objectionable features if taken out at the younger ages, or even before age 50. But short-term insurance, coupled with endowment, is a specious delusion to those who do not look closely into its practical effect. In illustration of this, take a policy at age 30 to secure $10,000, to be paid to the policy-holder at age 40, in case he is alive at that time; or to his heirs in case of his death if prior. This forms two distinct agreements in one contract. Assuming that the insurance element of the policy is clearly understood in all its features, including the cost, we will consider the endowment element separately. The calculation of the net single premium to secure this endowment is made as follows (Actuaries' four per cent): The amount that will produce $1 in one year at this rate is $0.96153846; multiply this quantity by itself nine times, or raise it to the tenth power, and we have $0.67556417, and this is the amount that will produce $1 in 10 years, at four per cent, compounded annually. But the amount is only to be paid in case the insured is alive at the end of the ten years. From the mortality table we are now using, we find that out of 86,292 persons living at age 30, there will be 78,653 living at age 40; therefore, 78,653, divided by 86,292, expresses the fraction that at age 30 represents the probability that the person will be alive at age 40. Hence, $0.67556417, multiplied by this fraction, gives the amount which, if paid in hand at age 30, will insure an endowment of $1 to be paid to the insured at age 40, if he is alive. Multiply this by 10,000, and we have $6157.60, which is the net single premium for an endowment of $10,000 as above. This *net* single premium, invested for ten years at 4 per cent compound interest, will produce $9114.75 certain; at 6 per cent, $11,027.32; at 10 per cent, $15,971.22.

To provide for expenses, net premiums are increased. Suppose the loading in this case is 20 per cent; the actual premium paid in advance will then be $7389.12. This invested at 4 per cent compound interest amounts in 10 years to $10,937.70; at 6 per cent, $13,232.78; at 10 per cent, $19,165.47; and the endowment of $10,000 is not to be paid to the insured unless he is alive at age 40. No prudent man who needs insurance should ever allow it to be coupled with short-term endowment. This remark applies in good degree to the "return premium plan," as it is called, by which the company obtains the use of a large amount of the policy-holder's money in excess of that needed to effect the insurance proper, and agrees to return all the policy-holder has paid, *without interest.* Another objection to this "return premium plan" is the comparative complexity of the calculations. *Joint-life insurance* may be desirable, perhaps, in a few exceptional cases. The same may be said of survivorships. There is not much business of this kind done in the United States, and it will probably be well if the amount diminishes.

Tontine Life Insurance.—The tontine principle gives certain specified advantages to survivors at the cost of their associates. For instance, one hundred persons may put up one thousand dollars each in the hands of trustees; the condition being that, at the end of twenty years, the whole fund and its accumulations shall be divided equally among the survivors. Tontines are of great variety in terms and conditions. Those policy-holders of a regular company who insure on this plan are placed in groups or classes by themselves. All of each group who allow their policies to lapse before the end of the tontine period forfeit the accrued deposit and accumulations. Those who die in that time receive the amount of the policy without increase from over-payments. No return of over-payments is made to any holders of these tontine policies before the expiration of the period. This leaves until that time a large amount in the hands of the company that would in other kinds of insurance be returned yearly to the policy-holders.

It is believed that the tontine principle had better not be mixed up with life insurance proper. Whenever it is so mixed, the groups should at least be clearly defined, so that all may know, from time to time, just how the accounts in these groups stand.

The Co-operative Plan.—This system or scheme is based upon *entrance fees* to pay expenses, and *voluntary contributions* after death has occurred, to pay losses. Considered as benevolent and charitable institutions amongst certain professions or brotherhoods, these co-operative associations may, under certain circumstances, be of great benefit to a few individuals. But there is no business basis in it, and not a single feature that entitles such an organization to be called an insurance company. They, however, often assume the name and claim to furnish insurance with more certainty and at less cost than can be done by the largest and best conducted purely mutual company that demands money in advance before contracting to insure lives and return all surplus.

These co-operatives usually die out soon, but new ones spring up, and this will no doubt continue until business men find out that to secure *real* life insurance it *must be paid for* in advance. As a rule, it will not do, in the long run, to trust this matter to *contributions* to be made, if at all, sixty days after the policy-holder is dead.

CHAPTER XI.

GROSS VALUATIONS—NET VALUATIONS.

By the gross method of valuing life policies, it is assumed that the future expenses will be less than the loading; and that, after making a reasonable estimate for these expenses, the remainder of the loading may be considered as profit, and the present value thereof entered in the assets of the company. The expenses may, for purposes of illustration, be fairly estimated at 15 per cent, and the loading at 30 per cent of the net premium.

In case the net annual premium at age 30 for a whole-life policy is $100, and the loading is $30, the expenses being $15 each year, there will then be $15 paid each year in excess of what is required to effect the insurance and pay expenses. Calculate the value at age 30 of a life series of annual payments of $15 each. To do this, divide N at age 30 by D at the same age. This will give, by the American Experience Table of Mortality, and 4½ per cent interest, $17.12 as the value at age 30 of a life series of payments of $1 each. Multiply this by 15, and we have the value at age 30 of a life series of annual payments of $15 each. This value is $256.80. By considering this as a realized asset, the accounts would seem to show that the company in making this contract had immediately become $256.80 richer by this operation; because it has received sufficient to effect the insurance it has contracted to furnish, pay expenses, and, in addition, is to receive $15 a year for life from the insured.

Thirty thousand such policies as the above would, by this method of gross valuation, result in entering at once among the assets $7,704,000 clear profit. This too, notwithstanding the fact that the whole sum received by the company is but $3,900,000 out of which to pay death losses and expenses during the year, and provide for the deposit that must be held at the end of the year.

In this connection, attention is called to the following extract from the report of a committee of the British Parliament in 1853. (The party under examination was the actuary of the "Royal Exchange Assurance Office.")

Question: "Do you think there is any thing peculiar in the character of life assurance business which would justify the legislature in interfering with it in a way different from other business?"

Answer: "Yes; both on account of the long period over which the contracts extend, and especially for this reason: that life assurance offices are now taking to make up their accounts on principles that would be scouted from any other department of commercial enterprise."

Question: "Will you explain what principle you mean?"

Answer: "The practice of anticipating future profits and treating them as assets. Allow me to suppose the case of a bank making up its accounts: it owes to its depositors £1,000,000; it has on hand £900,000; it puts down as an additional item of assets, profits, we will say, at the rate of £10,000 a year, valued at twenty years' purchase; by that means, it makes its assets £1,100,000 against £1,000,000, and the result is stated to be a surplus of £100,000. That principle would never be adopted in a bank, and I think it ought not to be adopted in an assurance company."

Question: "But does it exist in assurance companies?"

Answer: "It is done."

Question: "Is it done by assurance companies generally, or only in particular cases?"

Answer: "It is in considerable use, and the practice is extending."

It is a safe business rule not to estimate your present wealth and regulate your present expenses by what you suppose your clear profits will be in future years. When the first payment of $15 in excess of the net premium and expenses has been realized by the company out of the premiums paid by each of the thirty thousand policy-holders, the profits from this source, namely, $450,000, may be entered in the assets. The remainder of the $7,704,000 should not be counted as assets before it is realized.

In case the "loading" and other resources of a company should prove to be in excess of expenses, and all claims other than those provided for by *net* premiums and *net* interest thereon, profit will result. But in view of the great and increasing number of policies that lapse or are surrendered, it would be dangerous to permit companies to assume that all their existing policies will continue in the company to maturity, and that their future yearly expenses will be certainly a given amount less than the loading, and place in their accounts, under the guise of assets realized and on hand, the amount of *supposed* profits the company *may* make in the future.

Lapsed Policies.—Policies are often allowed to lapse from inability to pay the premium. Sometimes this occurs because the policy-holder no longer needs to insure his life. But it is believed that much the larger portion of surrendered and lapsed policies arise from misapprehension on the part of policy-holders at the time of taking out the policy in regard to its precise nature and effect. It is not harsh to say that this arises often from the fact that agents do not take the pains to explain, even when they themselves understand, the exact nature of the policy they sell.

The companies have not, as a rule, shown any over-anxiety to have other than favorable views presented to the policy-holder at the time of signing the contract.

Full information, fair and candid dealing at the time the policy is issued is absolutely essential, if companies desire to diminish the number of polices surrendered and allowed to lapse.

This general principle is applicable to all kinds of business. Life insurance forms no exception to this rule, nor to the fact that success in business does not necessarily depend upon the amount of business done. The terms of the contract—the policy—should be made explicit and fair.

Knowledge of life insurance, full and exact information, is what is needed. It will not hurt officers of companies, directors, trustees, or agents, and it is essential that some of the policy-holders should understand this subject.

The Legal Standard of Safety.—"Something more than bare commercial solvency is required of life insurance companies." The laws of many of the States are intended to guard with especial care these trust funds held by corporations for future widows and orphans. The character of the securities in which these funds may be invested is prescribed; a deposit of one hundred thousand dollars with a principal financial officer of the State is required; the law determines the various items that may be admitted as assets, and designates the table of mortality and rate of interest to be used as a basis for calculating the liability of the company on account of the deposit that must be held for all policies the company has in force. On this point, the law in one or more of the States provides that—

"When the actual funds of any life insurance company doing business in this Commonwealth are not of a net cash value equal to its liabilities, counting as such the net value of its policies, according to the 'American Experience' rate of mortality, with interest at four and one half per centum per annum, it shall be the duty of the Insurance Commissioner to give notice to such company and its agents to discontinue issuing new policies within this Commonwealth until such time as its funds have become equal to its liabilities, valuing its policies as aforesaid."

The question of commercial solvency is not raised by carrying into effect the foregoing requirements of law. But it is made the duty of the commissioner, after giving notice to the company to cease issuing new policies, to examine all its affairs, and if he is "of opinion," after such examination, that "a company is insolvent, or that its condition is such as to render its further proceedings hazardous to the public, or to those holding its policies, he shall report to the Attorney-General, who shall bring the matter before a court of competent jurisdiction; and the court, after full hearing, shall make such orders and decrees as may be needful, according to the usual course of proceedings in equity."

In strictly adhering to the system of net valuation as the legal standard of safety for a life insurance company, and requiring that the admitted assets of such a company shall be held in the securities prescribed by law, it does not follow that when a company fails to come up to this standard it should necessarily be given over to be divided in pieces, and its funds absorbed in the never-ending expenses of a chancery court.

The failure of a company to stand the test of net valuation computed upon data designated by the State, is an alarm-bell that should be heeded by all. In case it is, on close examination of all the facts, clear that the difficulty can not be remedied, then the assets of the company should be equitably and promptly distributed to the legal owners thereof. In case it is clear that a company may recuperate, by reducing expenses below the loading, and giving time for improvement in the condition of its affairs, arising from a rate of mortality that may be less, and a rate of interest greater than that upon which the net premiums are based, it will be well to allow the company time to endeavor to retrieve its lost ground, and re-establish its impaired deposit. But this should only be done when there is good reason to believe that the interests of the policy-holders will be benefited thereby, and not for the purpose of permitting companies to continue in business, merely because it is assumed by them that they will, in the future, make great profits.

In at least one State the law requires that a life insurance company shall cease to issue new policies whenever the admitted assets are twenty thousand dollars less than its liabilities, including in the latter the one hundred thousand dollars deposited with a principal financial officer of the State. It would seem that this should be the law in all the States, because there is an evident absurdity in requiring this amount to be deposited with the treasurer or other State officer for the better security of all the policy-holders of the company in the United States, and then permitting the company to at once incur liabilities for the whole of this amount.

But existing laws in nearly all of the States authorize life insurance companies to continue issuing new policies until the whole capital, including the one hundred thousand dollars deposited with the State, is exhausted.

Net Valuation.—The "loading" upon net premiums is, as previously stated, intended to provide for expenses, profits, and adverse contingencies. The State, in prescribing a table of mortality and rate of interest upon which to calculate net values in life insurance, designates the amount that will on these data safely effect the insurance. In calculating the deposit or reserve that must be held by a company at any time to the credit of a policy, the law authorizes the value of the future net premiums to be deducted from the net single premium. This is done because these net premiums together are, upon the data originally assumed, just sufficient to effect the insurance. If the insured at any future time fails to pay his net premiums, the insurance ceases, and no harm results from having at a previous time credited the company with the value of these future net premiums. This does not, however, hold good in case a company has been credited with that part of the loading on these future net premiums, not required for expenses, simply because in failing to receive this part of the loading, the company is not relieved from any equivalent obligation, and this item, previously admitted as a valid credit, falls to zero in case future premiums are not paid. And as this contingency may happen with respect to any policy—and often does occur—the State has fixed upon the method of net valuation as the standard of safety.

Some companies that base their net premiums on six per cent, maintain that they fully comply with the four and a half per cent standard, when they have a deposit for each policy equal to that called for by the valuation tables computed upon the four and a half per cent basis. In this they ignore the fact that these tables assume that the future net premiums the company has contracted to receive are those called for by the State standard of safety. Therefore, the results given in these tables are not correct, in case the company has contracted to furnish insurance for future net premiums less than those called for by the State standard.

Whole-Life Policy for $1000, *taken out at Age* 20, *paid for by equal annual Premiums of* $10.364 *each. American Experience, six per cent. The net annual Premium required by Law on the American Experience, four and a half per cent, is* $11.966. *The difference between the legal net annual Premium and that which the Company agrees to receive is* $1.602.

Age.	Net value at the beginning year.	Increased by seven per cent for one year, amounts at the end of the year to	Deposit or reserve on a six per cent valuation, (which, deducted from $1000, gives amount at risk each year.)	Cost of insurance on amount at risk on a six per cent deposit.	Amount of policy-holder's money available for deposit, after paying cost of insurance.	Deposit on data designated by law, (4½%.)	Value of a life series of annual premiums, each equal to $1.602, the difference between net 4½% and net 6%.	Deposit the company must have, according to the legal standard of safety.	Amount the capitalist has to put up, in order to make the deposit conform to the legal standard of safety.	Amount the capitalist is out of pocket, considering the first deposit and compound interest thereon at 7%, after allowing for amounts returned.	Amount returned each year to the capitalist.	Clear gain to the capitalist at the end of each respective year, after his money and compound interest thereon has been returned to him.	Age.
20	$10.364	$11.089	$3.206	$7.780	$3.309	$4.736	$28.943	$33.679	$30.370	$30.370	....	......	20
21	13.673	14.630	6.691	7.802	6.828	9.675	28.831	38.506	......	31.678	$0.818	......	21
22	17.192	18.395	10.399	7.825	10.570	14.825	28.681	43.506	......	32.936	.959	......	22
23	20.934	22.399	14.346	7.844	14.555	20.199	28.524	48.723	......	34.168	1.081	......	23
24	24.919	26.663	18.552	7.862	18.801	25.807	28.361	54.168	......	35.367	1.193	......	24
25	29.165	31.207	23.036	7.879	23.328	31.664	28.191	59.855	......	36.527	1.316	......	25
26	33.692	36.050	27.809	7.905	28.145	37.770	28.013	65.783	......	37.638	1.446	......	26
27	38.509	41.205	32.892	7.928	33 277	44.139	27.828	71.967	......	38.690	1.583	......	27
28	43.641	46.696	38.312	7.947	38.749	50.784	27.634	78.418	......	39.669	1.729	......	28
29	49.113	52.551	44.083	7.977	44.574	57.710	27.432	85.142	......	40.568	1.878	......	29
30	54.938	78.784	50.231	8.003	50.781	64.932	27.222	92.154	......	41.373	2.035	......	30
31	61.145	65.425	56.787	8.027	57.398	72.464	27.003	99.467	......	42.069	2.200	......	31
32	67.762	72.505	63.769	8.059	64.446	80.313	26.774	107.087	......	42.641	2.373	......	32
33	74.810	80.047	71.201	8.098	71.949	88.485	26.536	115.021	......	43.072	2.554	......	33
34	82.313	88.075	79.120	8.132	79.943	96.997	26.289	123.286	......	43.343	2.744	......	34
35	90.307	96.623	87.562	8.163	88.465	105.867	26.030	131.897	......	43.432	2.944	......	35
36	98.829	105.747	96.548	8.211	97.536	115.093	25.762	140.855	......	43.319	3.153	......	36
37	107.900	115.453	106.120	8.254	107.199	124.693	25.482	150.175	......	42.976	3.375	......	37
38	117.563	125.792	116.303	8.314	117.478	134.667	25.192	159.859	......	42.381	3.603	......	38
39	127 842	136.791	127.145	8.368	128.423	145.035	24.890	169.925	......	41.502	3.846	......	39
40	138.787	148.502	138.678	8.436	140.066	155.797	24.577	180.374	......	40.308	4.099	......	40
41	150.430	160.960	150.959	8.497	152.463	166.976	24.251	191.227	......	38.764	4.366	......	41
42	162.827	174.225	164.026	8.571	165.654	178.572	23.914	202.486	......	36.832	4.645	......	42
43	176.018	188.339	177.933	8.646	179.693	190.600	23.564	214.164	......	34.471	4.939	......	43
44	190.057	203.361	192.719	8.741	194.620	203.051	23.201	226.252	......	31.632	5.252	......	44
45	204.984	219.333	208.447	8.831	210.497	215.941	22.826	238.767	......	28.270	5.576	......	45
46	220.861	236.321	225.154	8.959	227.362	229.250	22.438	251.688	......	24 326	5.924	......	46
47	237.726	254.367	242.904	9.086	245.281	242.986	22.039	265.025	......	19.744	6.285	......	47
48	255.645	273.540	261.749	9.235	264.305	257.132	21.627	278.759	......	14.454	6.672	......	48

49	274.669	293.896	281.736	9.413	284.483	271.001	21.204	292.865	......	8.382	7.084	......	49
50	294.847	315.486	302.931	*9.607	305.879	286.558	20.770	307.328	......	1.449	7.520	......	50
51	316.243	338.380	......	9.856	328.524	301.805	20.326	322.131	......	......	7.943	$6.393	51
52	332.495	355.770	......	10.199	345.571	317.387	19.873	337.260	......	......	8.311	15.152	52
53	347.624	371.958	......	10.572	361.386	333.283	19.410	352.693	......	......	8.698	24.906	53
54	363.057	388.471	......	10.987	377.484	349.469	18.939	368.408	......	......	9.076	35.725	54
55	378.772	405.286	......	11.433	393.853	365.923	18.460	384.383	......	......	9.470	47.696	55
56	394.747	422.379	......	11.920	410.459	382.617	17.974	400.591	......	......	9.868	60.903	56
57	410.955	439.722	......	12.438	427.284	399.528	17.481	417.009	......	......	10.275	75.441	57
58	427.373	457.289	......	12.990	444.299	416.631	16.983	433.614	......	......	10.685	91.407	58
59	443.978	475.056	......	13.587	461.469	433.890	16.481	450.371	......	......	11.098	108.903	59
60	460.735	492.986	......	14.221	478.765	451.271	15.975	467.246	......	......	11.519	128.045	60
61	477.610	511.043	......	14.896	496.147	468.740	15.466	484.206	......	......	11.941	148.949	61
62	494.570	529.190	......	15.607	513 583	486.261	14.956	501.217	......	......	12.366	171.741	62
63	511.581	547.392	......	16.353	531.089	503.805	14.445	518.250	......	......	12.789	196.552	63
64	528.614	565.617	......	17.136	548.481	521.330	13.935	535.265	......	......	13.216	223.527	64
65	545.629	583.823	......	17.969	565.854	538.786	13.427	552.213	......	......	13.641	252.815	65
66	562.577	601.947	......	18.835	583.112	556.136	12.922	569.058	......	......	14.054	284.566	66
67	579.422	619.982	......	19.737	600.245	573.337	12.421	585.758	......	......	14.487	318.973	67
68	596.122	637.851	......	20.683	617.168	590.338	11.926	602.264	......	......	14.904	356.205	68
69	612.628	655.512	......	21.653	633.859	607.106	11.438	618.544	......	......	15.315	396.454	69
70	628.908	672.932	......	22.655	650.277	623.596	10.958	634.554	......	......	15.723	439.929	70
71	644.918	690.062	......	23.664	666.398	639.787	10.487	650.274	......	......	16.124	486.848	71
72	660.638	706.883	......	24.647	682.236	655.696	10.024	665.720	......	......	16.516	537.443	72
73	676.084	723.410	......	25.583	697.827	671.356	9.568	680.924	......	......	16.903	591.967	73
74	691.288	739.678	......	26.462	713.216	686.816	9.118	695.934	......	......	17.282	650.687	74
75	706.298	755.739	......	27.293	728.446	702.115	8.672	710.787	......	......	17.658	713.893	75
76	721.151	771.632	......	28.083	743.549	717.290	8.230	725.520	......	......	18.029	781.895	76
77	735.884	787.396	......	28.862	758.534	732.345	7.792	740.137	......	......	18.403	855.031	77
78	750.501	803.036	......	29.648	773.388	747.268	7.358	754.626	......	......	18.762	933.645	78
79	764.990	818.539	......	30.433	788 106	762.054	6.927	768.981	......	......	19.125	1018.125	79
80	779.345	833.899	......	31.338	802.561	776.573	6.505	783.078	......	......	19.483	1108.877	80
81	793.442	848 983	......	32.206	816.777	790.851	6.089	796.940	......	......	19.837	1206 335	81
82	807.304	863.815	......	33.007	830.808	804.947	5.678	810.625	......	......	20.183	1310.961	82
83	820.981	878.458	......	33.663	844.795	819.001	5.269	824.270	......	......	20.525	1423.253	83
84	834.634	893.058	......	34.253	858.805	833.081	4.859	837.940	......	......	20.865	1543.746	84
85	848.304	907.685	......	34.980	872.705	847.045	4.453	851.498	......	......	21.207	1673.015	85
86	861.862	922.192	......	35.947	886.245	860.641	4.057	864.698	......	......	21.547	1811.673	86
87	875.062	936.316	......	37.199	899.117	873.560	3.681	877.241	......	......	21.876	1960.366	87
88	887.605	949.737	......	38.448	911.289	885.773	3.325	889.098	......	......	22.191	2119.783	88
89	899.462	962.424	......	39.356	923.068	897.601	2.981	900.582	......	......	22.486	2290.654	89
90	910.946	974.712	......	40.051	934.661	909.245	2.642	911.887	......	......	22.774	2473.774	90
91	922.251	986.809	......	41.283	945.526	920.144	2.325	922.469	......	......	23.057	2669.995	91
92	932.833	998.131	......	43 685	954 446	929.060	2.065	931.125	......	......	23.321	2880.216	92
93	941.489	1007.393	......	44.586	962.807	937.450	1.821	939.271	......	......	23.536	3105.367	93
94	949.635	1016.109	......	45.794	970.815	944.972	1.602	946.574	......	......	23.741	3346.484	94
95	956.938	1023.924	......	00.000	1023.924	1000.000	0.000	1000.000	......	......	23.924	3604.662	95

* NOTE.—The amounts in the column headed, "Cost of insurance on amount at risk on a six per cent deposit," are calculated on this basis each year, up to and including age 50. At age 51, and each following year, to include age 95, the amounts in the same column are calculated on the basis of a four and a half per cent deposit, increased each year by the value at that time of a life series of annual premiums, each premium being equal to the difference between the net premium on a six per cent basis and the net premium called for by the legal standard of safety.

The table on pages 134 and 135 is intended to illustrate the case in which the net premium charged by a company is based upon the American Experience Table of Mortality and six per cent interest. A whole-life policy for $1000 is assumed to be taken out at age 20, paid for by equal net annual premiums of $10.364 each—this being the amount called for by the above-named table of mortality and rate of interest. The net annual premium to insure $1000 for whole life at age 20, American Experience four and a half per cent, is $11.966. Therefore the net annual premium which the company, on a six per cent basis, agrees to receive, is $1.602 less than the legal net annual premium on the four and a half per cent basis. In the table on pages 134 and 135, the deposit or "reserve" at the end of each year held by the company to the credit of this policy is brought up to that called for by the legal standard of safety established by the State, by adding the value at that age of a life series of annual premiums, each equal to $1.602. It will be seen that at the end of the first year the company will have to place $30.37 in deposit to the credit of this policy, in order to conform to the established legal four and a half per cent standard. The next year a portion of this amount can be withdrawn by the company, and so on increasing the amount withdrawn each successive year. At age 51, the amount so withdrawn will be more than the whole amount originally deposited by the company and seven per cent interest thereon. From that time the amounts that may be withdrawn each year on account of this policy continue to increase, and at 95 these yearly sums and interest thereon at seven per cent per annum amount to $3604.662, after having paid back to the company its original deposit, $30.37 and interest.

Suppose that a company had insured as above ten thousand policy-holders. It would be required to deposit to the credit of these policies, at the end of the first year, out of its own resources, $303,700 in order to bring the deposit resulting from a six per cent premium up to the legal 4½ per cent standard. When a company does this, it can not be fairly said that its capital is impaired in a sense affecting injuriously the real security of the policies. The established standard of safety is maintained, and the table shows clearly that if the policy continues, so far from requiring more capital to be deposited to its credit by the company, this amount becomes less and less, until the special original deposit made by the company is safely withdrawn; and on the data assumed, capital begins rapidly to make large profits, in addition to affording all the security required by the established legal standard. On net calculations, the company will not only get back the original deposit with interest thereon, but it will make a clear profit on the policy that persists to the table limit, $3604.66, besides paying the policy of $1000 at age 96.

It will be noticed that the table is constructed upon net values, and it should be borne in mind that the net premiums are in practice loaded in order to provided for expenses and contingencies; that the loading is generally more than enough to pay expenses, and that when a limited number of shareholders receive profits yearly, arising from the excess of loading over expenses, on a large number of premiums, the profits from this source alone may well be very great.

It is maintained by those who are believed to know, that the tables of mortality in use show a higher death-rate than will actually occur amongst well-selected lives, which, if true, will be a large additional source of profit to the shareholders, besides profits that may and do often arise from surrender charges and forfeitures.

It is claimed by some that human lives of the same age can be classed in such a manner that the long-lived may be assured at one price, and the short-lived at another and greater price, a good deal in the manner in which different kinds of property are classified in fire insurance. In short, they insure certain classes at a higher and others at a lower rate than the medium or average risk. It has, however, not yet been found generally practicable and safe to regulate the net price of life insurance on the assumed individual longevity of each isolated policy-holder.

The representatives of some companies insist that it is not just or reasonable to apply to them the test prescribed by the State, of net values based upon a designated table of mortality and rate of interest, because, they say, they have selected extra good risks, and that the death-rate amongst the insured in their companies will certainly be less than that given by the table of mortality. If their estimates prove to be correct in this respect, the company will eventually reap the benefit arising from a lower death-rate amongst its policy-holders. But the State assumes that it is safer for all companies to be held, at the end of each year, to a designated general standard based upon observation and experience.

CHAPTER XII.

THE DEPOSIT WHEN A RENEWAL PREMIUM IS NOT PAID SHOULD BE USED FOR EFFECTING FULL-PAID INSURANCE—ANNUAL STATEMENTS.

In case a life policy is not renewed by the payment of the annual premium when due, the company has in its hands the deposit intended solely for the *future* insurance of this policy. The policy-holder has paid for all the insurance the company has previously furnished him; paid his share of the previous expenses; contributed his proportion toward the profits, and the company holds a deposit paid by him for future insurance. It is claimed by some that the withdrawal of a policy-holder is an injury to those who remain in the company, and that on the non-payment of a renewal premium, he should forfeit the deposit held by the company.

The justice of this forfeiture is denied. So long as the death rate among the insured conforms to that given in the table of mortality, and the interest realized is that assumed, the net premiums are just sufficient to pay death losses year by year, and provide the requisite deposit for each policy.

Therefore, so far as paying death losses is concerned, and considering the *net* premiums only, it makes no difference to the company whether it has a greater or less number of policies in force, *provided* the mortality conforms to the rate designated in the table. The number insured may be 100,000 or 1,000,000; the company with one million of policy-holders would make no more out of the normal net contributions of each policy-holder to pay death-claims than the company with one hundred thousand policy-holders would make out of the net premiums of each of its policy-holders.

In other words, in case 900,000 policy-holders withdraw from a company containing 1,000,000, so far as net values are concerned, the company, when reduced to 100,000 policy-holders, is just exactly as strong in resources for paying death-claims as it was before the 900,000 withdrew. This is so, because when nine tenths of them withdraw, and diminish the net premiums of the company 90 per cent, their withdrawal diminishes the death-claims in just the same proportion. *Expense* incurred in the transaction of the business of a company is a different thing. The working expenses of a company consisting of 100,000 policy-holders ought to be less on each policy than that of a company consisting of 1000 policy-holders should be on each of its policies.

In estimating "the value of a policy-holder to a company to keep," we pass from the theory of net values to the consideration of ordinary business matters, such as expenses, loading, interest realized in excess of table rate, the health of the policy-holder at the time of proposed withdrawal, the cost of getting a policy-holder into the company, and whatever may have a practical bearing on the particular case. In determining what should be done with the accrued deposit in case the contract for insurance is not renewed at the beginning of any policy year, it should not be forgotten that the insurance the company furnishes is not the amount called for by the policy—it is the amount at risk, which is the face of the policy, less this deposit.

Until a very recent period, it was the custom of life insurance companies to appropriate to themselves the whole of the accrued deposit, in case the insured failed to renew the contract by paying the annual premium when due. The rights of withdrawing policy-holders in this regard are getting to be somewhat better understood, and many of the companies show a willingness, at least in part, to respect them.

The insured has no right, in equity, at his own option, to demand, at the time of withdrawal, the return to him of any portion of the deposit accrued on his policy. The original contract was for insurance; the deposit is intended to provide for future insurance; and all that the policy-holder is in equity entitled to is the insurance that this deposit will at that time effect.

In determining this amount, the future *expenses* of the policy must be provided for; and the remainder of the deposit only can be properly used as a net single premium for full-paid insurance. No further collections of premiums have to be made, and no agent's commissions thereon paid; therefore the expense will probably be little else than that attendant upon the investment and keeping of the funds. The interest actually received being usually more than the table net rate, this excess of interest might well be more than enough to cover the necessary expense upon the policy. When the accrued deposit is large, and the amount at risk consequently small compared with the policy, it seems absurd, as authorized by law in some States, to allow the company to deduct 20 per cent of the deposit, and furnish full-paid insurance for the remainder only.

This, however, is greatly better for the withdrawing policy-holders than the former system under which the company appropriated to itself the whole of the deposit in case of the non-payment of a renewal premium when due. If those who procured the passage of the State laws, just referred to, had based the deductions on the amount at risk, instead of on the amount of the deposit, it would have been more equitable.

Take, for instance, the deduction of 20 per cent of the deposit at the end of the first year; find what per cent this sum is of the amount at risk the first year. Having thus fixed the rate per cent of the amount at risk to be used in computing the sum to be deducted from the deposit, the deduction will be less as the policy grows older, instead of increasing as it does under existing laws, above referred to. For example, the deposit at the end of the first year for an ordinary life policy of $10,000, issued at age 20 (Am. Ex. $4\frac{1}{2}$) is $47.36. Therefore the amount at risk the first year is $9952.64.

Twenty per cent of the deposit at the end of the first year is $9.472. This sum is equivalent to $\frac{952}{1000000}$ (which is a small fraction less than one tenth of one per cent) of the amount at risk the first year. At the end of the first year, then, the deduction of twenty per cent from the deposit gives substantially the same as a deduction of one tenth of one per cent of the amount at risk. At the end of the fiftieth policy year, the deposit is $6235.96. Therefore the amount at risk that year is $3764.04. The 20 per cent deducted before applying this deposit to the purchase of full-paid insurance is $1247.19. One tenth of one per cent of the amount at risk is $3.76.

At age 94, the deposit is $9449.72. The amount at risk during the year is $550.28. Twenty per cent, to be deducted before applying this deposit to the purchase of full-paid insurance, is $1889.94. One tenth of one per cent of the amount at risk is $0.55.

The glaring inequity of a rule that allows a deduction of $1889.94 to be made from the deposit when the whole amount at risk during the year is but $550.28 needs no comment.

It is maintained by some that the policy-holders who cease to pay renewal premiums when due are nearly always in sound health, with fair prospects for long life, and that the unhealthy policy-holders remain. This selection against the company will, it is claimed, result in a very high rate of mortality amongst those that continue.

It is not at all clear that any large proportion of policy-holders cease to pay renewal premiums merely because they are in good health. But, be this as it may, existing legal contracts must stand unless modified with the consent of all the parties; but in contracts yet to be made the companies should not be permitted to seize upon and appropriate to themselves the accrued net value of life insurance policies. After making a deduction therefrom for future expenses, and fair compensation for diminished vitality in the company, caused by the failure to pay a renewal premium, the remainder should be used as a net single premium for full-paid insurance—the *term* of this full-paid insurance being that named in the original contract, the *amount* being determined by the net single premium.

ANNUAL STATEMENTS.

In many of the States, all the companies that do business therein are required by law to make annual statements to the insurance commissioner.

These statements give the assets and liabilities at the end of the year, and income and expenditures during the year, in full detail; and in addition a balance-sheet, taking as a basis the assets of the company at the beginning of the year.

The balance-sheet is an effective probe, often resisted by those who do not care to fully expose all the details of the business of a company, or take the trouble to explain them. It is believed that the following explanation will illustrate to policy-holders the importance of having this requirement of the law enforced upon those who hold these trust funds.

In the balance-sheet, for the end of any year, the assets on hand at the beginning of the year are taken as the basis; add to this the income during the year, and gains, if any, in market value of securities and other property; gains from accrued interest; gains in amount of uncollected premiums, in rents, and in any other item not included, either in assets at the beginning of the year or in income during the year. This gives the amount to be accounted for at the end of the year. From this deduct the expenditures—deduct the depreciation, if any, during the year, in market value of securities and other property—and deduct all other losses or depreciations in market value. When these deductions are made from the amount to be accounted for, the result gives the market value of the assets that ought to be on hand. If the required assets are on hand, the account is correct; but if the assets on hand at the end of the year are either more or less than the amount called for after the specified deductions are made, there is an error which should be found and corrected. The details of gains and depreciations are required to be given in explanatory schedules, the form of which each company arranges to suit its own business and books. In illustration, suppose the result as given by a detailed schedule of the investment account made out by a company shows a gain of $10,000. This would be added to the assets at the beginning of the year, and indicated in the balance-sheet under the head of "Balance of investment account, credit side;" but if the detailed schedule of the investment account showed a loss during the year of $10,000, this in the balance-sheet would be added to the expenditures, and indicated by "Balance of investment account, debit side." The blank form of balance-sheet provides, on both the credit and debit sides, for "*balance* of investment account;" so that if the balance, as shown by the schedule, is *gain*, it may be added to the assets on hand at the beginning of the year; or if the balance is *loss*, it may be added to the expenditures. The same applies to the schedule of profit and loss, showing this detailed account. If this account shows a *gain* of $10,000, the form of balance-sheet provides under the heading, "Balance of profit and loss account, credit side," for adding this to the assets on hand at the beginning of the year; but if this detailed schedule shows a *loss* of $10,000, the blank form of balance-sheet provides that this be added to the expenditures, and it is entered on that side of the balance-sheet, under the heading, "Balance of profit and loss account, debit side."

For instance, suppose the assets at the beginning of the year amount to $500,000, the cash income is $1,000,000; gains in market value and other gains, $100,000. This gives $1,600,000 to be accounted for. Suppose the expenditures to have been $700,000. This indicates that there should be $900,000 assets at the end of the year. Suppose the assets are only worth $800,000, the balance-sheet and its explanatory schedules must account, item by item, for the missing $100,000.

These annual statements are required to be made in the form that may be prescribed by the commissioner, and give all the information asked for by him in regard to the business and affairs of the company, the whole verified by the signature and oath of the president and secretary of the company.

The law further provides that whenever the commissioner suspects the correctness of any annual statement, or that the affairs of any company making such statement are in an unsound condition, he shall visit and examine such company. At such times, he shall have access to its books and papers, and shall thoroughly inspect and examine all its affairs, and he may summon and examine, under oath, the directors, officers, and agents of any insurance company, and such other persons as he may think proper, in relation to the affairs, transactions, and condition of said company.

The law in many of the States has imposed the foregoing and other important conditions upon life insurance companies; but, after all, a great deal is left to the judgment and discretion of the policy-holder in selecting the kind of insurance he needs, and the company in whose hands he proposes to place funds in trust for the benefit of his heirs. No person should make an application to a company for insurance on his life until he has carefully read the form of the policy which is to be the contract between himself and the company.

Life insurance will bear the closest scrutiny. *It needs it.* The most important element in the accounts is an accurate registry, or descriptive list of the policies in force. Without this, no computation can be made of the accrued liability of a company, on account of the net value of its policies, which is the amount the company should have on hand *deposited* to the credit of the policies.

"In some cases, life policies have been reported not in force, the "company thereby escaping liability for the net value thereof, when, "in fact, the terms of these policies obligated the company for a specific amount of full-paid insurance in lieu of the policy reported "not in force." After getting an exact description of all the policies in force, and calculating the liability of the company on account of the accrued net value of these policies, and adding thereto all other liabilities of the company, it becomes important to know the nature and amount of assets held by the company to meet its liabilities. Even mortgages, on improved, productive, unencumbered real estate, worth more than double the amount loaned thereon, have been made *delusive.*

Well might Mr. Gladstone, in a speech delivered March 7th, 1864, in the British House of Commons, state, "I dare say there are "not many members of this house who know to what an extraordi-"nary extent the public are dependent on the prudence, the high "honor, and the character of those concerned in the management of "these institutions."

APPENDIX.

APPENDIX.

CHAPTER XIII.

EXTRACTS FROM MASSERES ON ANNUITIES, LONDON, 1783, AND QUOTATIONS FROM AMERICAN ACTUARIES, 1870, 1853, AND 1871.

THESE extracts show an earnest desire on the part of Masseres to convey to his readers a thorough understanding of the principles on which calculations of the "True Value" or "Fair Price" of annuities are based.

EXTRACTS—MASSERES, 1783.

An explanation of the *data* or grounds upon which the computations of the values of annuities for lives are built. These are, first, the decrease of the present value of a future sum of money arising from the mere distance of time at which it is to be paid, and the consequent discount that is to be allowed to the purchaser of it for prompt payment (the quantity of which discount, it is evident, will depend on the rate of interest of money); and, secondly, the chance which, when the payment of such future sum is not made certain, but is to depend on the continuance of the life of a person of a given age, the grantor of it has of escaping the necessity of paying it at all by means of the death of the said person before it becomes due, in order to determine which chance, it is necessary to have recourse to certain tables of the several probabilities of the duration of human life at every different year of age, which have been formed from observations of the numbers of persons who have died every year, in the course of a long series of years, at different ages, in divers cities and parishes, and other numerous bodies of men.

The doctrine of life annuities is by no means of so abstruse and difficult a nature as many people are apt to imagine. A moderate share of common sense, or capacity to reason justly, and a knowledge of common arithmetic, are all the qualities that are necessary to a right understanding of the principles on which it is founded, even so far as to be able to compute the value of any proposed annuity for any given life or number of lives, if a person is disposed to undergo the labor of performing all the necessary arithmetical operations that arise in such a computation.

TABLE

Representing the probabilities of the duration of human life at the several ages therein mentioned, from the age of three years to the age of 95, grounded on lists of the French TONTINES or LONG ANNUITIES, and verified by a comparison thereof with the necrologies, or mortuary registers, of several religious houses of both sexes.

BY MONSIEUR DE PARCIEUX.

Age.	Persons Living.	Age.	Persons Living.	Age.	Persons Living.	Age.	Persons Living.	Age.	Persons Living.
3	1000	22	798	41	650	60	463	79	136
4	970	23	790	42	643	61	450	80	118
5	948	24	782	43	636	62	437	81	101
6	930	25	774	44	629	63	423	82	85
7	915	26	766	45	622	64	409	83	71
8	902	27	758	46	615	65	395	84	59
9	890	28	750	47	607	66	380	85	48
10	880	29	742	48	599	67	364	86	38
11	872	30	734	49	590	68	347	87	29
12	866	31	726	50	581	69	329	88	22
13	860	32	718	51	571	70	310	89	16
14	854	33	710	52	560	71	291	90	11
15	848	34	702	53	549	72	271	91	7
16	842	35	694	54	538	73	251	92	4
17	835	36	686	55	526	74	231	93	2
18	828	37	678	56	514	75	211	94	1
19	821	38	671	57	502	76	192	95	0
20	814	39	664	58	489	77	173		
21	8.6	40	657	59	476	78	154		

The Fundamental Maxim of the Doctrine of Life Annuities.—In every bargain between two persons concerning a grant of a sum of money to be paid by the one to the other at a given future time, in case the grantee or purchaser shall be then alive, or in case the grantee and one or more other persons of given ages shall be then alive, the fair price of such future sum of money, according to a given rate of the interest of money and a given table of the probabilities of the duration of human life, is to be ascertained in the following manner: We must suppose, in the first place, that the grantor of the future sum of money makes several hundred grants of the same kind, and upon exactly the same conditions, to as many different grantees, or purchasers, all of the same age with the first grantee; and, in the second place, that these several purchasers and their companions (or the persons upon the continuance of whose lives, as well as their own, their right to the said future sums depends) die off in the interval between the time of making the grants and the time of payment, in the same proportion as persons of the same ages respectively are represented to do in the table of the probabilities of the duration of human life by which the calculation is to be governed ; and, in the third place, we must suppose that the several sums of money paid by the several grantees of these future payments to the grantor of them as the price thereof, are improved by the said grantor, at compound interest, at the rate supposed in the question, during the whole interval of time between the time of making the grants and the time at which the payments become due. And then we must inquire what sum each of the said grantees ought to pay to the grantor, to the end that, upon these three suppositions, he may, at the end of the said interval, or when the said payments become due, be neither a gainer nor a loser by the sum total of all his bargains, but be possessed of just enough money, arising from the sums formerly paid him by the said grantees, to satisfy all the demands which will then be made upon him. And the sum which ought thus to be paid him by each of the said grantees, when he makes a great number of said grants to different persons, is the fair price which a single grantee ought to pay him for a grant for the said future sum of money, subject to the same conditions and contingencies, when he makes only one such grant.

This is a maxim which, I presume, will be admitted as self-evident, it being hardly possible to doubt of its truth. But if the reader should not admit it upon its own evidence, I confess I am unable to demonstrate it by means of any other proposition more evident than itself. And, therefore, in this case, I must desire him to consider it as a definition of what is meant in the following pages by the expressions of the *fair price* or *true value* of such a future contingent payment, since it is only in that sense that the fair price or true value of such a future contingent payment can be collected from the tables of the probabilities of the duration of human life above described.

The first problem is, "To find the present value of a future sum of money, which is certainly to be paid at the end of one or more years, according to any given rate of interest."

PROBLEM I.

To find the present value of any given sum of money which is payable at the end of any given number of years, according to any given rate of interest.

SOLUTION. (Omitted.)

PROBLEM II.

To find the sum of money which the purchaser of a future payment of one pound sterling, to be received at the end of any given number of years, provided the said purchaser shall then be living, ought to pay for it—the age of the said purchaser, and the rate of interest of money, and the probabilities of the duration of human life, being all given.

A Solution of this Problem in the Case of a Particular Example.

Let the rate of interest of money be supposed to be 3 per cent, and the probabilities of the duration of human life such as they are represented to be in Monsieur de Parcieux's table above mentioned; and let the number of years at the end of which the said sum of one pound is to be paid to the grantee, or purchaser of it, if he be then alive, be 30, and the age of the said grantee, or purchaser, 25 years.

Then, in the first place, we must look into M. de Parcieux's table to see how many persons of 25 years of age are there supposed to be all living at the same time. This number we shall find to be 774. We must therefore suppose that the grantor of the one pound to the purchaser, proposed in the question, does not confine himself to that single grant, but makes 773 more such grants, of one pound each, to as many different persons of the same age of 25 years, to be paid to them at the end of 30 years, or when they shall be 55 years old, if they shall then be living, but not to be paid to their executors, or other representatives, if they shall then be dead; that is, we must suppose that he makes 774 such grants in all, including that of the purchaser proposed in the question. And we must likewise suppose that all these 774 purchasers have the same chance, one with the other, of living any given number of years, or that there is no apparent reason for supposing that any one of them is more likely to live to any given future age than any other. This done, we must inquire how many of these 774 purchasers of one pound each will be alive at the end of 30 years, supposing them to die off in the proportion mentioned in M. de Parcieux's table. Now, it appears by M. de Parcieux's table, that out of 774 persons of the age of 25 years, all living at the same time, 526 will be alive at the age of 55 years, or at the distance of 30 years. Therefore, out of the said 774 purchasers of these future payments of one pound, to be received at the end of 30 years, 526 will live to be entitled to them.

Therefore at the end of the said 30 years, the grantor of these future payments will have 526 sums, of one pound each, to pay to the said surviving purchasers. And consequently, to the end that the said grantor may be neither a gainer nor a loser by the sum total of all his bargains, it is necessary that he should receive at the time of making the said grants 526 times the present value of one pound, payable at the end of 30 years, when the interest of money is 3 per cent, or 526 times the sum which, being improved continually at compound interest during the said term of 30 years at the said rate of interest, will at the end of that time amount to one pound; because, in that case, if he improves the said sum (of 526 times the present value of one pound) so received, at compound interest, at the said rate of 3 per cent, during the whole 30 years, it will in that time increase to just 526 pounds, which is the sum he will then be obliged to pay to the surviving purchasers. The present value of one pound, payable at the end of 30 years, without being liable to any contingency, when the interest of money is 3 per cent, is .41198676 of a pound. Therefore 526 times .41198676 of a pound, or £216.70503576, is the sum which the said grantor ought to receive, at the time of making the said grants, from all the 774 purchasers of them. Therefore, the sum which each of them ought then to pay him is the 774th part of £216.70503576, or .27998066 of a pound, or nearly .28 of a pound, or 5*s.* 7¼*d.* And consequently when he makes only one such grant to a purchaser of 25 years of age, he ought to receive for it the same sum of .27998066 of a pound, or .28 of a pound, or 5*s.* 7¼*d.*

I have solved the foregoing problem, in the case of a particular example, for the sake of making the method of solution as clear and familiar as possible. But it is easy to see that the reasonings used in it extend to all other cases whatsoever, and consequently that the solution is really general.

Problem 3d relates to the computation of the present value of a future sum of one pound sterling, that is to take place at the end of a certain number of years, provided two persons of given ages shall then be living, and upon the supposition of a given rate of interest of money.

PROBLEM III.

To find the sum of money which the purchaser of a future payment of one pound sterling, to be received at the end of any given number of years, provided the said purchaser and another person (who may be called *his companion*) shall be then living, ought to pay for such future sum; the ages of the said purchaser and his companion, and the rate of interest of money, and the probabilities of the duration of human life, being all given

A Solution of this Problem in the Case of a Particular Example.

Let the rate of interest of money be supposed to be 3 per cent, and the probabilities of the duration of human life to be such as they are represented to be in M. de Parcieux's table above mentioned, and let the number of years at the end of which the said sum of one pound is to be paid to the purchaser of it, in case not only the said purchaser himself, but likewise his companion aforesaid, shall be then alive, be 30; and the age of the said purchaser be 25 years; and that of his said companion be 20 years.

Then, in the first place, we must look into M. de Parcieux's table to see how many persons of 25 years of age are there represented as all living at the same time. This number is 774. We must therefore suppose that the grantor of the one pound to the purchaser proposed in the question makes at the same time 773 more such grants of one pound to as many different persons all of the same age of 25 years, to be paid to them at the end of 30 years, or when they shall be 55 years old, if not only the grantees themselves shall then be living, but certain other persons, who may be called *their companions*, who are of the same age of 20 years with the companion of the purchaser mentioned in the question; that is, we must suppose that the grantor makes 774 such grants in all, including that of the purchaser proposed in the question. And we must likewise suppose that all these 774 purchasers of these future payments of one pound have the same chance, one with another, of living any given number of years, or that there is no apparent reason for supposing that any one of them is more likely to live to any given future age than any other. This done, we must inquire how many of these 774 purchasers of these remote payments will be alive at the end of 30 years, supposing them to die off in that interval of time in the proportion mentioned in M. de Parcieux's table. Now, it appears by M. de Parcieux's table, that out of 774 persons of the age of 25 years, all living at the same time, 526 will be alive at the age of 55 years, or at the end of 30 years. Therefore out of the said 774 purchasers of these future payments of one pound each, only 526 will live to the end of the 30 years. And of these 526 surviving purchasers, only some part will be entitled to demand these payments—to wit, those whose companions, who were of the age of 20 years at the time of making the grants, are likewise living at the end of 30 years. For the other surviving purchasers, whose companions are then dead, will, by the conditions of this problem, have no right to them. We must therefore, in the next place, inquire how many of the companions of the said 526 surviving purchasers will also be alive at the end of the said 30 years. Now, the companions of these 526 surviving purchasers were at the time of making the grants just as many as those purchasers themselves—that is, 526. We must therefore inquire, by M. de Parcieux's table, how many of these 526 companions of the said 526 surviving purchasers, who were all living and of the age of 20 years at the time of making the grants, will be alive at the end of the said 30 years. Now, it appears by M. de Parcieux's table that out of 814 persons at the age of 20 years, all living at the same time, only 581 will be living at the age of 50 years; and consequently out of 526 persons of the age of 20 years, all living at the same time, only $526 \times \frac{581}{814}$, or 375, will be alive at the age of 50 years. Therefore, of the 526 companions of the 526 surviving purchasers, only 375 will be living at the end of the said 30 years. Therefore, only 375 out of the said 526 surviving purchasers will be entitled to receive the said payments of one pound each. Therefore, at the end of the said 30 years, the grantor of the said future payments will have only 375 sums of one pound each to pay to the surviving purchasers, which will be due to those 375 of them whose companions will be then alive. And consequently, to the end that the said grantor may be neither a gainer nor a loser by the sum total of all his bargains, it is necessary that he should receive at the time of making the said grants 375 times the present value of one pound, payable at the end of 30 years, or, when the interest of money is 3 per cent, or 375 times the sum which, being continually improved at compound interest, during the said term of 30 years, at that rate of interest, will, at the end of that time, amount to one pound; because, in that case, if he improves the said sum of 375 times the present value of one pound, so received, at compound interest, at the said rate of 3 per cent, during the whole 30 years, it will in that time increase to just 375 pounds, which is the sum which he will then be obliged to pay to the 375 surviving purchasers, who, by the continuance of the lives of their respective companions, will be entitled to their several payments of one pound apiece. The present value of one pound payable at the end of 30 years, when the interest of money is 3 per cent, is .4119 of a pound. Therefore, 375 times £.4119, or £154.4625, is the sum which the said grantor of those future payments ought to receive, at the time of making the said grants, from all the 774 purchasers of them. Therefore, the sum which he ought then to receive from each of the said purchasers is the 774th part of £154.4625—that is, £.1995, or nearly 4 shillings. And consequently when he makes only one such grant of one pound, payable at the end of 30 years, to a purchaser of 25 years of age, provided a companion of the purchaser who is of the age of 20 years at the time of making the grant shall also be living at the end of the said 30 years, he ought to receive for it the same sum of $\frac{2}{10}$ of a pound, or 4 shillings.

Problem IV.

To find the sum of money which a purchaser ought to pay for a future sum of one pound sterling, to be received at the end of any given number of years, if either the said purchaser or another certain person (who may be called his companion) shall be then living; the age of the said purchaser and his companion, and the rate of interest of money, and the probabilities of the duration of human life, being all given.

A Solution of this Problem in the Case of a Particular Example. —Let the rate of interest of money be supposed to be 3 per cent, and the probabilities of the duration of human life to be such as they are represented to be in M. de Parcieux's table above mentioned; and let the space of time at the end of which the said sum of one pound is to be paid to the purchaser of it, if he is then living, or to his companion, if the purchaser himself is then deceased, and his said companion is still alive, be 30 years, and the age of the said purchaser 25 years, and that of his said companion 20 years. Then, in the first place, we must look into M. de Parcieux's table to see how many persons of 25 years of age are there represented to be all living at the same time. This number is 774. We must therefore suppose that the grantor of the future payments of one pound to the purchaser proposed in the question makes at the same time 773 more such grants of one pound to as many different purchasers, all of the same age of 25 years, to be paid to them at the end of 30 years, or when they shall be 55 years old, if they shall then be living: and if they shall then be dead, but certain other persons (who may be called their companions), who are of the same age of 20 years with the companion of the purchaser mentioned in the question shall be then alive: to be paid to their said companions respectively—that is, we must suppose that the grantor makes 774 such grants in all, including that to the purchaser proposed in the question; and we must likewise suppose that all these 774 purchasers of these future payments of one pound have the same chance, one with another, of living any given number of years, or that there is no apparent reason for supposing that any one of them is more likely to live to any given future age than any other. This done, we must inquire how many of these 774 purchasers of these remote payments will be alive at the end of 30 years, supposing them to die off in that interval of time in the proportion mentioned in M. de Parcieux's table. Now, it appears by M. de Parcieux's table, that out of 774 persons of the age of 25 years, all living at the same time, 526 will be alive at the age of 55 years, or at the end of 30 years. Therefore, out of said 774 purchasers of these future payments of one pound each, 526 will live to the end of the said 30 years; and, consequently, 248 will have died in the mean time. But by the conditions of this problem (which differ widely from those of the last problem), all these 526 surviving purchasers of these future payments will be entitled to receive them, and likewise all the surviving companions of the deceased 248 purchasers. We must therefore inquire, by means of M. de Parcieux's table, how many of the companions of the said deceased 248 purchasers will be alive at the end of the said 30 years. Now, the number of the companions of the said deceased 248 purchasers, at the time of making the grant, was 248, each of the said purchasers having had one companion, and their age at the time of making the grants was 20 years. Now, it appears, from M. de Parcieux's table, that out of 814 persons of the age of 20 years, all living at the same time, 581 will be living at the age of 50 years, or at the end of 30 years. Therefore, out of the 248 companions of the deceased purchasers (who were all living at the time of making the said grants, and were then 20 years of age), $248 \times \frac{581}{814}$, or 177 will be living at the end of the said 30 years. Therefore, the grantor, at the end of the said 30 years, will have 526 pounds to pay to the 526 surviving purchasers, and 177 pounds to pay to the 177 surviving companions of the 248 deceased purchasers—that is, he will have, in all, 526 and 177 pounds, or 703 pounds, to pay to both. To the end, therefore, that the said grantor may be neither a gainer nor a loser by the sum total of all his bargains, it is necessary that he should receive from all the purchasers of the said future payments, at the time of making the grants, 703 times the value of one pound, payable at the end of 30 years, when the interest of money is 3 per cent—that is, 703 times .4119 of a pound, or £289.5657. Therefore, the sum which he ought to receive, at the time of making the said grants, from each of the said purchasers, who are 774 in number, is the 774th part of £289.5657, or .3741 of a pound. Therefore, the sum which he ought to receive from a single purchaser, as the price of such a future payment of one pound, when he makes only one such grant, is likewise £.3741, or 7*s.* 5¾*d.*

The reasoning used in the solution of the foregoing problem may be extended to the valuation of a future payment, to be received at the end of a given number of years in case any one of three persons, or more, whose ages are given, shall be then alive. In the case of three lives, the additions necessary to be made to the preceding solution will be as follows:

An Investigation of the said Value in the Case of a Particular Example.—In the particular example solved, let the right of the purchaser, of 25 years of age, to the future payment of one pound, at the end of 30 years, be extended to two other persons besides himself, instead of one; so that, if either the purchaser himself or either of his said companions shall be then alive, the said future sum shall be payable by the grantor of it to one of the said three persons; and to make the case more clear and definite, let it be supposed that the older of these two persons is called his *first companion* and the younger his *second companion;* and that, if the purchaser himself is alive at the end of the said 30 years, the said sum of one pound shall be payable to him alone, though either or both of his said companions should be also living at the same time; and that, if he is then dead, but his companions are both alive, it shall be paid to the elder of the two, or his first companion; and that, if only one of them is then alive, it shall be paid to the said only surviving companion. And let the age of the said purchaser's older or first companion be 20 years, as was supposed in the foregoing example; and that of his younger or second companion, 10 years, at the time of making the grant. And further, let it be supposed that the grantor of the said future payment of one pound makes 774 such grants of one pound each, to be received at the end of 30 years, to as many different purchasers, all of the same age of 25 years as the purchaser proposed in the question; and that the grant to the purchaser proposed in the question is one of those 774 grants; and that each of these purchasers has two companions, to wit, an older, or first, companion of 20 years of age, and a younger, or second, companion of 10 years of age; and that each of the sums so granted is to be paid by the said grantor, at the end of the said space of 30 years, provided the purchaser himself, or either of his two companions, is then alive—namely, to the purchaser himself, if he is then alive; or otherwise to the older of his two companions, if they are then both alive; or if only one of them is then alive, to the said only surviving companion.

These things being supposed, it is evident that the number of persons that will be entitled to receive these payments of one pound each, at the end of the said 30 years, will be greater than in the case supposed in the solution of the foregoing problem, because not only all the 526 surviving purchasers themselves, together with the 177 surviving first companions of the 248 deceased purchasers, making in all 703 persons, will be entitled to these payments, as they were in that solution, but there will also be some surviving second companions of the deceased purchasers, who will also have a right to them. What the number of these will be, we must now proceed to inquire.

Now, it is evident, in the first place, from the conditions of this question, that the surviving second companions of the 526 surviving purchasers can have no claim to these payments of one pound; because they are to be made to the said surviving purchasers themselves. And, for the like reason, it is evident, in the second place, that the second companions of those deceased purchasers whose first companions are alive at the end of the said 30 years can have no claim to these payments; because it is provided that when both the companions of a deceased purchaser are alive at the time his payment becomes due, it shall be made to the said purchaser's first companion, and not to his second companion. Now, it has been shown, that out of the 248 purchasers who will have died in the course of the said 30 years, there will be 177 whose first companions (who were 20 years old at the time of making the grants) will be alive at the end of the said 30 years. Therefore, the number of the said deceased purchasers whose first companions will also be dead before the end of the said 30 years is the excess of 248 above 177 persons—that is, 71 persons. There are therefore 71 deceased purchasers, whose second companions will have a right to receive these payments of one pound each, if they live to the end of the said 30 years. We must therefore inquire how many of the second companions of these 71 deceased purchasers will live to the end of the said 30 years, supposing them to die off in the proportion set forth in M. de Parcieux's table of the probabilities of the duration of human life.

Now, these companions are evidently 71 in number, because each of the said 71 deceased purchasers had one second as well as one first companion; and the age of these second companions, at the time of making the grants, is supposed to be 10 years. Now, it appears from M. de Parcieux's table, that out of 880 persons of the age of ten years, all living at the same time, 657 will live to the age of 40 years, or to the end of the term of 30 years. Therefore, out of the said 71 second companions of the said deceased purchasers, there will be 71 × $\frac{657}{880}$, or 53, who will live to the end of the said 30 years. Therefore, the whole number of persons entitled to receive the said payments of one pound each, at the end of the said 30 years, will be, first, the 526 surviving purchasers, and, secondly, the 177 surviving first companions of the 248 deceased purchasers, and, thirdly, the said 53 surviving second companions of those 71 of the said 248 deceased purchasers, whose first companions will have died before the end of the said 30 years—that is, in all, 756 persons. Therefore, at the end of the said 30 years, the aforesaid grantor will be obliged to pay to the said surviving purchasers, and to the said first and second companions of the purchasers that are deceased, the sum of 756 pounds. Therefore, to the end that, when the said payments become due, the said grantor may be neither a gainer nor a loser by the sum total of all his bargains, it is necessary that he should receive, at the time of making said grants, 756 times the present value of one pound certain, payable at the end of 30 years, when the interest of money is three per cent—that is, 756 times .4119 of a pound, or £311.3964, from all the 774 purchasers of these future payments. Therefore, the sum which each of the said purchasers ought then to pay him, as the price of the said future payment of one pound to be received at the end of the said 30 years, is the 774th part of £311.3964, or .4023, or 8*s.* ½*d.* And, consequently, this sum of 8*s.* ½*d.* is likewise the price which a single purchaser ought to pay for a grant of such a future payment of one pound, to be received at the end of 30 years, if either himself or either of his two companions aforesaid shall be then alive, when the grantor of it makes only one such grant.

METHOD OF COMPUTING ANNUITIES.

"A very easy and convenient method of deducing the value of a life annuity of one pound a year for a life of any given age from the value of the same annuity for a life that is older than the former by one year: by the help of which method, a whole table of the values of a life annuity of one pound a year for every age of human life, proceeding from the older ages to the younger by the constant difference of a year, may be computed with nearly the same labor as is necessary to obtain the value of the same annuity for the first, or youngest, life in the table. This method was first communicated to me by Dr. Price; but it was published in the year 1779 by Mr. William Morgan, the actuary to the Society for Equitable Assurances near Blackfriars Bridge, in his treatise on the Doctrine of Annuities and Assurances on Lives, pages 56, 57; and it had been published before by Dr. Price himself in his Treatise on Reversionary Payments, Note O of the Appendix, and likewise by Mr. Thomas Simpson, in his book of Life Annuities, Prob. I., Coroll. 7; which last book was published so long ago as the year 1742. But I should suspect that it was not known to Mr. De Moivre, when he calculated his tables of the values of life annuities; for, if it had, I should imagine he would hardly have thought it necessary to have recourse to a certain inaccurate hypothesis concerning the probabilities of life, in order to diminish the labor of his computations, which would have been almost equally facilitated by the use of this excellent method."—*Masseres*, 1783.

TETENS, OF KIEL.

In 1785, Prof. Tetens, of the University of Kiel, published a method of computing commutation columns for use in making life insurance calculations. In this he introduced the device of multiplying both the numerator and denominator of the fraction which at each age represents the amount that will effect insurance for life, by v raised to a power equal to the ages of the insured; v being equal to $\frac{1}{1+r}$, and r being the rate of interest. Tetens commenced the computations at the oldest age in the table of mortality, and in regular order took an age one year younger to the youngest age given in the table. This method was first used in calculating the value of a life series of annual payments; but the principles apply equally to insurance.

The method of Tetens makes these calculations simple and easy. But if the real meaning of the commutation columns is not understood, they are of no use whatever to an ordinary business man. Masseres was not acquainted with this method, it being introduced after he wrote; but the clearness with which he explains, and his evident determination to make himself understood by his readers, form a marked contrast with the writings and publications of some actuaries in these days.

QUOTATION—1870.

A life insurance actuary says, in a work published in 1870: "The object of this treatise is to explain the science of life insurance, so that its main features can be easily understood by any one having an ordinary knowledge of arithmetic." In explaining the commutation columns, he says, "In this treatise, D represents the number of the living at any age, discounted, at four per cent, for the number of years corresponding to that age. For the sake of convenience and uniformity, we employ that power of $\frac{1}{1.04}$ in computing the D column which corresponds to the given ages; N represents the sums of the discounted numbers of the living from ninety-nine up to any given age; C denotes the number of the dying, discounted by the same power of $\frac{1}{1.04}$ increased by one, as in the D column; and M, computed like the N column, is the discounted numbers of the dying at the various ages. In computing the C column, we use a power of $\frac{1}{1.04}$ greater by one than the corresponding age, since the losses by death are regarded as taking place at the end of the year. The numbers in these columns have the same relative value to each other, and the same results are produced as if we took the first power of $\frac{1}{1.04}$ for the age ten, or any required age, and so on."

Reflect upon this. "Discount the number living." Remember that the avowed object of this actuary was "to explain the science of life insurance," so that it can be understood by any one having an ordinary knowledge of arithmetic. Read again his explanation of the commutation columns; and then consider the following statement, published in 1853, by a distinguished actuary: "It is not to be expected that men who enjoy honor and emolument from being considered the exclusive depositaries of a science so useful to the world, should so popularize and simplify it as to remove the bread from their own mouths and the glory from their own wigs."

The same distinguished actuary, in 1871, says in substance:

Having curtate commutation columns in which $x+n$ is the age at which a policy becomes certainly payable, a constant annual premium being payable till that age, and writing $x+n$ as the "argument of the summation" when we assume $l_{x+n}=0$. The expression for the net single premium at age x in this case is $1-(1-v)\frac{{}_{x+n}N_x}{D_x}$, and that for the net annual premium is $\frac{D_x}{{}_{x+n}N_x}-(1-v)$.

The reserve at the end of t years is expressed by ${}_{x+n}H_{x+t}$. This is equal to the net single premium at age $x+t$, less the value at that age of the net annual premiums yet to be paid. Hence,

$$ {}_{x+n}H_{x+t}=1-(1-v)\frac{{}_{x+n}N_{x+t}}{D_{x+t}}-\left(\frac{D_x}{{}_{x+n}N_x}-(1-v)\right)\times\frac{{}_{x+n}N_{x+t}}{D_{x+t}}. $$

From which:

$$ {}_{x+n}H_{x+t}=1-\frac{D_x}{{}_{x+n}N_x}\times\frac{{}_{x+n}N_{x+t}}{D_{x+t}}. \quad (6) $$

We now quote his exact words, 1871:

"SELF-INSURANCE.

"Since the normal reserve which will exist on a policy at the end of any year is just so much more in the hands of the company towards the payment of the claim that might have occurred in that year than if the insured had each year paid only its risk, it may properly be called a *self-insurance*. Hence H_{x+t} may be called the self-insurance value of the policy. It may be regarded as a savings-bank deposit, with only this difference, that it can not be withdrawn till the expiration of the policy by death, or what, in case of an endowment policy, we have assumed to be death. If $x+n$ is the limiting age up to which some may live, but none beyond, by the assumption we should have $H_{x+n}=1$. And if S is the sum insured, the self-insurance will begin with SH_{x+1} the first year, and increase from year to year until it is S in the last year. Consequently the insurance done by the company per dollar of the policy is a series of complementary risks, $1-H_{x+1}$, $1-H_{x+2}$, $1-H_{x+3}$, ... O. The normal cost or contribution to claims of each of these risks, at the end of the year in which it takes effect, is,

$$ \frac{d_x}{l_x}(1-H_{x+1}),\ \frac{d_{x+1}}{l_{x+1}}(1-H_{x+2}),\ \text{etc.} $$

"This is what becomes of the net premiums and assumed interest thereon, so far as they do not go to form the self-insurance deposits aforesaid; that is, H_{x+1}, H_{x+2}, etc. Hence the present value of all the normal contributions, which a policy is liable to make for the settlement of claims other than its own, may be called the

INSURANCE VALUE.

"To conduct a company either with reference to permanent profit as a stock company, or equity and stability as a mutual one, *with the present great variety of policies*, it is almost as important to know this value as the self-insurance or reserve. The new tables, which will assist in calculating this value for all single-life policies, are constructed on the following principles, and their use will be presently illustrated:

"If $x+n$ be the age at which a policy becomes certainly payable, a constant annual premium being payable till that age, referring to the D and N columns (see tables), we shall have the successive self-insurance values in terms of these tables, thus:

1st. $${}_{x+n}H_{x+1}=1-\frac{D_x}{{}_{x+n}N_x}\times\frac{{}_{x+n}N_{x+1}}{D_{x+1}}.$$

2d. $${}_{x+n}H_{x+2}=1-\frac{D_x}{{}_{x+n}N_x}\times\frac{{}_{x+n}N_{x+2}}{D_{x+2}},$$

etc., etc.

Consequently we have the insurance done by the company each year:

1st. $$1-{}_{x+n}H_{x+1}=\frac{D_x}{{}_{x+n}N_x}\times\frac{{}_{x+n}N_{x+1}}{D_{x+1}}.$$

2d. $$1-{}_{x+n}H_{x+2}=\frac{D_x}{{}_{x+n}N_x}\times\frac{{}_{x+n}N_{x+2}}{D_{x+2}},$$

etc., etc.

The values of these risks will be,

1st. $$\frac{d_x}{l_x}\left(1-{}_{x+n}H_{x+1}\right)=\frac{D_x}{{}_{x+n}N_x}\times\frac{{}_{x+n}N_{x+1}}{D_{x+1}}\times\frac{d_x}{l_x}.$$

2d. $$\frac{d_{x+1}}{l_{x+1}}\left(1-{}_{x+n}H_{x+2}\right)=\frac{D_x}{{}_{x+n}N_x}\times\frac{{}_{x+n}N_{x+2}}{D_{x+2}}\times\frac{d_{x+1}}{l_{x+1}},$$

etc., etc.

"The first of these is certain because the premium is paid in advance, but must be discounted by the factor v to refer it to the beginning of the year. The second must not only be discounted two years, but must be multiplied by the fraction $\frac{l_{x+1}}{l_x}$, expressing the probability of the party being alive to pay the second premium. Hence, the discount factor will be $v^2\frac{l_{x+1}}{l_x}$. In like manner, the discount factor for the third year will be $v^3\frac{l_{x+2}}{l_x}$, and so on. Observing that $\frac{D_x}{{}_{x+n}N_x}$ is a factor common to every term of the series to be discounted, and substituting for D_{x+1}, D_{x+2}, etc., their values, $v^{x+1}l_{x+1}$, $v^{x+2}l_{x+2}$, etc., and applying the discount factors above explained, we have the insurance value, which we will designate by the symbol I.

$${}_{x+n}I_x = \frac{D_x}{{}_{x+n}N_x}\left(\frac{{}_{x+n}N_{x+1}}{v^{x+1}l_{x+1}} \times \frac{vd_x}{l_x} + \frac{{}_{x+n}N_{x+2}}{v^{x+2}l_{x+2}} \times \frac{v^2 d_{x+1} \times l_{x+1}}{l_{x+1} \times l_x} + \text{etc.}\right)$$

"Multiplying numerators and denominators by v^x,

$${}_{x+n}I_x = \frac{D_x}{{}_{x+n}N_x}\left(\frac{{}_{x+n}N_{x+1}}{v^{x+1}l_{x+1}} \times \frac{v^{x+1}d_x}{v^x l_x} + \frac{{}_{x+n}N_{x+2}}{v^{x+2}l_{x+2}} \times \frac{v^{x+2} d_{x+1} \times l_{x+1}}{v^x l_x \times l_{x+1}} + \text{etc.}\right).$$

Canceling like factors in numerator and denominator, and substituting D_x for $v^x l_x$, we have,

$${}_{x+n}I_x = \frac{D_x}{{}_{x+n}N_x} \times \frac{{}_{x+n}N_{x+1} \times \frac{d_x}{l_{x+1}} + {}_{x+n}N_{x+2} \times \frac{d_{x+1}}{l_{x+2}} + \text{etc.}}{D_x}. \qquad (7)$$

"Obviously, if we assume $x=10$ and perform all the multiplications of $\frac{d_{10}}{l_{11}}$ into N_{11}, $\frac{d_{11}}{l_{12}}$ into N_{12}, etc., as indicated in the numerator of the last factor of (7), the summation of the products (after the manner in which the N column is produced from the D) will produce a column of *numerators* which we will call Δ (*lucus a non*), and this will give us, instead of (7),

$${}_{x+n}I_x = \frac{D_x}{{}_{x+n}N_x} \times \frac{{}_{x+n}\Delta_x}{D_x}, \text{ and } (8)\ {}_{x+n}I_{x+t} = \frac{D_x}{{}_{x+n}N_x} \times \frac{{}_{x+n}\Delta_{x+t}}{D_{x+t}},$$

when the policy has completed t years and the $(t+1)^{\text{th}}$ premium is just paid.

"Similarly, to find the insurance value of a paid-up policy, expressing the self-insurance values in terms of the D and N columns, we shall find the aggregate of the discounted future costs of insurance reduce itself to ${}_{x+n}I_{x+t} = (1-v)\,\frac{{}_{x+n}\Delta_{x+t}}{D_{x+t}}$.

"To get the insurance values of limited-premium life or endowment policies, let ϕ_x be the premium to be paid q times, and $v - \phi_x = c_1$, $c_1 - H_{x+1} = c_2$, $c_1 - H_{x+2} = c_3$ . . . . . . $c_1 - H_{x+q-1} = c_q$. Then referring to Table XXII., p. 200, column δ_x, and denoting the insurance value when the first premium is just paid by ${}_{x+n}I_{x\,|\,q}$, we shall have ${}_{x+n}I_{x\,|\,q} = \frac{\delta_x c_1 + \delta_{x+1}c_2 \ . \ . \ . \ . \ + \delta_{x+q-1}c_q}{D_x} + \frac{D_{x+q}}{D_x} \times \frac{{}_{x+n}\Delta_{x+q}}{D_{x+q}}$. After having thus found the initial insurance value, we may find that of the succeeding years by applying the coefficient of accumulation, thus:

$${}_{x+n}I_{x+1\,|\,q} = \frac{rl_x}{l_{x+1}}\left({}_{x+n}I_{x\,|\,q} - \frac{d_x}{l_{x+1}}c_1\right)$$

$${}_{x+n}I_{x+2\,|\,q} = r\frac{l_{x+1}}{l_{x+2}}\left({}_{x+n}I_{x+1\,|\,q} - \frac{d_{x+1}}{l_{x+2}}c_2\right),$$

etc., etc., etc.

"For the following briefer process applicable to any policy payable at the age $x+n$ or previous death, including, of course, the ordinary whole-life policy, the public are indebted to the keen analysis of Mr. * * * *. His notation is slightly modified to adapt it to the tables.

"Let ϕ_x be the annual premium to be paid q times, and when the first premium is just paid, we have:

$$_{x+n}I_{x\,|\,q}=d\frac{_{x+n}\varDelta_x}{D_x}+\phi_x\frac{_{x+q}\varDelta_x}{D_x},$$

and when the $(t+1)^{\text{th}}$ premium has just been paid,

$$_{x+n}I_{x+t\,|\,q}=d\frac{_{x+n}\varDelta_{x+t}}{D_{x+t}}+\phi_x\frac{_{x+q}\varDelta_{x+t}}{D_{x+t}}.$$

Though the insurance value of an annual premium term policy is greater than that of an endowment policy for the same term and amount, there is, except for a very long term, too little reserve on it to secure a proper surrender charge. Therefore, unless the premium is extravagantly loaded, the company is not sufficiently secured against loss by lapse after having paid the usual commission. For this reason, and because this sort of policy is little sought by the public which fails to see value, except in the indemnity or endowment, it is hardly necessary to insert any formulas for the insurance values of term policies. But as these policies are really valuable, and when paid for by single or a limited number of annual premiums, the reserves afford sufficient security to the company paying a moderate commission, it may be well to provide for business which may arise. Putting K for the insurance value of policies of this class, we have for the ordinary term policy of n years when the $(t+1)^{\text{th}}$ premium is just paid,

$$_{x+n}K_{x+t}=\frac{_{x+n+1}\varDelta_{x+t}}{D_{x+t}}-(v-{_{x+n}\gamma_x})\frac{_{x+n}\varDelta_{x+t}}{D_{x+t}}. \qquad (9)$$

"If the premium is limited to q payments, in which case it is

$$_{x+n}\gamma_x\frac{_{x+n}N_x}{_{x+q}N_x}=\rho_x,$$

the value is,

$$_{x+n}K_{x+t\,|\,q}=\frac{_{x+n+1}\varDelta_{x+t}}{D_{x+t}}-v\frac{_{x+n}\varDelta_{x+t}}{D_{x+t}}+\rho_x\frac{_{x+q}\varDelta_{x+t}}{D_{x+t}},$$

and a single premium term policy is,

$$_{x+n}K_{x+t}=\frac{_{x+n+1}\varDelta_{x+t}}{D_{x+t}}-v\frac{_{x+n}\varDelta_{x+t}}{D_{x+t}}.$$

"The insurance value of a pure endowment or tontine policy is, of course, negative, the operation being wholly the exact reverse of insurance, to wit, of term insurance. For example: if T be the insurance value of a tontine, or pure endowment policy, at annual premium, we have, by substituting in (8) for $\frac{D_x}{{}_{x+n}N_x}$, its value $=d+{}_{x+n}\pi_x=d+{}_{x+n}\gamma_x+{}_{x+n}e_x$, and subtracting (9)

$${}_{x+n}T_{x+t}=(1+{}_{x+n}e_x)\frac{{}_{x+n}\Delta_{x+t}}{D_{x+t}}-\frac{{}_{x+n+1}\Delta_{x+t}}{D_{x+t}},$$

which is always negative, and if paid up it becomes,

$${}_{x+n}T_{x+t}=\frac{{}_{x+n}\Delta_{x+t}}{D_{x+t}}-\frac{{}_{x+n+1}\Delta_{x+t}}{D_{x+t}}.$$

"It must not be inferred from the negativeness of the insurance value of endowment that the company loses or is weakened by it. The mortality being normal, it neither gains nor loses. It gains if the mortality is greater, and loses if it is less. But the insurance of pure endowment being inverted, its negativeness indicates that the interest of the policy-holder as a probable survivor is to have the vitality of the company diminished. *He* can afford to pay less than nothing to increase it. Hence, *a fortiori*, he can not be satisfied if he is charged for expenses more than his ${}_{x+n}H_{x+t}$ would cost him in a savings-bank, unless there should have occurred in the company that extraordinary mortality which is the only source of prosperity to pure tontine companies. This is not to be hoped or wished for when endowment is coupled with insurance in the same policy."

CHAPTER XIV.

ALGEBRAIC SUMMARY AND FORMULAS.

l_x=tabular number living at any age, x.

l_{x+n}=tabular number living n years after the policy was issued at age x.

d_x=tabular number of deaths between age x and age $x+1$.

d_{x+n}=tabular number of deaths between age $x+n$ and age $x+n+1$.

r=rate of interest per annum.

$v=\frac{1}{1+r}$=the sum that will, if invested at the rate r, amount to \$1 in one year.

$v^x=\left(\frac{1}{1+r}\right)^x$=the sum that will, if invested at the rate r, compounded annually, amount to \$1 in x years.

NET PREMIUMS.

$v\frac{d_x}{l_x}$=the amount that will at age x insure \$1 for one year.

$v\frac{d_x}{l_x}+v^2\frac{d_{x+1}}{l_x}$=the amount that will at age x insure \$1 for two years.

$v\frac{d_x}{l_x}+v^2\frac{d_{x+1}}{l_x}$+other similar terms to table limit=the amount that will at age x insure \$1 for life. Continuing these yearly terms to age 95 (American Experience oldest table age), and introducing the factor v^x in both numerator and denominator, we have,

$\frac{v^{x+1}d_x+v^{x+2}d_{x+1}+\ \ldots\ldots\ +v^{96}d_{95}}{v^x l_x}$=the amount that will at age x insure \$1 for whole life. Designating the terms of the numerator by C_x, C_{x+1} . . . . . C_{95}, and the denominator by D_x, we have,

$\frac{C_x+C_{x+1}+\ \ldots\ldots\ C_{95}}{D_x}$=the amount that will at age x insure \$1 for whole life. Call the sum of all the terms of the numerator M_x and the expression becomes $\frac{M_x}{D_x}$. The net single premium that will at age $x+n$ insure \$1 for whole life $=\frac{M_{x+n}}{D_{x+n}}$.

The amount that will at age x insure \$1, the insurance to commence at age $x+1$, and continue for one year, is $\frac{v^2 d_{x+1}}{l_x}=\frac{v^{x+2} d_{x+1}}{v^x l_x}=\frac{C_{x+1}}{D_x}$. The amount that will at age x insure \$1, the insurance to commence at age $x+2$, and continue for one year, is $\frac{v^3 d_{x+2}}{l_x}=\frac{v^{x+3} d_{x+2}}{v^x l_x}=\frac{C_{x+2}}{D_x}$. The amount that will at age x insure \$1, the insurance to commence at age $x+1$ and continue for whole life, is expressed by $\frac{C_{x+1}+C_{x+2}+\ldots\ldots+C_{95}}{D_x}=\frac{M_{x+1}}{D_x}$. In like manner, the amount that will at age x insure \$1, to commence at age $x+2$, and continue for whole life, is $\frac{C_{x+2}+C_{x+3}+\ldots\ldots+C_{95}}{D_x}=\frac{M_{x+2}}{D_x}$. Therefore the amount that will at age x insure \$1, to commence at age x; \$2, to commence at age $x+1$; and so on, increasing the amount insured for whole life \$1 each year, is expressed by $\frac{M_x+M_{x+1}+\ldots\ldots+M_{95}}{D_x}$. Call the sum of all the terms of the numerator R_x, and we have $\frac{R_x}{D_x}=$ the amount that will at age x insure \$1 the first year, \$2 the second, \$3 the third, and so on each year, increasing the amount insured \$1 each year to the table limit of age.

The amount that will at age x insure \$1 for life, the insurance to begin at the end of n years, is $\frac{M_{x+n}}{D_x}$; therefore the amount that will at age x insure \$1 for n years only is $\frac{M_x-M_{x+n}}{D_x}$.

The amount that will at age x insure \$1 at age $x+n$, \$2 at age $x+n+1$, and so on, increasing the amount insured \$1 each year to the table limit, is $\frac{R_{x+n}}{D_x}$. The amount that will at age x insure \$1 the first year, \$2 the second, and so on, increasing the amount insured \$1 each year for n years, after which the insurance is to cease increasing and remain equal to n times \$1 to the table limit, is $\frac{R_x}{D_x}-\frac{R_{x+n}}{D_x}$. The amount that will at age x insure n times \$1, the insurance to commence at age $x+n$ and continue to the table limit, is $\frac{n\times M_{x+n}}{D_x}$. Therefore $\frac{R_x}{D_x}-\frac{R_{x+n}}{D_x}-\frac{n\times M_{x+n}}{D_x}=$ the amount that will insure \$1 the first year, \$2 the second, and so on, increasing the insurance \$1 each year for n years, the insurance to cease at that time.

Designate by Z_x the net single premium that will at age x insure \$1 + this premium. Then since $\frac{M_x}{D_x}$ is the amount that will insure \$1; $(1+Z_x)\frac{M_x}{D_x}$ is the amount that will insure $1+Z_x$. Hence $Z_x = (1+Z_x)\frac{M_x}{D_x}$; from which $Z_x = \frac{M_x}{D_x - M_x}$.

The net single premium that will provide the insurance of \$1 for life, and return this net premium plus m per cent thereof, is expressed by $\frac{M_x}{D_x - \overline{1+m}M_x}$.

The net single premium that will at age x secure the payment of \$1 at age $x+z$, in case the insured is then alive, is expressed by $\frac{v^z l_{x+z}}{l_x} = \frac{v^{x+z} l_{x+z}}{v^x l_x} = \frac{D_{x+z}}{D_x}$.

$\frac{M_x - M_{x+z} + D_{x+z}}{D_x}$ = net single premium at age x to secure \$1 at age $x+z$, or at death if prior.

$\frac{M_x - M_{x+z} + D_{x+z}}{D_x - \overline{1+m}(M_x - M_{x+z} + D_{x+z})}$ = net single premium at age x to secure \$1 at age $x+z$, or at death if prior, and return this premium plus m per cent of itself.

Value at age x of a Life Series of Annual Payments of \$1 *each, the first in advance.*—The value at age x of \$1, to be paid in one year, provided the person is alive to make the payment, is expressed by $v\frac{l_{x+1}}{l_x}$. The value at age x of \$1, to be paid in two years, provided the person is then alive to make the payment, is $v^2\frac{l_{x+2}}{l_x}$. And in like manner for each succeeding year to the table limit. Adding together all these yearly values, noting the condition that the first payment of \$1 is to be made immediately, and we have,

$$\frac{l_x + vl_{x+1} + v^2 l_{x+2} + \ . \ . \ . \text{ to table limit}}{l_x}.$$

This is the amount that will if paid at age x be the equivalent of a life series of annual payments of \$1 each, the first in advance.

Multiplying the numerator and denominator by v^x, the expression becomes,

$$\frac{v^x l_x + v^{x+1} l_{x+1} + v^{x+2} l_{x+2} \ldots\ldots + v^{95} l_{95}}{v^x l_x}.$$

Designating the numerator of this fraction by N_x, and noting that the denominator has already been designated by D_x, and we have $\frac{N_x}{D_x}$=the value at age x of a life series of annual payments of \$1 each, the first being made in advance.

The value at age x of a life series of annual payments of \$1 each, the first payment to be made at age $x+1$, is expressed by,

$$\frac{v^{x+1} l_{x+1} + v^{x+2} l_{x+2} + \ldots\ldots + v^{95} l_{95}}{v^x l_x} = \frac{N_{x+1}}{D_x}.$$

In like manner, the value at age x of a life series of annual payments of \$1 each, the first to be made at age $x+2$, is $\frac{N_{x+2}}{D_x}$, and so on for each succeeding year to the table limit. Adding together all these respective values, and designating the sum of the terms of the numerator by S_x, we have,

$$\frac{S_x}{D_x} = \frac{N_x + N_{x+1} + N_{x+2} + \ldots\ldots + N_{95}}{D_x} = 1$$

The value at age x of a life series of annual payments of \$1 immediate, \$2 at the beginning of the second year, \$3 the third, etc., increasing the payments \$1 each year to table limit.

NET ANNUAL PREMIUM.

The amount that will at age x insure \$1 for whole life has been found to be equal to $\frac{M_x}{D_x}$. The amount in hand that is the equivalent of a life series of annual payments of \$1 each is equal to $\frac{N_x}{D_x}$. Designate the net annual premium that is the equivalent of the net single premium $\frac{M_x}{D_x}$ by aP_x, and we have the proportion $\frac{N_x}{D_x} : \frac{M_x}{D_x} :: \$1 : aP_x$, or $aP_x = \frac{M_x}{N_x}$=net annual premium to secure \$1 at death or table limit.

The value at age x of a series of annual payments of \$1 each for a years is expressed by $\frac{N_x - N_{x+a}}{D_x}$. From the following proportion, we find $\frac{N_x-N_{x+a}}{D_x}:\frac{M_x}{D_x}::\$1:\frac{M_x}{N_x-N_{x+a}}$. Therefore $\frac{M_x}{N_x-N_{x+a}}$ is the net annual premium for a years to secure \$1 at death, or at table limit of age.

$\frac{M_x-M_{x+z}}{N_x-N_{x+z}}$=net annual premium to insure \$1 for z years, the insurance to cease at the end of that time.

Designate by Z'_x the net annual premium to secure \$1 at death and a return of all the net annual premiums paid. Then, since $\frac{R_x}{D_x}$ is the amount that will insure \$1 the first year, \$2 the second, and so on, $\frac{Z'_xR_x}{D_x}$ will insure Z'_x the first year, $2Z'_x$ the second, and so on, increasing the insurance by Z'_x each year to table limit; therefore $\frac{M_x}{D_x}+\frac{Z'_xR_x}{D_x}=Z'_x\times\frac{N_x}{D_x}$, or $Z'_x=\frac{M_x}{N_x-R_x}$.

The net annual premium that will insure \$1 at death, and return all the net annual premiums paid plus m per cent thereof, is $\frac{M_x}{N_x-(1+m)R_x}$.

$\frac{M_x}{N_x-N_{x+a}-(1+m)(R_x-R_{x+a})}$ = net annual premium for a years to secure \$1 at death, and the return of all these net premiums plus m per cent thereof.

$\frac{D_{x+z}}{N_x-N_{x+z}}$ =net annual premium to secure \$1 at age $x+z$ if the assured is then alive.

$\frac{D_{x+z}}{N_x-N_{x+a}}$ =net annual premium for a years to secure \$1 at age $x+z$ if the insured is then alive.

$\frac{D_{x+z}}{N_x-N_{x+z}-(1+m)(R_x-R_{x+z}-zM_{x+z})}$ = net annual premium at age x, to secure \$1 at age $x+z$, if the assured is then alive, and to return the loaded premiums in case of death prior to age $x+z$.

$\frac{M_x - M_{x+z} + D_{x+z}}{N_x - N_{x+a}}$ = net annual premium for a years, to secure \$1 at age $x+z$, or at death, if prior.

$\frac{M_x - M_{x+z} + D_{x+z}}{N_x - N_{x+z} - (1+m)(R_x - R_{x+z} - zM_{x+z} + zD_{x+z})}$ = net annual premium to secure \$1 at age $x+z$, or at death, if prior, and in either event to return these premiums plus m per cent thereof.

FORMULAS FOR THE DEPOSIT OR "RESERVE."

The net value of a policy at the end of any policy year may be found, in case the net value at the end of the preceding year is known, by either of the three following general formulas:

1. $H_{x+n} = u_{x+n-1}\,(H_{x+n-1} + aP_x - c_{x+n-1})$. (See page 96.)

2. $H_{x+n} = u_{x+n-1}\,(H_{x+n-1} + aP_x) - k_{x+n-1}$. (See page 97.)

3. $H_{x+n} = 1 - u_{x+n-1}\,(v - aP_x - H_{x+n-1})$. (See page 98.)

In case the deposit at the end of the preceding year is not known, it may be calculated directly in different cases by the following formulas:

4. $\dfrac{M_{x+n}}{D_{x+n}}$ = net value at the end of n years of a full-paid whole-life policy.

5. $\dfrac{M_{x+n}D_x}{D_{x+n}\,[D_x-(1+m)\,M_x]}$ = net value at the end of n years of a full-paid whole-life policy, to secure $1 and the return of the premiums paid; m being the percentage, or loading, added to the net premiums.

6. $\dfrac{M_{x+n} - M_{x+z}}{D_{x+n}}$ = net value at the end of n years, term policy for z years, full paid.

7. $\dfrac{D_{x+z}}{D_{x+n}}$ = reserve at the end of n years, to secure $1 at age $x+z$, if the insured is then alive, full paid.

8. $\dfrac{D_{x+z}}{D_x-(1+m)(M_x-M_{x+z})} \times \dfrac{D_x-(1+m)\,M_x+(1+m)\,M_{x+n}}{D_{x+n}}$ = reserve at the end of n years, full paid, to secure $1 at age $x+z$, if the insured is then alive, and in case of prior death, the premium actually paid to be returned at the end of the year in which the insured dies.

9. $\dfrac{M_{x+n} - M_{x+z} + D_{x+z}}{D_{x+n}}$ = deposit at the end of n years, full paid, to secure $1 at age $x+n$, or at previous death.

10. $\dfrac{D_x}{D_{x+n}} \times \dfrac{M_{x+n} - M_{x+z} + D_{x+z}}{D_x-(1+m)\,(M_x-M_{x+z}+D_{x+z})}$ = reserve at end of n years, full paid, to secure $1 at age $x+z$, or previous death, in either event the premium actually paid to be returned.

11. $\dfrac{M_{x+n}}{D_{x+n}} - \dfrac{M_x}{N_x} \times \dfrac{N_{x+n}}{D_{x+n}} = 1 - \dfrac{A_{x+n}}{A_x}$ = reserve at age $x+n$, life policy, annual premiums.

12. $\dfrac{M_{x+n}}{D_{x+n}} - \dfrac{M_x}{N_x - N_{x+a}} \times \dfrac{N_{x+n} - N_{x+a}}{D_{x+n}}$ = reserve at age $x+n$, life policy, annual premiums for a years, and before a years have elapsed. After a years, the formula for full-paid applies.

13. $\dfrac{M_{x+n}}{D_{x+n}} - \dfrac{M_x}{N_x - (1+m)R_x} \left\{ \dfrac{N_{x+n} - (1+m)\ (R_{x+n} + nM_{x+n})}{D_{x+n}} \right\}$ = reserve at end of n years, annual premiums, to secure \$1 at death, and return all the premiums paid.

14.
$$\frac{M_{x+n}}{D_{x+n}} - \frac{M_x}{N_x - N_{x+a} - (1+m)\ (R_x - R_{x+a})} \times$$
$$\cdot \left\{ \frac{N_{x+n} - N_{x+a} - (1+m)(R_{x+n} - R_{x+a} + nM_{x+n}}{D_{x+n}} \right\} =$$

reserve at end of n years, and before a years have elapsed, annual premiums for a years, to secure \$1 at death, and return all the premiums actually paid.

15. $\dfrac{M_{x+n}}{D_{x+n}} \left\{ 1 + \dfrac{(1+m)\ aM_x}{N_x - N_{x+a} - (1+m)\ (R_x - R_{x+a})} \right\}$ = reserve for above policy when a or more years have elapsed.

16. $\dfrac{M_{x+n} - M_{x+z}}{D_{x+n}} - \dfrac{M_x - M_{x+z}}{N_x - N_{x+z}} \times \dfrac{N_{x+n} - N_{x+z}}{D_{x+n}}$ = reserve at end of n years, annual premiums for z years, insurance to cease at that time.

17. $\dfrac{D_{x+z}}{D_{x+n}} - \dfrac{D_{x+z}}{N_x - N_{x+z}} \times \dfrac{N_{x+n} - N_{x+z}}{D_{x+n}}$ = reserve at end of n years, annual premiums, to secure \$1 at age $x+z$, if the insured is then alive.

18. $\dfrac{D_{x+z}}{D_{x+n}} - \dfrac{D_{x+z}}{N_x - N_{x+a}} \times \dfrac{N_{x+n} - N_{x+a}}{D_{x+n}}$ = reserve at end of n years, before a years have elapsed, annual premiums for a years to secure \$1 as above.

19. $\dfrac{D_{x+z}}{D_{x+n}} \times \dfrac{N_x - N_{x+n} - (1+m)(R_x - R_{x+n} - nM_{x+n})}{N_x - N_{x+z} - (1+m)\ (R_x - R_{x+z} - zM_{x+z})}$ = reserve at end of n years, annual premiums to secure \$1 at age $x+z$, if the insured is then alive, the premiums paid to be returned if death occurs prior to age $x+z$.

20. $\frac{M_{x+n} - M_{x+z} + D_{x+z}}{D_{x+n}} - \frac{M_x - M_{x+z} + D_{x+z}}{N_x - N_{x+z}} \times \frac{N_{x+n} - N_{x+z}}{D_{x+n}} =$ reserve at end of n years, annual premiums for z years, to secure \$1 at age $x+z$, or at death, if prior.

21. $\frac{M_{x+n} - M_{x+z} + D_{x+z}}{D_{x+n}} - \frac{M_x - M_{x+z} + D_{x+z}}{N_x - N_{x+a}} \times \frac{N_{x+n} - N_{x+a}}{D_{x+n}} =$ reserve at end of n years, before a years have elapsed, annual premiums for a years to secure \$1 at age $x+z$, or at death, if prior. After a years, it becomes full paid.

ANNUITIES.

22. $\frac{N_x}{D_x} =$ net single premium at age x to secure \$1 annually for life. Payments to be made at beginning of each year; the first immediate.

23. $\frac{N_{x+n}}{D_{x+n}} =$ reserve on above at the end of n years, just before the $n+1$ payment of the annuity is made.

24. $\frac{N_x - N_{x+z}}{D_x} =$ net single premium to secure an annuity of \$1 for z years.

25. $\frac{N_{x+n} - N_{x+z}}{D_{x+n}} =$ reserve for above at end of n years.

26. $\frac{N_{x+z}}{D_x} =$ net single premium at age x, to secure an annuity of \$1; first payment to be made at the end of z years, and annually thereafter.

NOTE.—The formulas in use for calculating net premiums and net values for joint life and survivorship policies are quite similar to those for single lives. The commutation columns for joint lives are very voluminous. They are given, together with formulas used in their application, in a work entitled "Commutation Tables," published by C. & E. Layton, 150 Fleet street, London, England, 1858; and in "Commutation Tables," published by S. W. Green, 16 Jacob street, New-York, 1873; also in other life tables.

LIST OF TABLES.

Amount of $1 in any Number of Years.

	4 per cent.	4½ per cent.		4 per cent.	4½ per cent.
1	1.040 0000	1.045 0000	51	7.390 9507	9.439 1049
2	1.081 6000	1.092 0250	52	7.686 5887	9.863 8646
3	1.124 8640	1.141 1661	53	7.994 0523	10.307 7385
4	1.169 8586	1.192 5186	54	8.313 8143	10.771 5868
5	1.216 6529	1.246 1819	55	8.646 3669	11.256 3082
6	1.265 3190	1.302 2601	56	8.992 2216	11.762 8420
7	1.315 9318	1.360 8618	57	9.351 9105	12.292 1699
8	1.368 5690	1.422 1006	58	9.725 9869	12.845 3176
9	1.423 3118	1.486 0951	59	10.115 0264	13.423 3569
10	1.480 2443	1.552 9694	60	10.519 6274	14.027 4079
11	1.539 4541	1.622 8530	61	10.940 4125	14.658 6413
12	1.601 0322	1.695 8814	62	11.378 0290	15.318 2801
13	1.665 0735	1.772 1961	63	11.833 1502	16.007 6027
14	1.731 6764	1.851 9449	64	12.306 4762	16.727 9449
15	1.800 9435	1.935 2824	65	12.798 7352	17.480 7024
16	1.872 9812	2.022 3701	66	13.310 6846	18.267 3340
17	1.947 9005	2.113 3768	67	13.843 1120	19.089 3640
18	2.025 8165	2.208 4788	68	14.396 8365	19.948 3854
19	2.106 8492	2.307 8603	69	14.972 7099	20.846 0628
20	2.191 1231	2.411 7140	70	15.571 6183	21.784 1356
21	2.278 7681	2.520 2412	71	16.194 4831	22.764 4217
22	2.369 9188	2.633 6520	72	16.842 2624	23.788 8207
23	2.464 7155	2.752 1663	73	17.515 9529	24.859 3176
24	2.563 3042	2.876 0138	74	18.216 5910	25.977 9869
25	2.665 8363	3.005 4345	75	18.945 2547	27.146 9963
26	2.772 4698	3.140 6790	76	19.703 0648	28.368 6111
27	2.883 3686	3.282 0096	77	20.491 1874	29.645 1986
28	2.998 7033	3.429 7000	78	21.310 8349	30.979 2326
29	3.118 6514	3.584 0365	79	22.163 2683	32.373 2980
30	3.243 3975	3.745 3181	80	23.049 7991	33.830 0964
31	3.373 1334	3.913 8574	81	23.971 7910	35.352 4508
32	3.508 0588	4.089 9810	82	24.930 6627	36.943 3111
33	3.648 3811	4.274 0302	83	25.927 8892	38.605 7601
34	3.794 3163	4.466 3615	84	26.965 0047	40.343 0193
35	3.946 0890	4.667 3478	85	28.043 6049	42.158 4551
36	4.103 9325	4.877 3785	86	29.165 3491	44.055 5856
37	4.268 0899	5.096 8605	87	30.331 9631	46.038 0870
38	4.438 8134	5.326 2192	88	31.545 2416	48.109 8009
39	4.616 3660	5.565 8991	89	32.807 0513	50.274 7419
40	4.801 0206	5.816 3645	90	34.119 3333	52.537 1053
41	4.993 0614	6.078 1009	91	35.484 1067	54.901 2750
42	5.192 7839	6.351 6155	92	36.903 4709	57.371 8324
43	5.400 4953	6.637 4382	93	38.379 6098	59.953 5649
44	5.616 5151	6.936 1229	94	39.914 7942	62.651 4753
45	5.841 1757	7.248 2481	95	41.511 3859	65.470 7917
46	6.074 8227	7.574 4193	96	43.171 8414	68.416 9773
47	6.317 8156	7.915 2685	97	44.898 7150	71.495 7413
48	6.570 5282	8.271 4556	98	46.694 6636	74.713 0496
49	6.833 3494	8.643 6711	99	48.562 4502	78.075 1369
50	7.106 6833	9.032 6363	100	50.504 9482	81.588 5180

Present Value of a Dollar due in any Number of Years and corresponding Logarithm.

	v^x 4½ %.	λv^x 4½ %.	v^x 4 %.	λv^x 4 %.		v^x 4½ %.	λv^x 4½ %.	v^x 4 %.	λv^x 4 %.
1	.9569378	$\bar{1}$.9808837	.9615385	$\bar{1}$.9829667	51	.1059422	.0250692	.1353006	.1312997
2	.9157300	.9617674	.9245562	.9659333	52	.1013801	.0059529	.1300967	.1142664
3	.8762966	.9426511	.8889964	.9489000	53	.0970145	$\bar{2}$.9868366	.1250930	.0972330
4	.8385613	.9235348	.8548042	.9318666	54	.0928368	.9677203	.1202817	.0801997
5	.8024510	.9044185	.8219271	.9148333	55	.0888391	.9486040	.1156555	.0631663
6	.7678957	.8853022	.7903145	.8978000	56	.0850135	.9294877	.1112072	.0461330
7	.7348285	.8661859	.7599178	.8807666	57	.0813526	.9103714	.1069300	.0290997
8	.7031851	.8470696	.7306902	.8637333	58	.0778494	.8912552	.1028173	.0120663
9	.6729044	.8279533	.7025867	.8466999	59	.0744970	.8721389	.0988628	$\bar{2}$.9950330
10	.6439277	.8088371	.6755642	.8296666	60	.0712890	.8530226	.0950604	.9779996
11	.6161987	.7897208	.6495809	.8126333	61	.0682191	.8339063	.0914042	.9609663
12	.5896638	.7706045	.6245970	.7955999	62	.0652815	.8147900	.0878887	.9439330
13	.5642716	.7514882	.6005741	.7785666	63	.0624703	.7956737	.0845083	.9268996
14	.5399729	.7323719	.5774751	.7615332	64	.0597802	.7765574	.0812580	.9098663
15	.5167204	.7132556	.5552645	.7444999	65	.0572059	.7574411	.0781327	.8928329
16	.4944693	.6941394	.5339082	.7274666	66	.0547425	.7383248	.0751276	.8757996
17	.4731764	.6750231	.5133732	.7104332	67	.0523852	.7192085	.0722381	.8587663
18	.4528004	.6559068	.4936281	.6933999	68	.0501294	.7000922	.0694597	.8417329
19	.4333018	.6367905	.4746424	.6763666	69	.0479707	.6809760	.0667882	.8246996
20	.4146429	.6176742	.4563869	.6593332	70	.0459050	.6618597	.0642194	.8076662
21	.3967874	.5985579	.4388336	.6422999	71	.0439282	.6427434	.0617494	.7906329
22	.3797009	.5794416	.4219554	.6252665	72	.0420366	.6236271	.0593744	.7735996
23	.3633501	.5603253	.4057263	.6082332	73	.0402264	.6045108	.0570908	.7565662
24	.3477035	.5412090	.3901215	.5911999	74	.0384941	.5853945	.0548950	.7395329
25	.3327306	.5220927	.3751168	.5741665	75	.0368365	.5662782	.0527837	.7224996
26	.3184025	.5029764	.3606892	.5571332	76	.0352502	.5471619	.0507535	.7054662
27	.3046914	.4838602	.3468166	.5400998	77	.0337323	.5280456	.0488015	.6884329
28	.2915707	.4647439	.3334775	.5230665	78	.0322797	.5089293	.0469245	.6713995
29	.2790150	.4456276	.3206514	.5060332	79	.0308897	.4898131	.0451197	.6543662
30	.2670000	.4265113	.3083187	.4889998	80	.0295595	.4706968	.0433843	.6373329
31	.2555024	.4073950	.2964603	.4719665	81	.0282866	.4515805	.0417157	.6202995
32	.2444999	.3882787	.2850579	.4549331	82	.0270685	.4324642	.0401112	.6032662
33	.2339712	.3691624	.2740942	.4378998	83	.0259029	.4133479	.0385685	.5862328
34	.2238959	.3500461	.2635521	.4208665	84	.0247874	.3942316	.0370851	.5691995
35	.2142544	.3309298	.2534155	.4038331	85	.0237200	.3751153	.0356587	.5521662
36	.2050282	.3118135	.2436687	.3867998	86	.0226986	.3559990	.0342873	.5351328
37	.1961992	.2926973	.2342968	.3697664	87	.0217211	.3368827	.0329685	.5180995
38	.1877504	.2735810	.2252854	.3527331	88	.0207858	.3177664	.0317005	.5010661
39	.1796655	.2544647	.2166206	.3356998	89	.0198907	.2986502	.0304812	.4840328
40	.1719287	.2353484	.2082890	.3186664	90	.0190342	.2795339	.0293089	.4669995
41	.1645251	.2162321	.2002779	.3016331	91	.0182145	.2604176	.0281816	.4499661
42	.1574403	.1971158	.1925749	.2845997	92	.0174302	.2413013	.0270977	.4329328
43	.1506605	.1779995	.1851682	.2675664	93	.0166796	.2221850	.0260555	.4158994
44	.1441728	.1588832	.1780463	.2505331	94	.0159613	.2030687	.0250534	.3988661
45	.1379644	.1397669	.1711984	.2334997	95	.0152740	.1839524	.0240898	.3818328
46	.1320233	.1206506	.1646139	.2164664	96	.0146163	.1648361	.0231632	.3648000
47	.1263381	.1015343	.1582826	.1994331	97	.0139868	.1457198	.0222723	.3477667
48	.1208977	.0824181	.1521948	.1823997	98	.0133845	.1266035	.0214157	.3307333
49	.1156916	.0633018	.1463411	.1653664	99	.0128082	.1074872	.0205920	.3137000
50	.1107096	.0441855	.1407126	.1483330	100	.0122566	.0883710	.0198000	.2966667

Actuaries' Table of Mortality.

Age.	Living.	Deaths.	Percentage of deaths to number living.	Age.	Living.	Deaths.	Percent'ge of deaths to number living.
10	100000	676	.00676	55	63469	1375	.02166
11	99324	674	.00679	56	62094	1436	.02313
12	98650	672	.00681	57	60658	1497	.02468
13	97978	671	.00685	58	59161	1561	.02639
14	97307	671	.00690	59	57600	1627	.02825
15	96636	671	.00694	60	55973	1698	.03034
16	95965	672	.00700	61	54275	1770	.03261
17	95293	673	.00706	62	52505	1844	.03512
18	94620	675	.00713	63	50661	1917	.03784
19	93945	677	.00721	64	48744	1990	.04083
20	93268	680	.00729	65	46754	2061	.04408
21	92588	683	.00738	66	44693	2128	.04761
22	91905	686	.00746	67	42565	2191	.05147
23	91219	690	.00756	68	40374	2246	.05563
24	90529	694	.00767	69	38128	2291	.06009
25	89835	698	.00777	70	35837	2327	.06493
26	89137	703	00789	71	33510	2351	.07016
27	88434	708	.00801	72	31159	2362	.07580
28	87726	714	.00814	73	28797	2358	.08188
29	87012	720	.00827	74	26439	2339	.08847
30	86292	727	.00842	75	24100	2303	.09556
31	85565	734	.00858	76	21797	2249	.10318
32	84831	742	.00875	77	19548	2179	.11147
33	84089	750	.00892	78	17369	2092	.12044
34	83339	758	.00909	79	15277	1987	.13006
35	82581	767	.00929	80	13290	1866	.14041
36	81814	776	.00948	81	11424	1730	.15144
37	81038	785	.00969	82	9694	1582	.16319
38	80253	795	.00991	83	8112	1427	.17591
39	79458	805	.01013	84	6685	1268	.18968
40	78653	815	.01036	85	5417	1111	.20509
41	77838	826	.01061	86	4306	958	.22248
42	77012	839	.01089	87	3348	811	.24223
43	76173	857	.01125	88	2537	673	.26527
44	75316	881	.01170	89	1864	545	.29238
45	74435	909	.01221	90	1319	427	.32373
46	73526	944	.01284	91	892	322	.36099
47	72582	981	.01352	92	570	231	.40526
48	71601	1021	.01426	93	339	155	.45723
49	70580	1063	.01506	94	184	95	.51630
50	69517	1108	.01594	95	89	52	.58427
51	68409	1156	.01690	96	37	24	.64865
52	67253	1207	.01795	97	13	9	.69231
53	66046	1261	.01909	98	4	3	.75000
54	64785	1316	.02031	99	1	1	1.00000

American Experience Table of Mortality.

Age.	Number living.	Number of deaths.	Percentage of deaths to living.	Age.	Number living	Number of deaths.	Percentage of deaths to living.
10	100000	749	.00749	53	66797	1091	.01633
11	99251	746	.00752	54	65706	1143	.01735
12	98505	743	.00754	55	64563	1199	.01857
13	97762	740	.00757	56	63364	1260	.01988
14	97022	737	.00760	57	62104	1325	.02134
15	96285	735	.00763	58	60779	1394	.02293
16	95550	732	.00766	59	59385	1468	.02472
17	94818	729	.00769	60	57917	1546	.02669
18	94089	727	.00773	61	56371	1628	.02888
19	93362	725	.00777	62	54743	1713	.03129
20	92637	723	.00780	63	53030	1800	.03394
21	91914	722	.00786	64	51230	1889	.03687
22	91192	721	.00791	65	49341	1980	.04013
23	90471	720	.00796	66	47361	2070	.04371
24	89751	719	.00801	67	45291	2158	.04765
25	89032	718	.00806	68	43133	2243	.05200
26	88314	718	.00813	69	40890	2321	.05676
27	87596	718	.00820	70	38569	2391	.06199
28	86878	718	.00826	71	36178	2448	.06767
29	86160	719	.00834	72	33730	2487	.07373
30	85441	720	.00843	73	31243	2505	.08018
31	84721	721	.00851	74	28738	2501	.08703
32	84000	723	.00861	75	26237	2476	.09437
33	83277	726	.00892	76	23761	2431	.10231
34	82551	729	.00883	77	21330	2369	.11102
35	81822	732	.00895	78	18961	2291	.12083
36	81090	737	.00909	79	16670	2196	.13173
37	80353	742	.00923	80	14474	2091	.14447
38	79611	749	.00941	81	12383	1964	.15860
39	78862	756	.00959	82	10419	1816	.17429
40	78106	765	.00979	83	8603	1648	.19156
41	77341	774	.01001	84	6955	1470	.21136
42	76567	785	.01025	85	5485	1292	.23555
43	75782	797	.01052	86	4193	1114	.26568
44	74985	812	.01083	87	3079	933	.30302
45	74173	828	.01116	88	2146	744	.34669
46	73345	848	.01156	89	1402	555	.39515
47	72497	870	.01200	90	847	385	.45455
48	71627	896	.01251	91	462	246	.53247
49	70731	927	.01316	92	216	137	.63426
50	69804	962	.01378	93	79	58	.73418
51	68842	1001	.01454	94	21	18	.85714
52	67841	1044	.01539	95	3	3	1.00000

Commutation Columns.—Actuaries' four per cent.

	D_x.	N_x.	S_x.	C_x.	M_x.	R_x.
10	67556.42	1381771.3	24814821	439.117	14411.368	427355.215
11	64518.99	1314214.9	23433050	420.978	13972.251	412943.847
12	61616.50	1249695.9	22118835	403.586	13551.273	398971.596
13	58843.05	1188079.4	20869139	387.486	13147.687	385420.323
14	56192.36	1129236.4	19681059	372.582	12760.201	372272.636
15	53658.53	1073044.0	18551823	358.252	12387.619	359512.435
16	51236.51	1019385.5	17478779	344.987	12029.367	347124.816
17	48920.88	968149.0	16459394	332.212	11684.380	335095.449
18	46707.09	919228.1	15491245	320.384	11352.168	323411.069
19	44590.29	872521.0	14572017	308.974	11031.784	312058.901
20	42566.30	827930.7	13699496	298.407	10722.810	301027.117
21	40630.73	785364.4	12871565	288.195	10424.403	290304.307
22	38779.80	744733.7	12086201	278.328	10136.208	279879.904
23	37009.95	705953.9	11341467	269.184	9857.880	269743.696
24	35317.31	668943.9	10635513	260.331	9588.696	259885.816
25	33698.62	633626.6	9966568.7	251.761	9328.365	250297.120
26	32150.76	599928.0	9332942.1	243.812	9076.604	240968.755
27	30670.38	567777.2	8733014.1	236.102	8832.792	231892.151
28	29254.64	537106.8	8165236 9	228.945	8596.690	223059.359
29	27900.53	507852.2	7628130.1	221.989	8367.745	214462.669
30	26605.43	479951.7	7120277.9	215.527	8145.756	206094.924
31	25366.63	453346.3	6640326.2	209.233	7930.229	197949.168
32	24181.75	427979.7	6186979.9	203.378	7720.996	190018.939
33	23048.31	403797.9	5759000.2	197.664	7517.618	182297.943
34	21964.17	380749.6	5355202.3	192.089	7319.954	174780.325
35	20927.30	358785.4	4974452.7	186.894	7127.865	167460.371
36	19935.51	337858.1	4615667.3	181.814	6940.971	160332.506
37	18986.94	317922.6	4277809.2	176.849	6759.157	153391.535
38	18079.83	298935.7	3959886.6	172.213	6582.308	146632.378
39	17212.24	280855.9	3660950.9	167.673	6410.095	140050.070
40	16382.56	263643.6	3380095.0	163.227	6242.422	133639.975
41	15589.23	247261.0	3116451.4	159.067	6079.195	127397.553
42	14830.58	231671.8	2869190.4	155.356	5920.128	121318.358
43	14104.82	216841.2	2637518.6	152.586	5764.772	115398.230
44	13409.74	202736.4	2420677.4	150.826	5612.186	109633.458
45	12743.15	189326.7	2217941.0	149.634	5461.360	104021.272
46	12103.40	176583.6	2028614.3	149.419	5311.726	98559.912
47	11488.46	164480.2	1852030.7	149.303	5162.307	93248.186
48	10897.30	152991.7	1687550.5	149.414	5013.004	88085.879
49	10328.76	142094.4	1534558.8	149.578	4863.590	83072.875
50	9781.92	131765.6	1392464.4	149.913	4714.012	78209.285

51	9255.78	121983.7	1260698.8	150.392	4564.099	73495.273
52	8749.40	112727.9	1138715.1	150.987	4413.707	68931.174
53	8261.89	103978.5	1025987.2	151.675	4262.720	64517.467
54	7792.45	95716.64	922008.73	152.205	4111.045	60254.747
55	7340.54	87924.19	826292.09	152.910	3958.840	56143.702
56	6905.30	80583.65	738367.90	153.552	3805.930	52184.862
57	6486.16	73678.35	657784.25	153.918	3652.378	48378.932
58	6082.78	67192.19	584105.90	154.325	3498.460	44726.554
59	5694.50	61109.41	516913.71	154.663	3344.135	41228.094
60	5320.82	55414.91	455804.30	155.204	3189.472	37883.959
61	4960.96	50094.09	400389.39	155.563	3034 268	34694.487
62	4614.60	45133.13	350295.30	155 833	2878.705	31660.219
63	4281.28	40518.53	305162.17	155.772	2722.872	28781.514
64	3960.84	36237.25	264643.64	155.484	2567.100	26058.642
65	3653.02	32276 41	228406.39	154.838	2411.616	23491.542
66	3357.68	28623.39	196129.98	153.723	2256.778	21079.926
67	3074.81	25265.71	167506.59	152.186	2103.055	18823.148
68	2804.37	22190.90	142240.88	150.006	1950.869	16720.093
69	2546.50	19386.53	120049.98	147.127	1800.863	14769.224
70	2301.43	16840.03	100663.45	143.691	1653.736	12968.361
71	2069.22	14538.60	83823.42	139.589	1510.045	11314.625
72	1850.05	12469.38	69284.82	134.848	1370.456	9804.580
73	1644.04	10619.33	56815.44	129.442	1235.608	8434.124
74	1451.37	8975.290	46196.11	123.461	1106.166	7198.516
75	1272.09	7523.920	37220.82	116.885	982.7045	6092.350
76	1106.27	6251.830	29696.90	109.755	865.8195	5109.645
77	953.971	5145.560	23445.07	102.248	756.0645	4243.826
78	815.031	4191.589	18299.51	94.3904	653.8165	3487.761
79	689.294	3376.558	14107.92	86.2047	559.4261	2833.944
80	576.578	2687.264	10731.36	77.8415	473.2214	2274.518
81	476.560	2110.686	8044.103	69.3925	395.3799	1801.297
82	388.838	1634.126	5933.417	61.0124	325.9874	1405.917
83	312.868	1245.288	4299.291	52.9205	264.9720	1079.930
84	247.914	932.4199	3054.003	45.2153	212.0515	814.9579
85	193.163	684.5059	2121.583	38.0931	166.8362	602.9064
86	147.641	491.3429	1437.075	31.5838	128.7431	436.0702
87	110.379	343.7019	945.7318	25.7091	97.1593	307.3271
88	80.4242	233.3229	602.0299	20.5139	71.4502	210.1678
89	56.8171	152.8987	368.7070	15.9733	50.9363	138.7176
90	38.6584	96.08156	215.8083	12.0336	34.9630	87.7813
91	25.1380	57.42316	119.7267	8.72547	22.9294	52.8183
92	15.4457	32.28516	62.30357	6.01882	14.2040	29.8889
93	8.83281	16.83946	30.01841	3.88327	8.18515	15.6849
94	4.60982	8.006646	13.17895	2.28853	4.30188	7.49979
95	2.14399	3.396826	5.17231	1.20449	2.01335	3.19791
96	.857040	1.252836	1.77548	.53454	.80886	1.18456
97	.289541	.395796	.522643	.19274	.27432	.37570
98	.085663	.106255	.126847	.06178	.08158	.10138
99	.020592	.020592	.020592	.01980	.01980	.01980

Commutation Columns.—American Experience, four and one half per cent.

	D_x.	N_x.	S_x.		C_x.	M_x.	R_x.	
10	64392.76820 30043	1214144.09195 58226	20701126.40778 95886	10	461.53285 53498	12109.05132 45239	322708.02654 86155	10
11	61158.34102 31232	1149751.32375 28184	19486982.31583 37660	11	439.88924 31899	11647.51846 91741	310598.97522 40916	11
12	58084.83900 86027	1088592.98272 96952	18337230.99208 09476	12	419.25382 92778	11207.62922 59842	298951.45675 49175	12
13	55164.32416 93851	1030508.14372 10925	17248638.00935 12525	13	399.57991 80428	10788.37539 67065	287743.82752 89333	13
14	52389.24703 83066	975343.81955 17074	16218129.86563 01600	14	380.82296 59867	10388.79547 86637	276955.45213 22268	14
15	49752.42778 83736	922954.57251 34008	15242786.04607 84526	15	363.43495 22508	10007.97251 26770	266566.65665 35632	15
16	47246.54379 26044	873202.14472 50272	14319831.47356 50517	16	346.36511 41459	9644.53756 04262	256558.68414 08862	16
17	44865.63851 51406	825955.60093 24228	13446629.32884 00246	17	330.09146 88895	9298.17244 62803	246914.14658 04600	17
18	42603.53390 44508	781089.96241 72822	12620673.72790 76017	18	315.01040 01453	8968.08097 73908	237615.97413 41798	18
19	40453.92156 58363	738486.42851 28315	11839583.76549 03195	19	300.61607 32713	8653.07057 72455	228647.89315 67890	19
20	38411.27059 26008	698032.50694 69951	11101097.33697 74880	20	286.87730 86622	8352.45450 39742	219994.82257 95435	20
21	36470.31943 06687	659621.23635 43943	10403064.83003 04929	21	274.14403 94609	8065.57719 53120	211642.36807 55693	21
22	34625.68316 69207	623150.91692 37256	9743443.59367 60983	22	261.97544 36126	7791.43315 58511	203576.79088 02573	22
23	32872.64959 65028	588525.23375 68050	9120292.67675 23729	23	250.34650 09405	7529.45771 22385	195785.35772 44061	23
24	31206.73445 26508	555652.58416 03021	8531767.44299 55680	24	230.23329 90114	7279 11121 12980	188255 90001 21676	24
25	29623.67048 34295	524445.84970 76514	7976114.85883 52659	25	228.61298 41290	7039.87791 22866	180976.78880 08696	25
26	28119.39704 78610	494822.17922 42219	7451669.00912 76145	26	218.76840 58650	6811.26492 81577	173936.91088 85830	26
27	26689.74551 55330	466702.78217 63609	6956846.82990 33926	27	209.34775 68086	6592.49652 22926	167125.64596 04253	27
28	25331.07857 33450	440013.03666 08278	6490144.04772 70317	28	200.33278 16351	6383.14876 54840	160533.14943 81327	28
29	24039.93379 62070	414681.95808 69328	6050131.01106 62039	29	191.97301 11495	6182.81598 38489	154150.00067 26487	29
30	22812.74832 49338	390642.02429 07758	5635449.05297 92211	30	183.96173 31723	5990.84297 26994	147967.18468 87998	30
31	21646.41943 90131	367829.27596 58420	5244807.02868 84453	31	176.28443 59612	5806.88123 95271	141976.34171 61004	31
32	20537.99253 91710	346182.85652 68289	4876977.75272 26033	32	169.16118 25680	5630.59680 35659	136169.46047 65733	32
33	19484.42019 46291	325644.86398 76579	4530794.89619 57744	33	162.54841 74054	5461.43562 09979	130538.86367 30074	33
34	18482.82975 92732	306160.44379 30289	4205150.03220 81164	34	156.19148 81154	5298.88720 35925	125077.42805 20095	34
35	17530.72694 18110	287677.61403 37557	3898989.58841 50876	35	150.08062 33885	5142.69571 54771	119778.54084 84170	35
36	16625.73463 19330	270146.88709 19447	3611311.97438 13319	36	144.59881 74724	4992.61509 20885	114635.84513 29399	36
37	15765.19508 86836	253521.15246 00116	3341165.08728 93872	37	139.31082 63353	4848.01627 46161	109643.23004 08514	37
38	14947.00026 33141	237755.95737 13280	3087643.93482 93756	38	134.56945 39846	4708.70544 82808	104795.21376 62353	38
39	14168.78008 02873	222808.95710 80139	2849887.97745 80476	39	129.97809 80221	4574.13599 42962	100086.50831 79544	39
40	13428.66312 71332	208640.17702 77266	2627079.02035 00337	40	125.86168 07004	4444.15789 62741	95512.37232 36582	40
41	12724.53365 62692	195211.51390 05934	2418438.84332 23071	41	121.85876 20628	4318.29621 55738	91068.21442 73840	41
42	12054.72846 88168	182486.98024 43242	2223227.32942 17137	42	118.26852 14684	4196.43745 35110	86749.91821 18102	42
43	11417.35680 75429	170432.25177 55074	2040740.34917 73895	43	114.90569 17811	4078.16893 20425	82553.48075 82993	43
44	10810 79460 25183	159014.89496 79646	1870308.09740 18820	44	112.02706 52822	3963.26324 02614	78475.31182 62567	44
45	10233.23092 75582	148204.10036 54463	1711293.20243 39175	45	109.31530 63541	3851.23617 49792	74512.04858 59953	45
46	9683.25017 45629	137970.86943 78881	1563089.10206 84712	46	107.13471 07092	3741.92086 86252	70660.81241 10161	46
47	9159.13339 89204	128287.61926 33252	1425118.23263 05831	47	105.18100 37883	3634.78615 79160	66918.89154 23910	47
43	8659.53995 21164	119128.48586 44048	1296830.61336 72579	48	103.65965 94558	3529.60515 41277	63234.10538 44750	48

49	8182.98144 30479	110468.94591 22883	1177702.12750 28531	49	102.62784 55182	3425.94549 46719	59754.50023 03473	49
50	7727.97640 62023	102285.96446 92404	1067233.18159 05648	50	101.91644 33177	3323.31764 91537	56328 55473 56754	50
51	7293.27628 98903	94557.98806 30881	964947.21712 13244	51	101.48152 25069	3221.40120 58360	53005.23708 65217	51
52	6877.73023 81537	87264.71177 31478	870389.22905 82863	52	101.28312 78743	3119.91968 33291	49783.83588 06857	52
53	6480.27690 86364	80386.98153 49941	783124.51728 51385	53	101.28498 46109	3018.63655 54549	46663.91619 73566	53
54	6099 93693 75292	73906.70462 63577	702737.53575 01444	54	101.54306 21223	2917.35157 08440	43645.27964 19017	54
55	5735.71716 51784	67806.76768 88284	628830.83112 37867	55	101.93114 86055	2815.80850 87217	40727.92807 10577	55
56	5386.79341 13739	62071.05052 36500	561024.06343 49583	56	102.50427 76819	2713.87736 01162	37912.11956 23360	56
57	5052.32195 32979	56684.25711 22761	498953.01291 13083	57	103.15042 75298	2611.37308 24344	35198.24220 22198	57
58	4731.60742 25161	51631.93515 89782	442268.75579 90322	58	103.84883 70328	2508.22265 49046	32586.86911 97854	58
59	4424.00515 58055	46900.32773 64621	390636.82064 00540	59	104.65226 41561	2404.37381 78718	30078.64646 48809	59
60	4128.84549 25956	42476.32258 06566	343736.49290 35919	60	105.46680 07675	2299.72155 37156	27674.27264 70091	60
61	3845.58151 75058	38347.47708 80610	301260.17032 29353	61	106.27824 95648	2194.25475 29481	25374.55109 32935	61
62	3573.70406 38378	34501.89557 05552	262912.69323 48743	62	107 01165 10731	2087.97650 33833	23180.29634 03453	62
63	3312.80085 02072	30928.19150 67174	228410.79766 43190	63	107.60437 18212	1980.96485 23102	21092.31983 69620	63
64	3062.53998 24440	27615.39065 65102	197482.60615 76017	64	108.06201 93356	1873.36048 04891	19111.35498 46518	64
65	2822.59825 09458	24552.85067 40662	169867.21550 10914	65	108 39020 07768	1765.29846 11535	17237.99450 41627	65
66	2592.66075 70661	21730.25242 31204	145314.36482 70252	66	108 43734 74496	1656.90826 03767	15472.69604 30092	66
67	2372.57773 10825	19137.59166 60543	123584.11240 39049	67	108.17918 11924	1548.47091 29270	13815.78778 26326	67
68	2162.23013 08483	16765.01393 49718	104446.52073 78505	68	107.59825 61447	1440.29173 17347	12267.31686 97055	68
69	1961.52148 62938	14602.78380 41236	87681.50680 28787	69	106.54542 57528	1332.69347 55900	10827.02513 79709	69
70	1770.50862 81169	12641.26231 78297	73078.72299 87551	70	105.03231 90074	1226.14804 98372	9494.33166 23809	70
71	1589.23431 07695	10870.75368 97128	60437.46068 09254	71	102.90547 96516	1121.11573 08298	8268.18361 25437	71
72	1417.89290 38599	9281.51937 89432	49566.70699 12126	72	100.04297 14692	1018.21025 11781	7147.06788 17140	72
73	1256.79234 32293	7863.62647 50833	40285.18761 22694	73	96.42779 52647	918.16727 97090	6128.85763 05358	73
74	1106.24430 35194	6606.83413 18540	32421.56113 71861	74	92.12805 62156	821.73948 44443	5210.69035 08269	74
75	966.47893 27982	5500.58982 83347	25814.72700 53321	75	87.27956 36539	729.61142 82287	4388.95086 63826	75
76	837.58065 91195	4534.11089 55365	20314.13717 69974	76	82.00316 11577	642.33186 45748	3659.33943 81538	76
77	719.50943 13012	3696.53023 64170	15780.02628 14609	77	76.47058 38197	560.32870 34172	3017.00757 35790	77
78	612.05518 77604	2977.02080 51159	12083 49604 50439	78	70.76819 90991	483.85811 95975	2456.67887 01618	78
79	514.93054 51692	2364.96561 73554	9106.47523 99280	79	64.91261 42537	413.08992 04984	1972.82075 05643	79
80	427.84388 83006	1850.03507 21862	6741.50962 25726	80	59.14724 30973	348.17730 62447	1559.73083 00659	80
81	350.27274 57071	1422.19118 38857	4891.47455 03863	81	53.16253 31819	289.03006 31474	1211.55352 38212	81
82	282.02669 71598	1071.91843 81786	3469.28336 65007	82	47.03961 26732	235.86752 99655	922.52346 06738	82
83	222.84239 41783	789.89174 10188	2397.36492 83221	83	40.84969 42044	188.82791 72923	686.65598 07052	83
84	172.39661 60141	567.04934 68405	1607.47318 73033	84	34.86845 03649	147.97822 30880	497.82801 34159	84
85	130.10438 79261	394.65273 08264	1040.42384 04628	85	29.32658 78146	113.10977 27231	349.84979 03280	85
86	95.17521 88132	264.54834 29002	645.77110 96364	86	24.19735 64412	83.78318 49085	236.74001 76049	86
87	66.87940 79734	169.37312 40870	381.22276 67362	87	19 39313 78451	59.58582 84673	152.95683 26964	87
88	44.60629 56223	102.49371 61136	211.84964 26492	88	14.79868 36277	40.19269 06222	93.37100 42292	88
89	27.88676 67285	57.88742 04913	109.35592 65357	89	10.56396 23056	25.39400 69945	53.17831 36070	89
90	16.12193 88700	30.00065 37627	51.46850 60444	90	7.01258 75903	14.83004 46889	27.78420 66125	90
91	8.41510 51083	13.87871 48927	21.46785 22816	91	4.28781 84234	7.81745 70986	12.95426 19237	91
92	3.76491 37376	5.46360 97844	7.58913 73889	92	2.28510 18167	3.52963 86752	5.13680 48251	92
93	1.31768 64490	1.69869 60468	2.12552 76045	93	.92575 63327	1.24453 68585	1.60716 61499	93
94	.33518 76377	.38100 95977	0.42683 15578	94	.27493 17602	.31878 05258	.36262 92914	94
95	.04582 19600	.04582 19600	0.04582 19600	95	.04384 87656	.04384 87656	.04384 87656	95

A_x COLUMNS.

Value at Age x of a Life Series of Annual Payments of $1 each —the first immediate.

Age.	American Experience 4½ per cent.	Age.	Actuaries' 4 per cent.	Age.	American Experience 4½ per cent.	Age.	Actuaries' 4 per cent.
10	18.855 2865	10	20.4536	55	11.821 8465	55	11.9779
11	18.799 5832	11	20.3694	56	11.522 8199	56	11.6698
12	18.741 4307	12	20.2818	57	11.219 4467	57	11.3593
13	18.680 6991	13	20.1907	58	10.912 1342	58	11.0463
14	18.617 2521	14	20.0959	59	10.601 3275	59	10.7311
15	18.550 9454	15	19.9976	60	10.287 6997	60	10.4147
16	18.481 8206	16	19.8957	61	9.971 8279	61	10.0977
17	18.409 5363	17	19.7901	62	9.654 3796	62	9.7805
18	18.333 9242	18	19.6807	63	9.335 9646	63	9.4641
19	18.255 0022	19	19.5675	64	9.017 1527	64	9.1489
20	18.172 5961	20	19.4504	65	8.698 6699	65	8.8356
21	18.086 5220	21	19.3293	66	8.381 4484	66	8.5243
22	17.996 7833	22	19.2042	67	8.066 1600	67	8.2170
23	17.903 1882	23	19.0747	68	7.753 5753	68	7.9130
24	17.805 5344	24	18.9410	69	7.444 6209	69	7.6130
25	17.703 6080	25	18.8027	70	7.139 9044	70	7.3172
26	17.597 1831	26	18.6598	71	6.840 2460	71	7.0261
27	17.486 2208	27	18.5122	72	6.545 9947	72	6.7400
28	17.370 4817	28	18.3597	73	6.256 9020	73	6.4593
29	17.249 7130	29	18.2022	74	5.972 3102	74	6.1840
30	17.123 8475	30	18.0397	75	5.691 3706	75	5.9146
31	16.992 6152	31	17.8718	76	5.413 3424	76	5.6512
32	16.855 7300	32	17.6985	77	5.137 5702	77	5.3938
33	16.713 0898	33	17.5196	78	4.863 9745	78	5.1428
34	16.564 5871	34	17.3350	79	4.592 7856	79	4.8986
35	16.409 9079	35	17.1443	80	4.324 0890	80	4.6607
36	16.248 7188	36	16.9476	81	4.060 2393	81	4.4290
37	16.081 0666	37	16.7443	82	3.800 7694	82	4.2026
38	15.906 6002	38	16.5342	83	3.544 6260	83	3.9802
39	15.725 3451	39	16.3172	84	3.289 2139	84	3.7611
40	15.536 9284	40	16.0929	85	3.033 3545	85	3.5436
41	15.341 3492	41	15.8610	86	2.779 5927	86	3.3279
42	15.138 2074	42	15.6212	87	2.532 5153	87	3.1138
43	14.927 4700	43	15.3736	88	2.297 7410	88	2.9012
44	14.708 8998	44	15.1186	89	2.075 8025	89	2.6911
45	14.482 6303	45	14.8571	90	1.860 8589	90	2.4854
46	14.248 4049	46	14.5896	91	1.649 2622	91	2.2843
47	14.006 5237	47	14.3170	92	1.451 1912	92	2.0902
48	13.756 9070	48	14.0394	93	1.289 1504	93	1.9065
49	13.499 8407	49	13.7572	94	1.136 7054	94	1.7369
				95	1.000 0000		
50	13.235 8018	50	13.4703			95	1.5843
51	12.965 0906	51	13.1792			96	1.4618
52	12.688 0262	52	12.8841			97	1.3670
53	12.404 8683	53	12.5853			98	1.2404
54	12.115 9785	54	1[illegible].2832			99	1.0000

Actuaries' four per cent.

For Use in Accumulation Formulas.

Age.	u_x.	c_x.	k_x.	Age.	u_x.	c_x.	k_x.
10	1.04708	.006500	.006806	55	1.06303	.020831	.022144
11	1.04710	.006525	.006832	56	1.06462	.022237	.023674
12	1.04713	.006550	.006859	57	1.06632	.023730	.025304
13	1.04717	.006585	.006896	58	1.06819	.025371	.027101
14	1.04722	.006630	.006944	59	1.07023	.027160	.029068
15	1.04727	.006677	.006992	60	1.07254	.029169	.031285
16	1.04733	.006733	.007052	61	1.07506	.031357	.033711
17	1.04740	.006791	.007113	62	1.07786	.033770	.036399
18	1.04747	.006860	.007185	63	1.08090	.036384	.039328
19	1.04755	.006929	.007259	64	1.08427	.039255	.042563
20	1.04764	.007010	.007344	65	1.08796	.042386	.046115
21	1.04773	.007093	.007432	66	1.09199	.045782	.049994
22	1.04782	.007177	.007520	67	1.09644	.049494	.054268
23	1.04793	.007273	.007622	68	1.10126	.053490	.058907
24	1.04803	.007371	.007725	69	1.10648	.057776	.063928
25	1.04814	.007471	.007830	70	1.11222	.062436	.069442
26	1.04827	.007583	.007949	71	1.11847	.067460	.075452
27	1.04839	.007698	.008071	72	1.12530	.072889	.082022
28	1.04854	.007826	.008206	73	1.13275	.078734	.089186
29	1.04868	.007956	.008344	74	1.14093	.085065	.097054
30	1.04884	.008101	.008497	75	1.14988	.091885	.105657
31	1.04900	.008248	.008652	76	1.15965	.099211	.115050
32	1.04918	.008410	.008824	77	1.17047	.107182	.125453
33	1.04936	.008576	.008999	78	1.18242	.115812	.136938
34	1.04955	.008746	.009179	79	1.19549	.125062	.149511
35	1.04975	.008931	.009375	80	1.20987	.135006	.163340
36	1.04996	.009122	.009576	81	1.22560	.145611	.179492
37	1.05017	.009314	.009782	82	1.24282	.156917	.195020
38	1.05040	.009525	.010005	83	1.26200	.169146	.213463
39	1.05064	.009741	.010235	84	1.28344	.182383	.234078
40	1.05089	.009963	.010470	85	1.30833	.197207	.258012
41	1.05116	.010204	.010726	86	1.33759	.213923	.286141
42	1.05146	.010476	.011014	87	1.37246	.232917	.319669
43	1.05183	.010818	.011379	88	1.41549	.255071	.361052
44	1.05231	.011247	.011836	89	1.46972	.281137	.413192
45	1.05286	.011742	.012363	90	1.53785	.311279	.478700
46	1.05353	.012345	.013006	91	1.62751	.347103	.564912
47	1.05425	.012996	.013701	92	1.74867	.389676	.681416
48	1.05504	.013711	.014466	93	1.91609	.439641	.842391
49	1.05590	.014482	.015291	94	2.15011	.496446	1.067416
50	1.05684	.015326	.016197	95	2.50162	.561798	1.405405
51	1.05788	.016248	.017189	96	2.95999	.623701	1.846154
52	1.05901	.017257	.018275	97	3.37999	.665680	2.250000
53	1.06024	.018359	.019464	98	4.15999	.721154	3.000000
54	1.06156	.019532	.020735	99	....	.961538	....

American Experience Four and a half per cent.

For Use in Accumulation Formulas.

Age.	*ux.*	Age.	*cx.*	Age.	*kx.*
10	1.052886	10	.00716746	10	.0075465
11	1.052914	11	.00719261	11	.0075732
12	1.052942	12	.00721796	12	.0076001
13	1.052970	13	.00724345	13	.0076271
14	1.052999	14	.00726911	14	.0076544
15	1.053038	15	.00730487	15	.0076923
16	1.053067	16	.00733101	16	.0077201
17	1.053097	17	.00735733	17	.0077480
18	1.053137	18	.00739400	18	.0077869
19	1.053178	19	.00743107	19	.0078262
20	1.053220	20	.00746857	20	0078660
21	1.053274	21	.00751691	21	.0079174
22	1.053328	22	.00756593	22	.0079694
23	1.053383	23	.00761565	23	.0080222
24	1.053439	24	.00766608	24	.0080757
25	1.053496	25	.00771724	25	.0081301
26	1.053566	26	.00777998	26	.0081967
27	1.053636	27	.00784375	27	.0082645
28	1.053708	28	.00790858	28	.0083333
29	1.053794	29	.00798559	29	.0084152
30	1.053881	30	.00806399	30	.0084985
31	1.053970	31	.00814382	31	.0085833
32	1.054073	32	.00823650	32	.0086819
33	1.054190	33	.00834248	33	.0087946
34	1.054311	34	.00845063	34	.0089096
35	1.054433	35	.00856100	35	.0090270
36	1.054585	36	.00369729	36	.0091720
37	1.054740	37	.00883661	37	.0093203
38	1.054925	38	.00900311	38	.0094976
39	1.055115	39	.00917356	39	.0096792
40	1.055336	40	.00937261	40	.0098913
41	1.055564	41	.00957668	41	.0101088
42	1.055825	42	.00981097	42	.0103587
43	1.056107	43	.01006412	43	.0106288
44	1.056440	44	.01036252	44	.0109474
45	1.056797	45	.01068238	45	.0112891
46	1.057223	46	.01106392	46	.0116970
47	1.057693	47	.01148373	47	.0121463
48	1.058238	48	.01197057	48	.0126677
49	1.058878	49	.01254162	49	.0132800
50	1.059603	50	.01318799	50	.0139740
51	1.060419	51	.01391439	51	.0147551
52	1.061333	52	.01472624	52	.0156294

Age.	*ux.*	Age.	*cx.*	Age.	*kx.*
53	1.062351	53	.01562973	53	.0166043
54	1.063500	54	.01664658	54	.0177036
55	1.064774	55	.01777130	55	.0189224
56	1.066202	56	.01902881	56	.0202885
57	1.067781	57	.02041644	57	.0218003
58	1.069530	58	.02194790	58	.0234739
59	1.071487	59	.02365555	59	.0253466
60	1.073660	60	.02554390	60	.0274254
61	1.076077	61	.02763646	61	.0297390
62	1.078756	62	.02994418	62	.0323025
63	1.081717	63	.03248139	63	.0351357
64	1.085007	64	.03528510	64	.0382846
65	1.088688	65	.03840086	65	.0418042
66	1.092761	66	.04182473	66	.0457044
67	1.097283	67	.04559563	67	.0500313
68	1.102323	68	.04976263	68	.0548545
69	1.107886	69	.05431775	69	.0601779
70	1.114064	70	.05932325	70	.0660899
71	1.120842	71	.06475161	71	.0725763
72	1.128184	72	.07055749	72	.0796018
73	1.136089	73	.07672532	73	.0871668
74	1.144613	74	.08328003	74	.0953234
75	1.153894	75	.09030674	75	.1042044
76	1.164100	76	.09790479	76	.1139709
77	1.175563	77	.10628156	77	.1249407
78	1.188617	78	.11562389	78	.1374325
79	1.203548	79	.12606091	79	.1517203
80	1.221459	80	.13824492	80	.1688605
81	1.241984	81	.15177468	81	.1885018
82	1.265588	82	.16679135	82	.2110892
83	1.292615	83	.18331204	83	.2369518
84	1.325064	84	.20225716	84	.2680036
85	1.366999	85	.22540814	85	.3081324
86	1.423087	86	.25424009	86	.3618058
87	1.499327	87	.28997173	87	.4347624
88	1.599551	88	.33176222	88	.5306705
89	1.729740	89	.37881632	89	.6552533
90	1.915833	90	.43497173	90	.8333333
91	2.235139	91	.50953831	91	1.1388889
92	2.857215	92	.60694666	92	1.7341772
93	3.931190	93	.70256193	93	2.7619048
94	7.315000	94	.82023240	94	6.0000000
95	....	95	.95693780		

Decimals of a year from date to January 1st.

	Jan.	Feb.	Mar.	April.	May.	June.	July.	Aug.	Sept.	Oct.	Nov.	Dec.
1	1.00000	91507	83836	75342	67123	58630	50411	41918	33425	25205	16712	08493
2	99726	91233	83562	75068	66849	58356	50137	41644	33151	24932	16438	08219
3	99452	90959	83288	74795	66575	58082	49863	41370	32877	24658	16164	07945
4	99178	90685	83014	74521	66301	57808	49589	41096	32603	24384	15890	07671
5	98904	90411	82740	74247	66027	57534	49315	40822	32329	24110	15616	07397
6	98630	90137	82466	73973	65753	57260	49041	40548	32055	23836	15342	07123
7	98366	89863	82192	73699	65479	56986	48767	40274	31781	23562	15068	06849
8	98082	89589	81918	73425	65205	56712	48493	40000	31507	23288	14795	06575
9	97808	89315	81644	73151	64932	56438	48219	39726	31233	23014	14521	06301
10	97534	89041	81370	72877	64658	56164	47945	39452	30959	22740	14247	06027
11	97260	88767	81096	72603	64384	55890	47671	39178	30685	22466	13973	05753
12	96986	88493	80822	72329	64110	55616	47397	38904	30411	22192	13699	05479
13	96712	88219	80548	72055	63836	55342	47123	38630	30137	21918	13425	05205
14	96438	87945	80274	71781	63562	55068	46849	48356	29863	21644	13151	04932
15	96164	87671	80000	71507	63288	54795	46575	38082	29589	21370	12877	04658
16	95890	87397	79726	71233	63014	54521	46301	37808	29315	21096	12603	04384
17	95616	87123	79452	70959	62740	54247	46027	37534	29041	20822	12329	04110
18	95342	86849	79178	70685	62466	53973	45753	37260	28767	20548	12055	03836
19	95068	86575	78904	70411	62192	53699	45479	36986	28493	20274	11781	03562
20	94795	86301	78630	70137	61918	53425	45205	36712	28219	20000	11507	03288
21	94521	86027	78356	69863	61644	53151	44932	36438	27945	19726	11233	03014
22	94247	85753	78082	69589	61370	52877	44658	36164	27671	19452	10959	02740
23	93973	85479	77808	69315	61096	52603	44384	35890	27397	19178	10685	02466
24	93699	85205	77534	69041	60822	52329	44110	35616	27123	18904	10411	02192
25	93425	84932	77260	68767	60548	52055	43836	35342	26849	18630	10137	01918
26	93151	84658	76986	68493	60274	51781	43562	35068	26575	18356	09863	01644
27	92877	84384	76712	68219	60000	51507	44288	34795	26301	18082	09589	01370
28	92603	84110	76438	67945	59726	51233	43014	34521	26027	17808	09315	01096
29	92329	84110	76164	67671	59452	50959	42740	34247	25753	17534	09041	00822
30	92055		75890	67397	59178	50685	42466	33973	25479	17260	08767	00548
31	91781		75616		58904		42192	33699		16986		00274
	Jan.	Feb.	Mar.	April.	May.	June.	July.	Aug.	Sept.	Oct.	Nov.	Dec.

INDEX.

Printed in Dunstable, United Kingdom

82202496R00112